IN THE WAKE
OF DIAGHILEV

by the same author

THE MOST UPSETTING WOMAN: Autobiography 1
(Collins, London 1981)

BUCKLE AT THE BALLET
(Dance Books, London 1980)

DIAGHILEV
(Weidenfeld and Nicolson, London 1979)

NIJINSKY
(Penguin Books, London 1980)

RICHARD BUCKLE

IN THE WAKE OF DIAGHILEV

A William Abrahams Book

HOLT, RINEHART and WINSTON · NEW YORK

First published in the United States in 1983 by
Holt, Rinehart and Winston, 383 Madison Avenue,
New York, New York 10017.

Library of Congress Cataloging in Publication Data
Buckle, Richard.
In the wake of Diaghilev.
"A William Abrahams book."
Sequel to: The most upsetting woman.
1. Ballet—History.   2. Diaghilev, Serge,
1872–1929.   3. Impresarios—Russian S.F.S.R.—
Biography.   I. Title.
GV1787.B818 1983   792.8´09   82-12096
ISBN 0-3-062493-2

First American Edition

Printed in Great Britain
1 3 5 7 9 10 8 6 4 2

ISBN 0-03-062493-2

To Boris Kochno

whose help with my life of Diaghilev was beyond price, and whose account of the events following his friend's death are incorporated in the early part of this book;

To Jean Hugo

who knew Boris in 'the days of the Boeuf sur le toit' and who designed his ballets *Les Cent Baisers* and *Les Amours de Jupiter*, which I admired before I met either of them; and

To Lauretta Hugo

my dearest friend, who went with me to see the latter ballet at the Adelphi Theatre in 1946, and without whose prompt action on 31 May 1979, the day after I had handed Boris an advance copy of *Diaghilev*, I might not have survived to complete either this book or its predecessor.

Contents

Illustrations

—••—

9

Introduction

On Tuesday, 19 December 1933 I was on my way home from school for the Christmas holidays. I was sixteen. Since my school, Marlborough, was in the south-west of England, and my mother's house was in Norfolk, on the east coast, it was customary for me to come up on the special school train to Paddington Station, lunch in London with my grandmother Sandford or my aunt Violet Kinnaird, then catch the three-thirty train at Liverpool Street Station for Norwich, where I changed on to the local line for Cromer.

As I stood on the platform of Liverpool Street, scanning the display on Smith's bookstall, my eye was attracted to the photograph on a book-jacket. The book was *Nijinsky*, 'by Romola Nijinsky, his wife'. To me the name Nijinsky meant nothing. I had never heard of ballet, although the human figure idealized by sculpture had already made its impression on me. On my first visit to Paris in 1931 I had been transfixed by the breeze-blown beauty of the 'Winged Victory of Samothrace' in the Louvre, and in the art classroom at Marlborough I had drawn in pencil from a cast of Michelangelo's exquisitely weary 'Slave', the original of which I had also seen during that excursion. The dancer in this photograph on the book-jacket was suspended in motion like the former carving, and had something of the latter's voluptuous abandon. He also had the quality of appealing sweetness which had captivated me in Botticelli's 'Venus', when it was on loan in 1930 to the Italian Exhibition at Burlington House. Not only did his stubby hands curl most sculpturally, his

13

outline was so strangely drawn in the air, and his gaze was like an aphrodisiac scent. Why he was wearing a bodice made of rags – hardly identifiable in a black-and-white photograph as rose-petals – and more rags formed into a kind of airman's helmet, I neither knew nor cared. I longed to buy the book and to learn more about this Nijinsky and what he was up to: but something stopped me. I had an instinct that my mother might not approve; and I suppose I was shrewd enough to sense (for reasoning did not enter into it) that the equivocal 'something' which had drawn me to the image of Nijinsky on the book's cover, was the quality to which she might raise an objection.

So, putting Nijinsky out of my mind, I travelled through Essex, past the estuary of the Stour with its mud flats, across which could be seen the spire of Mistley Church where my parents had been married, through Suffolk into Norfolk; and scattered lights were twinkling through the dark before I arrived at Norwich, and crossed the platform to the little local train, which let off farmers or women day-shoppers at Salhouse, Wroxham, Worsted, North Walsham and Gunton, before depositing me at Cromer. My mother drove me back to Overstrand; Nanny was waiting at the door to be kissed; the fire was blazing. And there on the table beside my mother's arm-chair was the book, *Nijinsky*.

When I opened the mysterious volume there were more photographs of the dancer in other roles besides *Le Spectre de la rose* to excite my imagination: he was the Harlequin of *Carnaval*, mischief incarnate; in *Le Pavillon d'Armide* he was the embodiment of ineffable courtliness; *Scheherazade* revealed him shimmering with lust; for *L'Après-midi d'un faune*, his own invention, he had thought out a more formalized image of sensuality; he was the romantic dreamer of impossible loves in *Giselle*; and from the eyes peering through Petrushka's awkward puppet mask there glinted a spark of soul. Reading and re-reading the text – in which I could not yet detect Romola Nijinsky's distortions – I learned what

14

ballet was; how the genius of Nijinsky had transcended its bounds (for Romola gave a very good idea of his magic); how Diaghilev had loved and lost him; and of the madness which cut short his career. Naturally I was intrigued by the homosexual aspect of the story, by the realization that male dancers as well as female were available to be loved; but chiefly I was attracted to the idea of this touring company whose director was perpetually evolving new masterpieces in the course of his progress round the civilized world. Even if I had not yet learnt how many of the best things in life come from the south, I was already drawn there. (To this day, whether at my cottage in Wiltshire or in a characterless American-type hotel, I like to write facing Naples.) Just as my appreciation of the English Romantic poets had been enhanced by the fact that they travelled or died in Italy or Greece, so I envied Diaghilev, sitting at a table in the sun, surrounded by his 'committee of friends', hatching new ballets over delectable luncheons, on the shore of a Mediterranean which to me was still a distant dream.

My fascination by Diaghilev's Ballet, which appeared a legendary band of heroes, although he had died only in 1929, was doubled when I found, on a visit to Norwich during 1934, a large handsome illustrated pamphlet, *Les Ballets Russes de Serge de Diaghilew*, in the bookshop in Elm Hill where I had formerly bought the poems of Rupert Brooke. How this slim book reached Norwich I cannot imagine: it must have been rare in Paris. The colour reproductions of designs by Picasso for *Pulcinella*, by Larionov for *Contes russes*, by Gontcharova for *Coq d'or* went to my head. But there were also, in black and white, very different designs by Matisse, Marie Laurencin, Braque, Pruna, Derain, Yakoulov, de Chirico, Rouault and Bakst. For days I was imitating them in poster paint.

Later that year, after reading Haskell's *Balletomania*, which raised the curtain for me on the frantic game of musical chairs that had been played by Diaghilev's orphans since

1929, I realized that some of the fabled dancers of his company were still to be seen on the stage. It seemed too good to be true. Les Ballets de Monte Carlo, a largely Russian company, had already given two long successful seasons in London: Massine, who had followed Nijinsky as Diaghilev's leading dancer, choreographer and boy-friend, and Danilova, Diaghilev's last ballerina, were its stars, along with the 'baby ballerinas', Baronova and Toumanova, whom Haskell had described. In addition, Ninette de Valois, a former Diaghilev dancer, whose French name concealed her Anglo-Irish nationality and her Russian training, was running a company named the Vic-Wells Ballet after the Old Vic and Sadler's Wells, two unfashionable theatres where they performed alternately. At the end of 1934 I saw my first ballet, *Giselle*, at Sadler's Wells. It was danced by the elfin Alicia Markova, whom Diaghilev had taken on in 1924 when she was fourteen. In August 1936 I saw the Russians at Covent Garden and was bowled over by the subtle vulgarity of Danilova and the authority of Massine in *Le Beau Danube*. This work had been created by Massine in 1923, after his first parting with Diaghilev – who thought it sentimental rubbish, which of course it was: but I had not yet reached the stage when Viennese waltzes made me feel sick.

By the time of my first visit to Covent Garden I was living with my aunt and uncle, Violet and Patrick Kinnaird, in Regent's Park, attending an art school and learning to draw, with the aim of becoming a stage designer. Although Pat and Violet kept quiet about it, I suspect that they hoped I would sooner or later see the folly of my ways, lose confidence in my ability to make a living in the world of art and the theatre, and submit to 'starting at the bottom' in Barclay's Bank. Pat was local director of the branch at 1 Pall Mall East, near to the National Gallery – he was in 1944 to join the bank's board of directors – and this building is called Kinnaird House. Although the family of Lord Kinnaird of Rossie Priory had been landowners in Perthshire for six hundred years, they had 'married into' banking in the eighteenth century. Douglas Kinnaird, a younger son of the seventh baron, was Byron's friend and banker.

For that matter I myself had a little Scottish banking blood. Great-Grandma Sandford's maternal great-grandfather, Richard Bethel Cox, had married a grand-daughter of Andrew Drummond, who came south to found in 1717 the famous bank at Charing Cross. (The Scots were mainly poorer than the English, and younger sons, even of such great families as the Drummonds, had to make their way in the world and go into business.) Andrew set up in Charing Cross rather than the City because it was the quarter of expatriate Scots and had a traditional connection with visiting Kings of Scotland even before the widowed Queen Margaret, sister of King Henry VIII, had her residence there. The equestrian statue of King Charles I, which still looks down Whitehall towards the scene of his beheading, presided over this colony of exiles, many of whom had followed Charles's father south. (The name 'Scotland Yard' commemorates the Hibernian association.) My mother remembers Great-Grandma driving weekly to Drummond's Bank – between Whitehall and the Admiralty Arch – to draw her housekeeping money in gold or notes, and how the clerks used to smile and wink at each other when the old lady unbuttoned her bodice and hitched up her skirt to secrete the cash in mysterious receptacles.

After seeing Alicia Markova drifting like a fairy through the blue midnight of *Giselle*; and after watching Massine slowly raise his right hand in *Le Beau Danube* as a sign of his re-awakening love for the Street Dancer, stare over our heads as the music of the Blue Danube waltz, *lento, pianissimo*, began to play, then suddenly give a flourish in the air and sweep Danilova into an accelerating whirl, I was irretrievably lost to Barclay's Bank and committed to the ballet. Massine was a supreme artist and his simple gesture led me a dance which would last nearly fifty years.

Yet although I cannot believe I should have made a good

banker, I was not such a fool at business as my family came to think. I might have made a fortune out of buying and selling pictures. I had a knack for finding cheap, attractive houses, which I embellished and which went up in value. I should have had no trouble at all in becoming a millionaire in real estate. If only I had had the time – if only it had not been for that damned old Diaghilev and his dazzling inheritors – I could have made a lot of money.

CHAPTER 1

In the Wake of Diaghilev

When Nijinsky married Romola de Pulszky in Buenos Aires in September 1913 it was a severe blow to Diaghilev's pride: he must have kicked himself for shirking the South American tour and staying behind in Venice to plan his next season's repertory. The loving aspect of his relationship with Nijinsky had begun to change – and perhaps their physical relations had been given up a long time before – yet Nijinsky had become to him what he most needed, a son and pupil, besides being the principal dancer of his company and, latterly, since the angry withdrawal of Fokine, its choreographer. There could be no doubt that if Diaghilev had been on the ship which took the Ballet to South America, or if Nijinsky's sister Bronislava, who was having a baby in Russia, had been on it, or even if Nijinsky's partner Karsavina, who travelled separately, had been on it, the unworldly genius could easily have been dissuaded from attaching himself to a girl with whom he could converse only in broken French, and whose position as his wife must inevitably hinder the close daily communication with Diaghilev and his collaborators which was essential for the creation of works of art. If Diaghilev's first impulse was to expel Nijinsky from the Russian Ballet he curbed it. He could not risk endangering the South American tour and losing money. Nevertheless, when he was back in St Petersburg that winter and Nijinsky was visiting Romola's mother in Budapest Diaghilev sent him a telegram saying that his services were no longer required; and he sought a reconciliation with the touchy Fokine, whose revolutionary

19

ballets had first conquered Europe in 1909, but who had left the company in disgust when Diaghilev gave Nijinsky his first opportunity as a choreographer with *L'Après-midi d'un faune.*

Diaghilev did not like Fokine, whose innovations he already considered old-fashioned, and he probably regarded his re-engagement as a temporary expedient. The astonishing fact is that he found a replacement for Nijinsky – as a pupil, lover, dancer and choreographer – in February 1914. He was in Moscow looking for someone who could play the adolescent hero of the ballet about Joseph and Potiphar's wife which he had commissioned from Richard Strauss, and which Fokine was to stage. How could he tell that the dark-eyed youth whom he saw performing two minor roles at the Bolshoi Theatre would become – though not a transcendent dancer like Nijinsky – a performer of extraordinary power and a highly original choreographer? The sixteen-year-old Massine's technique was limited, he was thinking of giving up dancing for acting, and he had no notion of becoming a choreographer: but that is how it turned out.

Diaghilev's love for Massine and his increasing belief in his talent were two reasons for keeping the Russian Ballet going – in the face of appalling difficulties – throughout the war. Another was that Stravinsky was composing *Les Noces*. So between the ages of eighteen and twenty-two Massine, under the eye of Diaghilev, created his finest works. Then the time came when, like Nijinsky, he was attracted by a woman, and, like Nijinsky, he was sent packing. His dismissal took place in Rome in January 1921. Within a month Diaghilev had adopted a new 'son'. Boris Kochno was neither a dancer nor a choreographer: but he became Diaghilev's secretary and the librettist of his ballets.

As a youth in Moscow, during the First World War and throughout the Revolution, Boris Kochno had been fascinated by what he heard of Diaghilev's company – that Russian Ballet which never performed in Russia; and Boris used to cut photographs of Diaghilev out of the newspapers. When his school, the Lycée Impérial, was closed in 1917 he was at a loose end. A year or two after this, as he wandered the streets of Moscow, he came upon the nationalized collection of the merchant Shchukine. Staring at Picasso's cubist portrait of Vollard, he longed more than ever to see the work of Diaghilev's troupe, a company which could commission such an artist as Picasso to design its scenery. When Boris and his mother reached Paris *via* Constantinople in October 1920, he made friends with the painter Sudeikine, who had worked for Diaghilev in 1913, and with his wife Vera (later Mme Stravinsky). That December the Diaghilev Ballet were in Paris for a season at the Théâtre des Champs-Elysées, and were giving Stravinsky's *Le Sacre du printemps* (henceforward referred to as *The Rite of Spring*). As no one could remember the original choreography of Nijinsky, who had gone mad two years before, Leonide Massine had devised a new version, the staging of which was subsidized by the dressmaker Chanel. Boris saw this, and the dancing of the English-born Lydia Sokolova as the Chosen Virgin in *The Rite* was a landmark in his life, just as Picasso's portrait of Vollard had been.

During February 1921,* while Boris sat to Sudeikine for his portrait, the two of them worked out a plan for him to go to Diaghilev's hotel on the pretext of bearing a message from the painter. Neither man knew that the jealous Diaghilev had quarrelled with and dismissed Massine in Rome a month before. On the morning of Sunday, 27 February 1921 Boris arrived at the Hôtel Continental, and to his surprise was told to go straight upstairs. Diaghilev had been expecting someone else, who never turned up. Within two days Diaghilev invited the sixteen-year-old Boris to be his secretary. What would be his duties, the young man asked. '*Il faut qu'un secrétaire sache se rendre indispensable.*' Boris was never paid, but Diaghilev lodged and fed him at the

* Mrs Stravinsky swears she shaved Boris that Sunday morning.

Boris Kochno. Drawing by Pablo Picasso, c. 1924.

finest hotels in Europe, and dressed him at the best English tailors. He did not mind asking Diaghilev, from time to time, for a few francs to buy cigarettes. Kochno was not attracted by young men and he was prepared to love Diaghilev: but, although he was handsome in a classical way, he was not Diaghilev's type. As friends, however, they got on very well and remained inseparable.

Diaghilev was still without a choreographer, and he staged Petipa's old four-act classical ballet *The Sleeping Beauty*, to the unfashionable music of Tchaikovsky, in London. This nearly ruined him. His company was saved from destitution by an arrangement to perform in Monte Carlo for several months a year. Bronislava Nijinska, who had come out of Russia, was taken on as Diaghilev's choreographer, and before she left at the end of 1924 had created more than one outstanding ballet for the company. It was during her regime that the (partly Irish) Englishman Anton Dolin (*né* Patrick Kay) was sent to Diaghilev from a Russian dance studio in London and promoted at once to leading roles. Then Balanchine came from Russia and was choreographer in charge until Diaghilev's death. Diaghilev forgave Massine in time, as he had forgiven Nijinsky, and invited him more than once to return as guest-choreographer. Another Russian emigré, Serge Lifar, a pretty, lively boy, set out to replace Dolin in Diaghilev's affections, and succeeded: and the latter built him up, with Balanchine's help, to be the company's star, as he had built up Massine and Dolin before him. Less than a year before his death Diaghilev fell in love with the sixteen-year-old music student, Igor Markevitch, and had him play his Piano Concerto at Covent Garden. Throughout these changes of choreographer, principal dancer and favourite in the 1920s, Kochno remained Diaghilev's closest artistic collaborator and friend.

At the end of his last Paris season in June 1929, and again after his final London season in July, Diaghilev, whose body was covered in sores, was warned by his Paris doctor that he had diabetes. Insulin had been discovered, but was hard to come by. The Ballet were to dance in Vichy before going on holiday, and the doctor said this was just the place for his patient to rest and take care of himself: but immediately on leaving the consulting-room Diaghilev went to order his tickets for a trip to the music festivals at Baden-Baden, Munich and Salzburg, and he set off to meet his beloved Igor

23

Markevitch in Basle next day. Meanwhile Boris went to Toulon with the son of his half-sister. Telegrams began to arrive for him from Diaghilev, who was by then in Venice. The third read: 'Am ill. Come at once.'

On 16 August, as he travelled eastward, Boris hoped that in spite of Diaghilev's message, all might yet be well and life might take its course as on other happy summer visits to Venice, when so many ballets had been planned at leisure. Would not Diaghilev be waiting for him as usual at the station, fanning himself with his straw boater? He was not. Boris was met by a man from the Grand Hôtel des Bains de Mer, who took him by motorboat to the Lido. Serge Lifar was at the landing-stage.

As Boris entered Diaghilev's bedroom Diaghilev was talking to an Italian doctor, and seemed hardly to recognize him or to notice his arrival. Diaghilev later complained that the doctor had no idea what was the matter with him and merely returned to watch him getting worse and worse.

On the morning of the seventeenth Boris found Diaghilev 'smiling in bed, gay'. He spoke of his happy excursion with Markevitch, and said how overwhelmed he had been by Wagner's greatness and the performance of *Tristan* in Munich. He insisted that Boris was to get down to work at once on his libretto for the new Markevitch ballet. It must be unlike any other. '*L'Habit du roi* must inaugurate that new departure in the theatre which we talked about so much in London.' It was a day of dawning possibilities. The sunny room seemed to create an atmosphere of convalescence. In the evening Diaghilev said 'I have left 60,000 *lire* (then about £650 or $3150) in the *caisse*. It is the money for our summer holiday. Bring it to me. Here is the receipt.' When Boris returned and put the money on the bed, Diaghilev said 'Now go down and deposit it in your name. God knows what may happen to me.' (Boris later divided this money with Lifar.) While Boris was out of the room Diaghilev had a visit from Misia Sert, his dearest friend, and Coco Chanel, who were

24

cruising on the Duke of Westminster's yacht. That night Boris decided to give Lifar a rest and sleep in an armchair in the sick man's room. But Diaghilev did not sleep. He passed the night in a state of extreme agitation, alternately hot and cold, and complained continually of draughts.

On the morning of the eighteenth, Diaghilev was calm but weaker. He spoke not of work, but of rest. 'We'll go to Sicily. I'll get better next week and we'll go to the south of Italy.' Later that day a nurse was fetched. Diaghilev's fever had increased. He lay on his back with his eyes closed, breathing with difficulty. The nurse said, 'He will last till dawn.' Boris telephoned to Misia, who was sitting fully dressed in her drawing-room at the Danieli. Diaghilev groaned, and sweat poured from his forehead as he seemed to struggle with a giant seated on his chest. The doctor put away the thermometer. Misia summoned a priest. Diaghilev's breathing grew calmer and he ceased to struggle. The nurse was packing. Now the breath came too faintly, and after a long silence Boris knew that he would hear it no more. It was six o'clock in the morning.

Was Diaghilev irreplaceable? Although people outside his organization were aware that the man who harnessed such diverse talents to bring them yearly '*un frisson nouveau*' must have a magic touch, they cannot have known exactly what he did. Members of the company understood how everything depended on Diaghilev's decisions and on his drive: but even they took the process of combination and creation for granted. They knew from their salaries how small was Diaghilev's budget, but as he hid his financial anxieties from them few can have guessed what a tight-rope he had been walking for twenty years. One thing clear to every dancer was that even Diaghilev could not have remained in business without a choreographer.

Diaghilev had been lucky in having a series of choreographers outstanding in their different ways, whose works remained in his repertory even after they had left him. In 1929 Fokine, whose *Les Sylphides, Prince Igor, Firebird* and *Petrushka* were still given, was in America, and seemed to have exhausted his creative impulse. Nijinsky, of whose few ballets only *L'Après-midi d'un faune* had survived, was mad. Massine, creator of *Contes russes, Les Femmes de bonne humeur, La Boutique fantasque* and *Le Tricorne*, was, like Fokine, in America at the time of Diaghilev's death. Bronislava Nijinska, choreographer of Stravinsky's great choral ballet *Les Noces* and Poulenc's *Les Biches*, was working in Paris. Balanchine, who had created Stravinsky's *Apollo* and Prokofiev's *The Prodigal Son*, was on holiday, like the rest of the troupe, but working on a film near London. Lifar had only been allowed to try his hand at arranging one short ballet, in the final season, and had shown no outstanding gift.

Kochno's function as Diaghilev's secretary and the librettist of some of his most successful later ballets might seem of slight importance: but this was far from being the case. He had been closer than anyone to the great impresario and entered into the secret processes of his mind. Diaghilev had latterly begun to refer to Boris as his successor, 'the Young Oak'. Boris had served his apprenticeship; and Grigoriev, Diaghilev's *régisseur*, who since 1909 had conducted rehearsals, maintained discipline, paid the dancers, moved them from place to place and controlled everything except the invention of new ballets, clearly thought that Boris, back in Paris from the Venice funeral, would take command. Grigoriev returned from Monte Carlo to Paris with his wife Tchernicheva, confident that the Russian Ballet would fulfil its contract with Barcelona in October, that Balanchine would continue as the company's choreographer, with Lifar as its leading dancer. There were Danilova and Doubrovska, Diaghilev's last St Petersburg-trained ballerinas; the Pole Woizikovsky, who danced all Massine's former roles, and his English-born girl-friend Lydia Sokolova as chief character dancers; and the nineteen-year-old Alicia

Markova, a former infant-prodigy, also English by birth, who was almost ready to take over leading classical roles. It was Danilova who described to me in later years how Boris Kochno, with his good manners, patience and tact, had always been 'the peacemaker'. With Diaghilev dead, Kochno's vocation was to carry on his work.

Yet to the public the name of Boris Kochno was hardly known. Serge Lifar was the star of the Russian Ballet; and he was as ambitious as it is possible to be. In October 1929 he took advantage of his celebrity to insist that he should be co-director with Kochno of the reconstituted company. This might sound logical to the world at large, but it was for the other principal dancers of the troupe to decide whether it was a practical solution. They had watched Diaghilev's systematic building-up of his former favourite's reputation; they knew how Lifar had been given a short cut to fame; they had observed the skill with which Balanchine had created roles wherein Lifar's physical glamour could be shown to advantage in spite of his limited technique; and they had long suspected – correctly – that when Lifar was smothered in flowers or crowned with laurels before the crimson curtains it was Boris, more often than not, who had been sent out to buy these in Les Halles or in Covent Garden. Grigoriev's discussions with the other members of Diaghilev's troupe took several days. All the dancers he consulted refused to serve under Lifar. The latter was furious, but to save his face agreed to sign with Kochno a circular letter to the dancers announcing the closure of Diaghilev's company.

So what was to happen? Kochno and Lifar, who were almost the same age, did not like each other, but they depended to some extent on each other, just as, if a new company were formed, they would depend on the choreographer Balanchine. While Lifar could obviously count on getting work, Kochno was without a job. He was also without money, since Diaghilev had never paid him a salary. Boris continued to think out roles for Serge – there was the project for a spoken, mimed and danced version of *Hamlet*; and Serge bought from the penniless Boris a number of designs for ballets by the most distinguished artists of the day, which they or Diaghilev had given him. Unlike Lifar, Boris had the instincts of a real collector: he coveted works of art, and he gloated over those he managed to acquire during nine unpaid years with Diaghilev. It was painful to him to be obliged to give them up.*

Boris Kochno took the curious step of a man at a turning point in his life, a man in doubt or desperation who goes into the wilderness to think. He booked a room at the Hôtel de la Poste at Joinville, a suburb beyond the Bois de Vincennes, four kilometres outside the perimeter of the capital. Like the hero of a Romantic novel he spent his days there asleep, then travelled nightly into Paris, to wander about the streets alone – Edgar Allan Poe's 'Man of the Crowd' – until it was time to catch the first train back at dawn.

One night, near the Place Pigalle at Montmartre, Boris saw what he once described to me as *'un grand garçon rose'*, coming towards him. This plump young man with a pink complexion was the painter Christian Bérard, whom Kochno knew only slightly. Instead of expressing the usual polite condolences on the death of Diaghilev, Bérard spoke so understandingly about him, and about work, art and life in general, that he and Boris suddenly became close friends. Throughout the night the two men walked the streets of Paris, which was transformed for Boris, in the light of this new friendship, into an enchanted city. They parted at the Gare de la Bastille at six in the morning.

Jacques Rouché, Director of the Paris Opéra, had invited Balanchine to arrange a ballet to Beethoven's *Les Créatures de Prométhée*, which would be danced by Serge Lifar and Olga

---

* Lifar rubbed out the artists' inscriptions to Boris on the sketches he bought. It can be observed today, for instance, on the handsome design by Juan Gris for a Herald, made for the Fête de Versailles in 1924, how the pencilled signature alone remains. (This is at the Wadsworth Atheneum, Hartford, Connecticut.)

Spessivtseva. Two weeks after Balanchine began work on the ballet he developed pleurisy. When he showed signs of tuberculosis, it became clear that he could not finish the job, and he proposed to Rouché that Lifar should take over. Lying in bed, Balanchine explained to Lifar what he had worked out and how the ballet must be completed. It was agreed that Lifar should have the credit as choreographer while Balanchine kept the fee, which he needed to pay the bill of the sanatorium to which he was going in Haute Savoie. Lifar would, of course, be well paid for dancing in the ballet. The first night of *Les Créatures de Prométhée* passed off successfully on 30 December 1929. Shortly after Balanchine returned to Paris, with health improved, Serge Lifar was appointed ballet master of the Opéra.

Georgi Balantchivadze, whose name Diaghilev had simplified to George Balanchine, was a curiously quiet, composed and self-contained character. He was devoid both of Russian ebullience and Georgian swagger. His absorption in the dance and in music was total; and his double experience as dancer and musician had endowed him with an ability to relate one art to the other with a subtlety which appeared uncanny. From time to time he fell in love with a girl dancer, whom he moulded and for whom he created ballets. These romantic passions seldom brought him fulfilment, but they left the world richer. He adapted himself mildly to the vicissitudes of life, neither unduly depressed by hardship nor exalted by success.

In the autumn of 1931 René Blum, representing the Monte Carlo theatre, asked Balanchine to form a company which would give regular April seasons in the principality, as Diaghilev's had done from 1924 until 1929. This arrangement had afforded Diaghilev the leisure to evolve new works at Monte Carlo and the freedom to show them in Paris, London and elsewhere during the rest of the year. Balanchine had found two remarkable thirteen-year-old girls in the Paris dancing school of Preobrajenska, the expatriate Russian ballerina. He asked Boris Kochno to work with him. Boris saw the hope of a new start; and with Blum's business manager Vassili Vosskrezensky, who called himself Colonel de Basil, he signed a contract as artistic director. He set to work and devised four new ballets. For *Jeux d'enfants*, to Bizct's suite, he invited Massine to make the choreography. He first asked Giacometti to design this, then, when the sculptor refused, turned to the Catalan painter Mirò. The other three works were all by Balanchine. Boris had just heard the music of *Le Bourgeois Gentilhomme* by Richard Strauss, and he had it played to the choreographer. For this Alexandre Benois designed the décor. Georges Auric had already been commissioned by Blum to compose the score for *Concurrence*, for which Boris invited Derain to provide sketches. Several piano pieces by Emmanuel Chabrier were orchestrated by Vittorio Rieti to make up *Cotillon*, and this was designed by Christian Bérard. The company, with Grigoriev as *régisseur* and with its new repertory, was acclaimed in Monte Carlo during March and April, then opened at the Théâtre des Champs-Elysées in Paris in June. All four of the new ballets were successful, but *Le Bourgeois Gentilhomme* fell victim to the wrath of Richard Strauss, whose permission to use the music nobody had remembered to ask, and it was never given after the Paris season.

Vosskrezensky-de Basil had decided to take over control of the Ballets de Monte Carlo from the easy-going René Blum. He had a persuasive way of making people sign documents. One day Blum remarked to Balanchine, 'De Basil has just bought my car from me with my own money.' Moreover de Basil aimed at making the company popular with a larger public than that of *le tout Paris*, which Kochno, like Diaghilev, was above all anxious to surprise and delight: and he correctly diagnosed that the secret of box-office success was a staple diet of old favourites. After Diaghilev's death the American impresario Ray Goetz had bought all Diaghilev's stock-in-trade, his décors, costumes and musical scores, with the intention that he and Massine should carry on the Russian Ballet: but the Wall Street crash had put a stop to the project. De Basil arranged to buy these properties and to take on Massine, who was more famous both as choreographer and dancer than Balanchine, as ballet master to the company. In June, during the Paris season, Balanchine was dismissed; and Kochno, finding himself cold-shouldered, resigned.

Ten friends, among whom were Chanel and Cole Porter, gave 10,000 francs each so that Kochno and Balanchine could form a new company. The dark beautiful girl, Tamara Toumanova and a few other dancers left the Blum-de Basil troupe to work with Balanchine: the other child-ballerina, blonde Irina Baronova, remained behind. In an atmosphere of poverty and hope a new repertory was rehearsed. The ideas of Kochno and Balanchine were inexhaustible. Sauguet and Derain would work together on *Fastes*; Milhaud and Derain on *Songes*; Christian Bérard would design Tchaikovsky's *Mozartiana*. There was no money left for a theatre. Marie-Laure de Noailles, who with her husband Charles had assumed the leading position in the social world of Paris which had been held in the days of Diaghilev and Proust by Edith and Etienne de Beaumont (the latter being Radiguet's Comte d'Orgel), stepped into the breach. '*Tout va s'arranger*,' she told Kochno. '*Viens déjeuner*'. She invited him to meet a rich, original young Englishman, Edward James, who was a patron of the Surrealist painters, and who himself behaved in a surrealist manner. He established Les Ballets 1933, whose name hardly guaranteed longevity. He was married, rather surprisingly, to the pretty Viennese dancer Tilly Losch, whose speciality was to control trailing draperies. After the adoption of the new company by James two new ballets were planned to enlarge the repertory. Boris gave James the idea of *Les Sept Péchés Capitaux* (The Seven Deadly Sins), for which Bertolt Brecht and Kurt Weill, refugees from Hitler, were to provide words and music, and which would be danced by Tilly Losch and sung by Weill's wife, Lotte Lenya;

and Pavel Tchelitchev, who had designed *Ode* for Diaghilev in 1928, was to design *Errante*, which Balanchine would arrange to Schubert's *Wandererfantaisie*, orchestrated by Koechlin, for Tilly Losch.

In the spring of 1933, while Kochno and Balanchine were rehearsing their programme for Edward James's Ballets 1933, and the Ballets de Monte Carlo, with Massine now as ballet master, were about to follow their Monte Carlo season with one at the Châtelet in Paris before going on to London, Lincoln Kirstein, a young American, fresh from Harvard, where his literary magazine *Hound and Horn* had caused a stir, loomed shyly in the studios and drawing-rooms of Paris. His German–Jewish grandfather, a lens-grinder in Iena, had emigrated to America; his father had made a fortune and was director of Filene, a department store in Boston. Lincoln had been spellbound by the Diaghilev Ballet, which he had seen on visits to Europe in the 1920s, and had even been in Venice at the time of Diaghilev's funeral. He was wondering whether to be a writer or a painter, but he had also half formulated the idea of establishing the classical ballet in America. Anxious by whatever means to get his foot in the door of the ballet world, he had made friends in New York with Romola Nijinsky, wife of the sick Vaslav, and undertaken to help her write a book about her husband. He arrived in Paris in her wake, with several half-finished chapters of the biography in his luggage.

Romola, the daughter of a Hungarian nobleman and of Hungary's greatest actress, had been a pampered child. From her bohemian home, a hive of luxury, debts and celebrities, she had emerged in 1913, fascinating and wilful, to lay siege to Diaghilev's inaccessible favourite, Nijinsky, and had succeeded, in Diaghilev's absence, in marrying him. How her hopes of becoming a queen of international society (and outshining her famous mother) were dashed by Diaghilev's dismissal of Nijinsky, by the latter's inability to run a company of his own, and then – although the war brought a reunion between Diaghilev and her husband – by the madness which overcame Nijinsky in 1918, is a story too well known to need repeating here. Romola wanted money to support her husband in a sanatorium and, being accustomed to luxury, she wanted it to pay her bills in the best hotels. She was a lesbian, and had recently arrived in New York, with the coffined body of a Swedish girl-friend. She looked to Hollywood to make her fortune; and she regarded the book, which she was glad to have Kirstein to help her write, as the raw material for a film, which would solve all her problems. (She was not the only member of her family to suffer from a kind of megalomania. Her elder sister Tessa, on the strength of some expedition of an explorer uncle, called herself Princess of Madagascar.) Romola liked publicity for its own sake, but also as a means towards squeezing a living out of society. She was at that time a keen spiritualist and through her medium, Mrs Garrett, claimed to receive guidance – as well as missing information for her Life of Nijinsky – from a 'contact' in the next world called Little Blue Bell.

In Paris, Kirstein's American friends introduced him to at least one former member of Diaghilev's circle, the painter Pavel Tchelitchev, who was working on *Errante* for Edward James. On 15 June 1933 Kirstein wrote in his diary: 'I am undetermined as to whether to go off to Holland and help Romola finish her biography, or stay here and somehow insert myself into a situation with Kochno–Balanchine, but there's small chance of even approaching them.' It was in London, where Les Ballets 1933 at the Savoy Theatre proved quite unable to hold their own against the Monte Carlo Ballet at the Alhambra, that Lincoln Kirstein met George Balanchine at last. On 11 July 1933, at the rented house of a New York picture dealer, the American amateur tackled the Russian professional in the kitchen. 'He said he would like to come to America . . . seemed intense, concentrated, disinterested: not desperate exactly, but without any hope. I like to imagine we got on well; he said nothing about meeting again.' Yet meet again they did; and Kirstein began cabling his plans to America and trying to raise money from his friends.

On 19 July Gollancz accepted Romola's book, the finishing of which Kirstein handed over to Arnold Haskell. Balanchine lunched with Kirstein and Romola and pored over a big map of America. Romola had it on absolute authority from the medium Mrs Garrett that Balanchine would die within three years. 'However,' wrote Lincoln Kirstein in his diary, 'much can be done in three years.' When Les Ballets 1933 petered out Toumanova and her inseparable mother rejoined the Ballets de Monte Carlo. Kochno found himself out of work again. He returned to life in Paris with Bérard.

On 18 October 1933 Balanchine arrived in New York.

Balanchine's School of American Ballet opened in a studio on Madison Avenue, New York, in January 1934. With money from his father and from the father of a college friend, Lincoln Kirstein managed to pay the rent. It was the inconspicuous beginning of a great enterprise. Kirstein already dreamed of an American ballet company. In March, using as many students as turned up on successive days for his classes, Balanchine made his first American ballet, *Serenade*, to Tchaikovsky's 'Serenade for Strings'. Meanwhile de Basil's company had followed up their London success with a New York début at the St James Theater; and Massine's first 'symphonic ballet', *Les Présages*, to Tchaikovsky's Fifth Symphony, seemed to have made history on both sides of the Atlantic. Yet today (1982) *Les Présages* is forgotten, and *Serenade* is given by companies throughout the world.

After my first term at Balliol (during winter 1934–5) I was spending the vacation with my grandparents at Iffley outside Oxford. It was then that I met my first dancer. Living in Oxford was a White Russian photographer, Cyril Arapoff, whom I had run into and made friends with at an exhibition of his work at Ryman's gallery in the High. He was the first

34

real 'bohemian' I ever got to know. He had no sense of money
or time, was often drunk and often in despair: but Cyril was
a true artist. He taught me to look at photography with a
more discerning eye and we got on like a house on fire. It was
he who told me that Anton Dolin, whom Diaghilev had
loved briefly and made his principal dancer in 1924, was
appearing in a revue called *King Folly* at the New Theatre,
and he took me round in the interval to meet him. Pat Dolin
was glad to have an enthusiastic young undergraduate to
talk to and I was thrilled by his rendering of a dance to Ravel's
nightmare 'Bolero' – an endurance test at least. He was returning to London that night – in a huge cream-coloured
car borrowed from Lillian Harvey, star of the film *Congress
Dances* – and we went first to drink coffee with the Narish-
kines at Headington. Then, instead of dropping me at my
grandparents' house at Iffley, as had been planned, Dolin
swept me up to London, where I was obliged to stay the night
at the slightly raffish Mount Royal hotel, since demolished,
near Marble Arch. On my return to Oxford by train next
morning, I found my grandmother in a terrible state, and my
grandfather, who had informed the police of my disappearance, standing angrily on the doorstep.

After my three terms (only) at Oxford I was installed at
Violet Kinnaird's house in Regent's Park to attend an art
school, and I began to go regularly to the ballet. I became
familiar with the old favourites of the Diaghilev repertory,
'plugged' by de Basil, who had bestowed on the Ballets de
Monte Carlo his own fictitious name. By 1936 René Blum,
his former employer, had assembled a new Monte Carlo
company. That summer I saw the first performance of
Massine's *Symphonie fantastique* (de Basil) at Covent Garden
and Fokine's *L'Epreuve d' amour* (Blum) at the Alhambra. The
Berlioz symphony was designed by Christian Bérard and the
two best movements – the ballroom, with its whirl of white
dancers against scarlet arches, and the pastoral, with its broken
aqueduct in a nacreous Campagna, were also those whose

music most enchanted me. In his curtain speech Massine, wearing a green velvet 1830 coat, said, 'This is the happiest night of my life.' In Fokine's ballet, which was one of his few successful creations since he left Diaghilev in 1914 and which had a newly discovered score by Mozart and a fine *chinoiserie* décor by Derain, Vera Nemtchinova was the Mandarin's tiptoeing daughter and André Eglevsky as her poor lover had a grotesque role which suited him exactly. I was a warm admirer of the burly yet elegant Eglevsky, famous for his interminable slow *pirouettes*, and when I made friends with him and drew his portrait he used to tell me about rehearsals with Fokine. When André was learning the role of Negro Slave in *Scheherazade*, Fokine explained, 'He is glad of himself.' On the first night that André danced the Chief Warrior in *Prince Igor*, Dennis Stoll conducted the music so slowly that Fokine rushed down the central aisle and tried to snatch the baton from him. There was quite a struggle. A brief paean I wrote in praise of Eglevsky was accepted by the *Dancing Times*.

I should not have been able to afford to go to the ballet so often had it not been for Edalji Dinshaw, a handsome Parsee who had been at Oxford with me and who used to buy stalls almost nightly during the season. Edalji took ballet classes with Stanislas Idzikovsky, a former Diaghilev star, and aspired to be a dancer, though he confided in me that his arms were so weak he could never hope to support a ballerina. Why he could not have done exercises to strengthen them I do not know: but this was typical of his fatalistic attitude to life. I think Edalji saw himself as doomed – to dance without a future; to love without being loved in return; to fade overnight like a lotus, leaving no trace behind. He was indeed destined to die of vanity. I used to draw during Idzikovsky's classes in his studio above the motor-car sale-rooms of Great Portland Street. 'Stas' was Polish and in the years following the First War had been, as the partner of Lydia Lopoukhova, the toast of London. They danced the

Tamara Toumanova in Kochno's and Balanchine's *Cotillon*, with music by Chabrier and décor by Christian Bérard. Photograph by Merlyn Severn, c. 1937.

Bluebird *pas de deux* together in Diaghilev's *Sleeping Princess* at the Alhambra in 1921; and, before that, Massine had created for Stas little roles such as the Cat in *Contes russes*, Battista in *The Good-humoured Ladies*, the Snob in *La Boutique fantasque* and the Dandy in *Le Tricorne*, in which his amazing technique and quirky personality made up for his lack of inches. Had he not been so tiny he might have become in more ways than in mere physical skill the successor of Nijinsky. 'Might have' – but his low stature had given him such a complex that he appeared incredibly conceited: he had made a scene and walked out on Diaghilev more than once. His English girl-friend, faithful to him since his arrival in England from Poland in 1914, and who had joined Diaghilev with him a year later, taking the name of Wanda Evina, had been the original American Child in *La Boutique fantasque*. She played the piano for Idzikovsky's classes. The affectation of this sweet-natured Yorkshirewoman was to be as Russian as possible, while her lover (accepted as her husband) tried to be sporting and

English. Smiling and dapper in his natty suit, with a double-breasted waistcoat, watch-chain and tie-pin, the diminutive snub-nosed virtuoso, now a famous teacher and the heir of Maestro Cecchetti, asked in his reedy voice, 'Well, old boy, is Oxford going to win the boat-race?': while, at the piano, Evie, daintily got up, 'with a rose pinned neatly', and putting so much expression into her standardized accompaniment that her ear-rings danced to and fro, signalled tragically to me with her eyebrows that this was not as it had been in the days of Diaghilev.

Although Edalji and I often went to the ballet alone or with his sisters, he would sometimes invite Stas and Evie to come too. Dining at Claridge's or seated in the stalls at Covent Garden, we must have looked an unusual group. The outrageously scented Edalji, with his magnolia complexion, plucked eyebrows and carved emerald rings could make even a dinner jacket by Huntsman of Savile Row look like fancy dress. Idzikovsky's Polish pallor was of a more insipid kind, and his dinner jacket was part of him, like a doll's. Evina had applied just a little too much rouge. As for myself, I am not sure if it was already evident that I was hardly 'the best type of Englishman'. One night I saw my rather humourless Aunt Judith Thornton staring at us across the *foyer* at Covent Garden in a way that left no doubt she had come to her own conclusions.

On Sunday nights there were performances of Marie Rambert's Ballet Club at the little Mercury Theatre near Notting Hill Gate, which was not hard to fill: but Sadler's Wells, where Ninette de Valois's young company performed twice a week at the most during their intermittent seasons, was often half empty. Here I saw the first – or early – performances of several ballets that became famous: de Valois's *Rake's Progress* and *Checkmate*, Ashton's *Apparitions*, *Nocturne*, *Les Patineurs*, and *A Wedding Bouquet*. Edalji and I argued about the respective merits of Robert Helpmann and Harold Turner: Edalji admired Helpmann for his subtle artistry, while

I spoke up for Turner's ebullience and strong *pirouettes*. We watched the rising star of Margot Fonteyn. Though English choreographers and at least one dancer of genius were flowering, watered by their long-sighted gardeners, Rambert and de Valois, British ballet could not compete before the war with the visiting Russian companies.

Since I saw no other way of becoming Diaghilev's successor, which is what I should have loved to be, I aimed to become a ballet designer. At my art schools I neglected my drawing from life to sketch settings and costumes for imaginary ballets, or to make new and 'better' designs for ballets I had seen on the London stage.

If there had been anyone whose advice I was prepared to take, an older man on the same wave-length, I might have had guidance as to how to become a proper stage designer. If John Bryson, who had lectured me on Anglo-Saxon at Oxford, and with whom I had felt an affinity, had already been as close a friend as he became later, he might have said to me: 'Listen, you must study perspective, architecture, the history of painting, and the different schools of design – Islamic, eighteenth-century French, Robert Adam, William Morris; you must learn to draw; you must immerse yourself in the history of the theatre; you must be prepared to serve several years of rigorous apprenticeship'. Then I might indeed have turned out a stage designer of consequence. But there was no one. Indeed, I wonder if I should have taken the good advice even had there been the right person to give it, for I had not acquired the habit of hard work. Would the Slade or the Royal College have set me on the right path? I think there was nothing then comparable to the Department of Stage Design which flourished at the Slade in the 1960s and 1970s under Nicholas Georgiadis. Did I really believe that the crude sketches I produced were evidence of a born genius to whom solid work was unnecessary? The slapdash manner in which some of Diaghilev's great painters indicated on paper their

39

ideas for stage sets and costumes had misled me. I had made friends with the photographer Gordon Anthony, Ninette de Valois's brother, and in his studio opposite South Kensington Station he introduced me to that autocratic lady, and I showed her my designs. She was not impressed. In the same studio, which had once been Millais's and the photographer Hoppé's (and it may have been there that Hoppé photographed my mother in 1917), I first met Margot Fonteyn.

In the summer of 1938, when I had just returned from a brief abortive stay in Paris, during which I had not only failed to make any impression with my textile and fashion designs, but caught clap and fallen in love, the growing tribe of English balletomanes enjoyed the exceptional luxury of having de Basil's 'Russian' company at Covent Garden simultaneously with Blum's 'Russian' Monte Carlo company across the road at Drury Lane. Massine, whose Beethoven *Seventh Symphony* was danced by Markova and Youskevitch, was sueing de Basil for presenting his old ballets. Nemtchinova and Baronova alternated in the second act of *Swan Lake* at Covent Garden; Danilova and Toumanova danced it at Drury Lane. Then Lifar, whom I had already judged ridiculous on the stage of the Paris Opéra, came to Drury Lane to dance *Giselle* with Markova, and he was booed. This was either because of his exaggerated clutching and grimacing or because the gallery thought he was trying to steal Markova's curtain calls. Without Diaghilev to guide him he had allowed his personality to get out of control: yet his displays of Russian temperament seemed to delight the French.

Ballet-going in the 1930s could be combined with erotic adventures. Standing at the back of the circle at Sadler's Wells or of the Covent Garden gallery, I made a number of charming friends. The physical contiguity of close-packed balletomanes, as well as their shared enthusiasm, not infrequently led to lasting relationships.

On 22 May 1939 I decided on top of a bus to publish a ballet magazine; and the first very amateurishly edited number of this came out two months later. Old friends had been enlisted. Ronald Crichton, who had been at Oxford with me, wrote on music. I published photographs by Cyril Arapoff, who had introduced me to Dolin. Dolin contributed an article on Diaghilev's *Sleeping Princess* (of which the substance, I guessed, was supplied by his old crony Poppaea Vanda) which enabled him to get in a few cracks against Arnold Haskell. I cooked up an interview with Idzikovsky.

Some of the famous ballets with which I made acquaintance in those pre-war years later grew stale for me through too frequent repetition; others vanished from the repertory. One ballet never seen again after 1939 was *Cotillon*. Certainly no lack of merit caused its disappearance: but it has been said that the choreographer, Balanchine, who anyway prefers to regard ballets as ephemeral and cares little about prolonging their life, associates it so closely with the youth and beauty of Tamara Toumanova that he cannot bear to revive it. And perhaps it is because *Cotillon* has not been revived that it still seems so perfect in my mind. Sometimes one of Chabrier's short orchestral compositions or piano pieces which Rieti orchestrated specially for Kochno in 1932 – the 'Menuet Pompeux', the 'Marche Joyeuse', the 'Danse Villageoise' or, loveliest of all, the 'Idylle', which I later learned Poulenc had found as strangely affecting as I did – drifts from the radio, and I see the circling of those doomed butterflies again.

Like *Le Bal*, the slight libretto of which Boris Kochno had devised for Diaghilev in the last year of his life, *Cotillon* was on the surface merely a series of numbers, but the extent to which it became more than a *divertissement* was a measure of its author's art. There was no story, yet much happened; for Kochno knew that his work was not finished when a few words had been written on paper. He had learnt from Diaghilev that the flavour or atmosphere of a ballet depended on subtle juxtapositions, accents or eliminations, and on a pulling together of details at the last minute. It was this knowledge which made him the Shakespeare of the ballet scenario. When I first heard Chabrier's dance tunes I thought that one or two of them had the solemn, plaintive quality of a hymn. Today I reflect that Bérard's setting, which in the 1930s I merely admired for its simplicity and up-to-the-moment *chic*, was really very odd: for his high grey-and-white marbled walls, if they had not been pierced at the foot by boxes framed in stiff crimson drapery, would have been as anonymous as those of a bank. The plainness of this ball-room held a power of suggestion, like the ambiguous tent Bakst designed for *Carnaval*. How happily the girl, mirror in hand, prepared for her coming-out dance! Yet by the time we had witnessed the late arrival of the master of ceremonies, the introductions, the distribution of hats and guitars, the girl's disappointed search for a kindred spirit, episodes of drunkenness and vampirism, and a party game that ended badly, her happiness had turned into a kind of despair, which set her whirling at the heart of a maelstrom of dancers. We felt we had experienced as many conflicting emotions as Lensky at Mme Larina's, as Romeo, who had gone to the Capulets' party in pursuit of Rosaline, as Marcel at the house of the Princesse de Guermantes, or as François at the dinner when the good-mannered but insensitive Comte d'Orgel planned the *tableaux* for his ball.

When England went to war in 1939 the second number of my magazine was about to appear. Edalji made it possible for André Eglevsky to get a passage to America where, I think, his fine technique and undoubted virility set a standard of male dancing which was almost as important as – and fore-shadowed – that set by Nureyev twenty years later through-out the Western world. Colonel de Basil's company, by then renamed Original Ballet Russe, were subsequently obliged to tour first Australia, then Mexico and finally South America; while the former Blum company – without René Blum, who died in a German concentration camp – led by Massine and Danilova and still called Ballets Russes de Monte Carlo – perambulated the United States. Both these companies grew

less Russian as the years went by. Balanchine was in Hollywood, where he had turned his hand with ease to the arrangement of dances for musical films. (I had seen and loved his
Goldwyn Follies in Paris in 1938.) In occupied Paris Kochno
and his friend Christian Bérard lay low; while Lifar, who had
resolved that his Opéra Ballet must be kept going at all costs,
exposed himself, by suffering the patronage of Goebbels and
Hitler, to the inevitable fate of being called a collaborator
after the war. No Englishman has the right to judge whether
he did well or not.

In spite of the two pre-war numbers of *Ballet*, I had met
hardly any of the bearers of those famous names mentioned
above – not Massine, not de Basil, not Kochno, not Balanchine, not Lifar. I did somehow contrive an interview with
René Blum to show him my designs; and he was perfectly
charming. Eglevsky introduced me to Toumanova in her
dressing-room – and she opened her magnificent eyes very
wide and allowed me to bask briefly in their gaze. I told Vera
Nemtchinova how much I admired her *arabesque*. 'Yes, I
have very good *arabesque*,' she agreed. I got through to
Fokine on the telephone at the Waldorf Hotel to ask him a
few breathless questions: he sounded furious.

CHAPTER 2

An Idle Apprentice

Five years of war had hardly equipped me for life in London society, in the world of the arts or in the world of ballet. I had been an outsider in the army, and I was an outsider in the London of 1946. Almost my only link with the ballet community was Frederick Ashton. We had made friends on barstools during the blitz, when he wore RAF uniform.

Of my wartime friends Iain Moncreiffe, with whom I had shared the hardships and convivialities of winter 1943 north of Naples, remained constant. Realizing how limited was my acquaintance, he must have made a quiet resolution to include me in his busy London life and to introduce me to people who might be useful when I started my magazine *Ballet* again. This strategy, of which I was hardly conscious at the time, resulted in no social triumphs, for nothing could temper my shyness and awkwardness in society – and drink, which modified the former, accentuated the latter; but it was not wasted in professional circles, for Iain brought into my life at least two people who became close friends, Karsavina and Cecil Beaton.

I took lodgings in the Edgware Road; sought out the pre-war printers of *Ballet*; engaged a secretary for the magazine, Peggy Newman; and looked around me. During the war the Sadler's Wells Ballet had toured uncomfortably round the country and had held London seasons in defiance of German bombs. In the absence of 'Russian' companies, whose glamour in the 1930s distracted us from the achievements of these

44

natives in far-off Islington, the latter had become popular; and Lord Keynes, husband of Diaghilev's former ballerina, Lydia Lopoukhova, had installed them at the Royal Opera House, Covent Garden. Keynes had also founded the Arts Council, which grew to be the main support of so many national institutions, not least the Sadler's Wells Ballet and the new Covent Garden Opera, its fellow-occupant of the famous theatre under the administration of David Webster from Liverpool. The under-privileged troupe from Islington had become the Establishment. I was nothing to them and my two feeble pre-war numbers of *Ballet* magazine hardly entitled me to pipe up at Webster's first press conference to complain that he had not given me tickets for the great opening night of Sadler's Wells Ballet at Covent Garden on 20 February 1946; yet pipe up I did, and showed the chip on my shoulder. I never got my tickets, but Michael Wood, the newly appointed Public Relations Officer of the Sadler's Wells Ballet, took me under his wing and was a staunch friend for many years. I had known Michael, who had been a Grenadier, since Sandhurst days. His tall slender figure, clad in the most immaculately tailored suits, a billycock from Lock's, and shoes polished to shine like jet, could be seen moving at lunch time from the herbaceous hubbub of the Covent Garden Market to the eighteenth-century calm of Brooks's Club in St James's, accompanied by an almost invisible dog called Henry. Michael's well-kept moustache and temper gave Americans an impression – when the Ballet went over to win New York under the banner of Sol Hurok in 1949 – of the classic English gentleman; and when he was promoted to be General Manager of the Royal Ballet, as it had become in 1956, nobody did more to ensure its welfare and smooth running. It was he who proposed me for the job of ballet critic to the *Observer* in 1948.

Was Ninette de Valois, who had danced with Diaghilev from 1923 till 1925, destined to be the great Russian's successor? She had made far-reaching plans, she had established a school, and now that the Governors of Sadler's Wells had released her Ballet for Covent Garden she was to found a second younger company to perform and take part in opera performances at her old theatre. She had sat on committees; she had talked influential men into understanding her point of view and had obtained much of what she wanted from them. Now she had two theatres and a measure of national backing such as the Ishmael Diaghilev had never enjoyed; she had an English ballerina in Fonteyn, and in Frederick Ashton (released from the Royal Air Force) a choreographer who promised to be outstanding. Her troupe had been scorned in the thirties for being English not Russian, but she had turned this deficiency into a virtue. She had suffered from and fought against the English snobbery for things foreign: this had left her jealous of Diaghilev's legend. She remembered the inadequacies of his company in its latter days and his lack of understudies (which had once necessitated her 'helping him out' by rushing across Europe, when Sokolova was ill, to dance The Hostess in *Les Biches* for two performances). Of his post-*Sleeping Princess* period, 1922 to 1929, she said the only ballet worth reviving was Nijinska's *Les Noces*. This was an exaggeration.

De Valois was suspicious of 'critics'. She regarded me as a potential enemy, as an irresponsible amateur – which I was – whose judgement sometimes surprised her by coinciding with her own, and as a possibly demoralising influence on Fred Ashton, whose romanticism made him prone to hanker after alien gods. Nor was it in my favour that I had roped in the revered historian and bookseller Cyril Beaumont to write for *Ballet*, for he was always harking back to the great days of Diaghilev. When the designer Sophie Fedorovitch told me that Ninette had said of me, 'He's no fool,' I realized my prospects were improving. When Ninette and I began to lunch together in 1947 her longing to discuss her problems frankly (which I might have called 'girlish' if it were not exactly like my own) was held in check by fear of uttering a word that might be used in evidence against her. I submitted ideas for possible ballets to her, and as late as 1954 – although I had attacked her fiercely in the *Observer* and even, according to Osbert and Edith Sitwell, killed her colleague Constant Lambert by my harsh criticism of his *Tiresias* – she enlisted me at a time when she had to go into hospital as go-between with Osbert Lancaster, who was to make new designs for *Coppelia*. If she briefly considered me as an artistic collaborator on a more regular basis, she thought better of it: and by 1960, when I really had learnt something about the workings of ballet and might have been useful, it was too late, for I was installed – after a few years of 'giving up writing about ballet for ever' – at the *Sunday Times*, a 'critic' once more and consequently 'in opposition'.

Even though she had, as she liked to say, belittling her hard apprenticeship, 'danced on every pier in England', Ninette admitted that, as a child, when she and her family and friends had acted plays, she had tended to leave herself out of the distribution of roles as she felt 'someone must take control'. The exercise of this 'control' was said by close observers such as Margaret Power – an influential voice from 'the gods' and a haunter of dressing-rooms in the thirties – to have held back the full blooming of Fonteyn, whose early growth Ninette had so tenderly overseen. Being a 'lady' herself, daughter of an Anglo-Irish squire, Ninette encouraged reticence rather than 'temperament'. Fred Ashton was in awe of her: he knew she knew he was lazy, sociable and a dreamer, with a regrettable tendency to fall in love. Yet Fred, reared in the perfumed shadow of St Rose of Lima, then miserably transplanted to the rigours of Dover College and an office in the City of London, had shown the strength of character to break into the world of ballet. He had poetry, showmanship, theatricality, wit – a divine spark – and Ninette knew this too and backed him up during frequent spells of self-doubt when every morning seemed to him a black Monday. His early struggles had left him rather plaintive, but he was the life and soul of every party, famous for his imitations of Queen Alexandra and Isadora Duncan.

Ashton and I had much in common, and our gossipy suppers could have led to fruitful work together, but something about my character and something about his prevented this. Matters might have been different had I been older instead of younger than Fred. I had too many 'frightfully good ideas' which were destined to come to nothing; and I did not know enough about dancing or music to balance my poetical and visual day-dreams. When I urged on Ashton the engagement of a young French designer for his *Scènes de ballet*, the eccentricities, exigencies and inexperience of André Beaurepaire nearly led to disaster. I think Fred began to dread André's appearances; and at the dress rehearsal Ninette snapped at me, 'Now, don't *you* butt in: you've done enough damage already.' In 1949, when Ashton was planning to revive Delibes's *Sylvia*, I begged him to change the foolish mythological story into a charade played out in the period of the Second Empire, and to invite Jean Hugo (husband of my old girl-friend Lauretta Hope-Nicholson) to design it: but nothing came of this.

In 1926 Fred had been given his first chance as choreographer by Marie Rambert. This impetuous little Pole had been chosen by Diaghilev from the pupils of Dalcroze to help Nijinsky analyse the difficult score of Stravinsky's *The Rite of Spring* in 1913; but she had left the Russian Ballet before the year was out, settled in England and married the playwright Ashley Dukes. Then she had founded the Ballet Club, whose Sunday performances at the tiny Mercury Theatre at Notting Hill Gate I used to attend before the war. Ashton was only the first of her choreographers, for she became in turn the Muse of Antony Tudor, Andrée Howard, Walter Gore and Frank Staff, then in later years of Norman Morrice, John Chesworth and Christopher Bruce. Because Rambert's Ballet Club and her small post-war company were run on a shoe-string, and salaries were infinitesimal, her choreographers and dancers deserted her one by one. I admired her gift for animating, producing and drawing out her pupils, but when I expressed to Ashton my feeling that she had been badly treated in comparison with de Valois, he would point out that she had missed her chance in the late twenties by turning down the offer from Lilian Baylis to form a group of dancers to take part in plays and operas at the Old Vic. The chance had been seized and the offer taken up by Ninette de Valois.

Mim Rambert and I got along famously from the start. She had none of Ninette's reserve: she was the sort of warm-hearted, impulsive and confiding woman I could appreciate. Indeed, like Granny, she gave so free a rein to her self-expression that she could be called (in her own phrase) 'badly brought up', and accused (in the words of Karsavina) of 'going too far'. No critic could possibly equal Mim's own impassioned appraisals of her dancers, which were poured into my ear if I chanced to sit next to her during a performance. (Ninette, in similar circumstances, would have been tight-lipped. 'I'm not saying anything. You're a critic.') Even if Rambert's curtain speeches were too gushing – as my Granny's would have been, if I could imagine Granny on a stage – and her little runs and curtseys too arch, it was impossible for me to resist a woman who selected a phrase I had written to savour appreciatively, or who rang me up at midnight to declaim a Shakespeare sonnet.

Rambert's ambitions were selfish like those of a creative artist, like Diaghilev's. She wanted to see works of art take shape immediately before her eyes, and if she could not create them all on her own, anyone in whom she detected a ray of intelligence or hint of compliance – the man in the street, the woman she sat next to on a bus, a youth who yearned for dancing lessons – must be harnessed to her chariot and lashed onwards to the impossible goal. Ninette de Valois was an empire builder, Alexander: what Diaghilev had done was not nearly good enough for her, although she had quietly learnt what he had to teach. She wanted to establish an enduring dynasty. She combined the self-assurance of Queen Victoria with the doggedness of Florence Nightingale. It was only natural that the tentacles of her swelling enterprise should gather in one by one the choreographers and dancers whom Rambert had inspired and revealed to the world. Ninette could offer them larger stages and more regular employment – even pay them almost enough to live on. It seemed hard on Rambert at the time.

In early post-war days Rambert, desperate for backing, thought of me briefly as a potential fund-raiser. Had I not a house in Brompton? 'It is so much easier to ask for money for other people rather than for oneself' she said rightly: but my acquaintance among the rich was limited. On a mission to Leonide Massine, another and more internationally renowned heir of Diaghilev, who was appearing with Irina Baronova in a musical play in Liverpool, I improvised the idea that he might join forces with Rambert. Strange that it should have been among the blackened architectural fantasies of that city, in the dining-room of the Adelphi Hotel, outside which trams clanged and sirens hooted in the rain and fog, that I first looked into the inscrutable eyes of this famous man, who would become, in the course of years, almost a friend. After his wartime exile from Europe (and from his beloved home on those islands off the coast of the Sorrento peninsula which I had observed with interest during the war), Massine wanted nothing so much as a company of his own: so he was politely ready to negotiate. Rambert, however, knew very well that her troupe was not on the scale of Massine's ambitions; she feared his financial exactions; and she had no intention of abdicating to him her artistic control.

My magazine, with its neat appearance, served as a passport to the ballet world of Paris. I used to send it regularly to old Alexandre Benois. My first visit to this historic gentleman was in January 1947. Since I knew from his *Reminiscences of the Russian Ballet*, published in England in mid-war, how it was he who had first introduced the raw young provincial Diaghilev, two years his junior, to ballet, and that the success in St Petersburg of Benois' *Le Pavillon d'Armide* had been one of the reasons why Diaghilev had resolved to show Russian ballet in the West, I approached his home with reverent trepidation. It was a long trek out to Benois' studio in a gloomy district off the Quai de Javel, beyond the Eiffel Tower. The studio was vast, with an expanse of glass windows, a big work table and many portfolios of designs; and it was somehow divided by the barriers of bookcases and sofas and by the spiral staircase which led to the sleeping quarters (whither I never penetrated) into painting-room, sitting-room and library. I recorded our first meeting: 'Alexandre Benois, the father of modern ballet, received me at the door of his studio in a fur-collared overcoat and a blue knitted cap. Paris is short of fuel. "It was in your magazine that I first saw a photograph of the realization of the *Raymonda* designs I sent to America." He spoke of the ballet in Imperial Russia: "Guerdt [the original René in his first *Armide*] had a style and nobility which I have never seen since, although later dancers could boast a far more remarkable technique." Of the first production of *Le Spectre de la rose* – "Nobody wanted to do it. Fokine and Bakst were worn out with their other ballets that season, Nijinsky was tired . . ." He showed me sketches of a complete version of *Le Lac des Cygnes*, including a marvellous dappled dawn over the lake for the apotheosis. When I spoke of the future of ballet and speculated on the possibility of another golden age, he cried immediately, "*Il faut remonter* La Fille mal gardée." He explained to me how to get back to the centre of Paris by *métro*, and where to change trains, saying, "I shall give you the thread of Ariadne to lead you through the Labyrinth", and he handed me a *métro* ticket (which I shall always keep). Finally, a blessing – "*J'ai une grande sympathie pour votre revue*".'

That summer Benois came to see me in London, commented on the Italian baroque paintings and those of the Dutch Mannerists which I then collected, and recalled seeing a picture by Abraham Bloemaert hanging in a small hotel where he had stayed years ago near the church of St Mary, Wyndham Place. I visited him more than once during the next ten years. The old man was very bent, which accentuated his patriarchal aspect and made him appear all the more a benevolent magician. As I sat beside him on a formal French sofa he would pat my knee and sometimes, when he broke into English, would call me 'dear'. He always wore his wands of magical office – his pencils – in the breast pocket of his coat, as Fokine had noticed forty years before, 'signifying his immediate willingness to draw a bit of scenery or an architectural detail on any available piece of paper . . .'

In 1951 Benois painted me a Christmas card showing three mysterious characters from ballets he had designed. His inscription read: *Les trois Mages ayant d'autres obligations à remplir ces jours-ci, j'ai demandé à trois magiciens de mes amis de vous porter, cher Mister Buckle, mes meilleurs souhaits ainsi que l'assurance de ma très grande et sincère sympathie.* The three magicians, he went on to explain, in case I was in any doubt, were the Charlatan from *Petrushka*, Councillor Drosselmeyer from *Casse-Noisette*, and King Hydraot from *Le Pavillon d'Armide.* The first, with crafty eyes gleaming above his long white beard, brandished the flute with which to animate his puppets and charm the crowd; the second, patch over eye and parcel under arm, held up the big painted wooden nutcracker which would come to life and guide the child Clara through the snow kingdom to the land of gingerbread, sugarplums and candy; the third, with mantle, crown and staff, glanced sideways at the spectator, assessing his potential worth as a victim for the fair witch Armida. Did Benois see himself, as indeed I saw him, as one who, having learnt not the black arts but the crimson-and-gold trickery of these dead enchanters, brought them to life again in little watercolours of his own, and sent them forth through the fifth column of the world's theatres, to subject us by their potent spells until the end of time? Cocteau wrote of Diaghilev, '*Il avait beau chercher des mécènes, le mécène c'était lui*': and one might echo his paradox in writing of Alexandre Benois. To find a magician he only had to look in the glass. He seemed to me the ideal fairy godfather.

For a decade or more London was, or seemed to us to be, the capital of ballet: most of the world's principal ballet companies visited us, and we had a chance to decide which had inherited the pre-eminence that had once been Diaghilev's. All were either directed or influenced by men or women who had worked with him. Something of the excitement which I had found lacking in the Sadler's Wells Ballet was supplied by Les Ballets des Champs-Elysées, which broke out of long-occupied France to open at the Adelphi Theatre on 9 April 1946. This marked the renascence of Boris Kochno, whose alliance with the twenty-two-year-old choreographer Roland Petit, and whose use not only of Bérard but of other younger, eye-opening designers, was as exhilarating to me as must have been Diaghilev's presentation of Derain and Picasso to the war-weary London of 1919. I was excited too by the personality and dancing of faun-like Jean Babilée.

Then, on 4 July 1946, Ballet Theatre came from New York to Covent Garden. As early as 1940 Lucia Chase, a serious and able dancer as well as a rich woman (who tried to conceal her benefactions), had assembled a company which combined the best of the old world with the most promising elements of the new. Herself a pupil of Pavlova's one-time partner Mordkin, Lucia lassoed old Fokine and a series of fugitives from Hitler-threatened Europe – such as Rambert's thoughtful choreographer Antony Tudor, and the ex-Diaghilev dancers Alicia Markova and Anton Dolin, who had helped to draw audiences to the Sadler's Wells Ballet in its early difficult days – and she tried to make them all work together. To these she added the home-grown contributions of Agnes de Mille, Jerome Robbins and Michael Kidd. Her chief dancers were the Americans Nora Kaye and John Kriza, the Cuban Alicia Alonso and my old friend André Eglevsky, who was consequently the first I ever saw dance Balanchine's *Apollo*, which Colonel de Basil had been shy of including in his repertory. It was a remarkable troupe, of extraordinary range, but its very eclecticism proved a weakness, for the company lacked a unifying artistic policy and a single choreographer to give it style and direction.

When Serge Lifar brought a scratch troupe to the Cambridge Theatre on 17 July 1946, they had nothing of interest to offer except the lovely Yvette Chauviré and a few other fine dancers. Lifar had been 'purged', but he was back at the Opéra by September 1947 and remained there until 1958. I never admired the ballets I saw there on my visits to Paris, except for one or two which Balanchine was invited to stage. On 22 July 1947 Colonel de Basil brought to Covent Garden a company which bore the title of Original Ballet Russe: this was misleading, because in spite of a few faded replicas of Diaghilev's most popular old ballets, revived by Grigoriev, and the survival of Lichine and Riaboushinska from his pre-war company, his best young dancers were the French Jeanmaire and Franco-Russian Skouratoff. I got to know de Basil at this time and he brought me a huge salami for my birthday; but his most valued gift was a new great friend, John Taras, the ballet-master of Original Ballet Russe until it petered out later in the year. Taras, three years younger than I, was my first close American friend: we looked at life in a similar way and laughed at the same jokes. In 1948 he became ballet master to the Monte Carlo troupe, which the Marquis de Cuevas directed and which in 1951 took his name.

Another new company was the Festival Ballet, founded in London by Markova and Dolin in 1950, which built up a popular repertory and travelled more extensively in Britain and abroad than did Sadler's Wells. From 1949 onwards, however, the impresario Hurok, who controlled the USA ballet circuit, presented Sadler's Wells Ballet in New York and in other American cities, where they earned not only golden opinions but silver dollars. Then de Valois invited Balanchine to stage a ballet at Covent Garden: it was thus in 1950 that I got to know George Balanchine and Lincoln Kirstein. I had been exchanging intimate letters with Lincoln for a year before he came over to see how Balanchine's work was received at our Royal Opera House and to spy out the land for a visit of his own company; for I had asked him to write a criticism of Sadler's Wells in New York, and although he had understandably refused he wrote me his private thoughts at length, and we went on confiding in an almost involuntary way. He and Balanchine had endured many ordeals since the latter's crossing to America seventeen years before, and their latest company, which had evolved out of American Ballet, Ballet Caravan and Ballet Society, was called New York City Ballet and had recently staged Stravinsky's *Orpheus*. When Balanchine's (April 1950) production of *Ballet Imperial* for Sadler's Wells Ballet was followed at Covent Garden in August by the New York City Ballet's first season, I no longer had any doubt on whose shoulders the mantle of Diaghilev had fallen. In spite of my hitherto predominant interest in theatrical design Balanchine's stage, bare but for the dancers whom he had schooled to play every imaginable game to the music of Bach, Mozart, Tchaikovsky, Bizet and Stravinsky – except the too-obvious one of 'Follow My Leader' which Massine had attempted in his symphonic ballets – kindled in me such a blaze of glory that I was ready to sacrifice the invention, colour and pattern of all my favourite stage designers from Picasso to Bérard. Off with their heads! Lighting alone would suffice.

The School of American Ballet had produced a first generation of Russian-trained American dancers, among them Balanchine's then wife, the darting Firebird, Maria

Tallchief, and a future wife, the long-limbed, witty Tanaquil LeClercq. The company was still short of men (as was Sadler's Wells): but its growing fame over the following years would bring boys flocking to the School. The United States being so vast and so disunited, Kirstein's company could expect no federal subsidy, but it enjoyed a kind of municipal one in the form of the rent-free Mecca Temple, a shabby, inadequate old theatre on West 55th Street. The aesthetic Kirstein, who had given up almost all personal endeavours in the world of art in order to establish an arena for the genius of Balanchine, spent more time than he would have liked in the tedious pursuit of raising money. I was overwhelmed by his achievement and by the unlimited invention of Balanchine.

Lincoln, who had been since childhood in love with England and English history, knew I had served in the army, and I guess he had built up an heroic image of me which was bound to topple from its pedestal when we met. I was flabbier, boozier, lazier than he expected. I took my editorial duties too lightly, strove hardly perceptibly to master the technicalities of music and dancing, lay too long in bed. The showy *settecento* paintings of Pittoni and Sebastiano Ricci which covered the walls of my red drawing-room were to him symptoms of dire frivolity. (Alas, how rich I should be if I had them still!) Yet he had to admit I was funny, and although he often tried to 'give me up' he failed to disentangle himself for more than a year or two at a time from my persistent friendship, and our correspondence continued on and off for thirty years.

The entry of Andrew Sykes upon the stage of my life, which took place in 1937, has passed unremarked until now. Yet, had I not kept the spotlight off him, he would have been a conspicuous figure, not only because of our close friendship, but because of his great height and unusual character. Although Andrew's features were strongly marked, and his

George Balanchine. Drawing by Lucian Freud, 13 June 1952, made during the New York City Ballet's second London season.

high forehead had a projecting frontal bone over fine eyes, the space between his distinctive nose and his full lips was so great that it had to betoken some dire weakness, probably an excess of good nature or the inability to say No. His was the type of face which, seen above a crowd of heads in a pub at night, signalled to every villain within range that he was 'an easy touch', almost asking to be taken advantage of. I was one of those villains. Andrew and I had met, however, not in a pub, but at Heatherley's art school. The fact that he, who had no bent for drawing, painting or sculpture, should have been at an art school at all indicates the uncertainty of his vocation: and he had already proved his unfitness for work in the office of his father, a solicitor. After drawing a few caricatures of Marlene Dietrich with arched attenuated eyebrows and unnatural lashes – which is all he did at Heatherley's – Andrew settled down to learn the catering business, and at the time war broke out was running his own small country hotel in Sussex. In 1946 he put some money into Ballet Publications Ltd.

We are all composed of contradictory elements – for instance, I have always been both rash and timid, in disregard of the foolish Buckle motto, 'Nihil temere tenta nihil timide'. In Andrew Sykes the conflict between classic calm and turbulent romanticism, order and adventure, the City and the Sea, was unusually evident. This slow, hesitant creature, who began every sentence with 'Actually' to soften the blow, who took two hours or more to get up in the morning, and spent half a day in the kitchen preparing little snacks for old ladies he had invited to play bridge, yearned to be breasting the waves in the outposts of Empire on hulks of Britain's might. Indeed, when *Ballet* at last closed down, Andrew joined the Royal Fleet Auxiliary as a Ship's Writer (i.e. purser) and saw twenty years' service afloat. What is more, the gentle malleability which allowed him to be conned in pubs or robbed by me disappeared when he had a job to do in the Queen's service, and decisions to make. During the only day I spent with him on board one of his supply ships, moored at the time in Portland Harbour, it became clear to me that he kept firm control not only of the ship's accounts but also of the captain, officers and crew.

Chance had brought Andrew and me together – the utterly incongruous chance that he should have been sent to recover from an unhappy love affair at an art school where I just happened to be and at which he spent only one term: and laughter united us in friendship. We spent whole days laughing till tears poured down our faces. Women always struck Andrew as much funnier than men; he adored observing the self-sufficiency of cats; and he was for ever cutting out, neatly with nail scissors, snippets that amused him in *The Times*, which he read daily from cover to cover.

While I yearned in vain to devise, inspire or design ballets – as Lincoln Kirstein had yearned in 1933 – my magazine limped along. Everything was more difficult than before the war: paper and printing were dearer, advertising seemed impossible to sell. Every month Cyril Beaumont ground out his long pedestrian articles about the latest performances. He had no idea of being succinct, and he did not like to be cut. The fact that he covered the most important productions left me free to generalize or write nonsense in my editorials, which was a pity, for it would have been good for me to get my teeth into some solid criticism and formulate my standards. No one had ever taught me to organize my thoughts; the shallowness of my knowledge and limitations of my experience were all too obvious. Month by month, with the aid of the tall elegant Peter Williams, I put together and laid out the magazine. If my colleagues and I had been better critics and provided a core of more valuable commentary, my attempts to enlarge the horizons of ballet enthusiasts might have seemed less glaring irrelevancies. On the one hand, I scattered among the ballet photographs drawings by artists I admired, old engravings of circus performers or action photographs of airborne footballers cut from a popular paper: on the other hand, I took up a lot of space with learned and entertaining essays on Oriental rituals or Scottish ceremonies by such diverse scholars as Beryl de Zoete and Iain Moncreiffe.

Beryl, who lived with Arthur Waley, the revered translator of Chinese poetry and of Lady Murasaki's *Tale of Genji*, was my only link (apart from Duncan Grant and later Lydia Keynes) with Bloomsbury. With her stained ivory *netsuke* head, dyed fringe and clattering silver rings (one on every finger), she was an intense and possessive lady, a kind of intellectual Circe, whom many (including Edith Sitwell) found intolerable even before, in the late 1950s, she went round the bend. Yet her magic was not solely black, for when I had been posted abroad she had written in a copy of Arthur's *Monkey*, 'May *Monkey* keep you from harm,' and it had. She had amused me in a wartime letter by reporting how my old school-friend Derek Hill, who was a conscientious objector and worked on a farm, expressed his impatience at the slowness of our advance up Italy, complaining 'Why *can't* they get a move on!' With my naif eagerness to bring two disparate friends together I introduced Iain Moncreiffe to Beryl. How incongruous, this juxtaposition of the Scottish laird – a member of White's, Brooks's, Boodles' and The Turf, and who had just become engaged to Diana Hay, twenty-third Countess of Erroll, Hereditary High Constable of Scotland – with the Witch of Gordon Square! But Iain took Beryl quite seriously and was charming to her.

Beryl de Zoete wrote very well, in my opinion, but I am not sure whether she saw, as I did, the flicker of genius in Iain's witty expositions of ancient lore. I was proud to publish the articles of both friends, even if some readers of my magazine found them irrelevant. 'Tuesday, 2 April 1946. Iain calls office 6. To Yiddish play with Beryl, Arthur, Iain.'

If truth were told I took more interest in and was prouder of the drawings with which I embellished the pages of *Ballet* than of almost any article I published. Line drawings I valued higher than those in half-tone, and of course got most pleasure from those by artists I had commissioned. Although I reproduced existing works by acclaimed painters such as Picasso, Bérard, Hugo, Keith Vaughan or Robert Colquhoun, it was more of a feather in my cap if I could persuade the designer of a newly successful ballet or an admired artist to make some black-and-white drawings specially for me. Michel Larionov, Duncan Grant, Bernard Meninsky, Ceri Richards, Edward Burra, Leonard Rosoman, Cecil Beaton, Antoni Clavé, Léonor Fini and Tom Keogh were among those who obliged.

André Eglevsky introduced me to Larionov, Diaghilev's old colleague, in 1946, and my Nanny, on a rare visit to London, once slammed the front door of 6 Alexander Square (my first post-war home) in his face, thinking he was a beggar. Soon afterwards he sent me drawings done in the rehearsal room at Monte Carlo. I had met Duncan Grant on my first Channel crossing in 1931, and we had made friends in the shadier pubs of Soho during the war. I came to know Edward Burra, who designed several ballets for Fred Ashton and Ninette de Valois, through his devoted friend and dealer Gerald Corcoran, whose faith in Edward's talent won him in the course of thirty years the fame and prices he deserved. (A watercolour of Edward's which I bought from Gerald for £75 (about $300) in 1947, and which, alas! I was obliged to sell soon after, was worth £25,000 ($60,750) in 1980.) Cecil Beaton was one of the people Iain Moncreiffe brought into my life at a dinner party at the Tower of London, but although he made some pen-and-ink drawings for *Ballet*, he and I did not become close friends until the 1960s.

Perhaps the finest of all the line drawings I reproduced were a series by Lucian Freud in February 1950, including a self-portrait as Actaeon and beautiful studies of his favourite Cockney model Charlie as Narcissus and as the youthful Hercules; and although I certainly did not initiate these I am not sure if they were done expressly for *Ballet* or not.

Lucian merely arrived one morning with the drawings, in dire need of money, and I gave him £18 (about $30) for the right to reproduce them. The Greek Iannis Tsarouchis, who became an outstanding stage designer and one of the great painters of the century, told me forty years later that some sketches of his which I reproduced were the first to appear in any publication: I had not known this at the time. The credit for my coup must go, however, to Ronald Crichton, who was working for the British Council in Greece and who sent me a selection of drawings by Greek artists, including those of Iannis and one by a pupil of his, a youth called Nicholas Georgiadis, then unknown. A young Frenchman, Philippe Jullian, had done a cover for *Vogue* whose colouring I thought sentimental, and I persuaded him to make satirical pen-and-ink drawings for *Ballet*. He made more than one series of strip-cartoons in a suggestive Firbankian spirit which caused several respectable dance teachers (former members of Pavlova's *corps de ballet*) to cancel their sub-scriptions.

Because British opera was getting going at Covent Garden, and because of Benjamin Britten – and perhaps because I was feeling claustrophobic in the narrow world of ballet – I decided to include a monthly article on opera in my magazine. Who was to write it? The first candidate came for a drink on 7 July 1948 and was sick on the floor. Not a good beginning. I asked Eric Walter White of the Arts Council to introduce me to Lord Harewood, who had just written an intelligent article in *Tempo*, and whom, when he was Guardsman Lascelles, I had watched drilling on the square at Caterham six years before. On 30 July Eric had us both to lunch at the Etoile in Charlotte Street. The tall, fair, good-mannered and extremely articulate George Harewood was not sick. We must have got on reasonably well because he came to supper at Bloomfield Terrace that same night after the theatre. Peter Williams was there; and George showed no surprise to find I was living with a beautiful black boy.

The world of advertizing was foreign to me: but I always tried to be nice to the rather pathetic men who, one after the other and with the least possible success, endeavoured to sell advertising space in the pages of *Ballet* magazine. My niceness did not go very far, for the whole subject bored me: I would grin and nod, then run a mile. If I thought of *Ballet*'s 'representatives' at all it was to imagine them standing drinks in depressing pubs to equally dull men in the hope of selling half a page at twenty pounds or a quarter of a page at ten. It was, however, one of these doomed pub-crawlers who introduced me to Philip Dossé, who would play an important role in my life – several roles in fact, both good and bad. Our meeting took place on 20 September 1948, two months after I had met George Harewood for the first time.

Philip is hard to describe, although he appeared nothing out of the ordinary. Ten years younger than I, lower middle class, pale, with a nose that managed to be both sharp and *retroussé*, he was at home in a Fleet Street office but terrified in society. He worked for – and I believe, partly owned – a firm called Sport-in-Print, which published a small-scale newspaper and a magazine about greyhound racing. The bombing and the austerities of war had made everyone want to read Tolstoy or Keats, listen to Myra Hess playing Beethoven, gloat over the loaded riches of Samuel Palmer's little landscapes or go to the ballet: and Philip's probing nose had scented the possibility of money to be made from the post-war boom in the arts. My advertizing man, trying to give a leg-up to impecunious *Ballet*, encouraged his interest. Philip, who dreamed of being another Harmsworth or Hearst, overestimated the money-making potential of my magazine, and I overestimated the extent of his ability to back us, run us and make our fortune. I suppose that optimism of this kind is the basis for many business partnerships.

Philip lived with his old father and mother in a flat in Notting Hill. His father had been a chef and Philip had inherited his interest in cooking. However, even *pommes lyonnaise* and baked Alaska could not unite them, for during the last ten years of Mr Dossé's life he and Philip exchanged no word. Philip's grandfather had been a French courier who conducted Queen Victoria, George Harewood's great-great-grandmother, on her expeditions to France. Philip was homosexual. He clearly found me entertaining as a person and as a writer. In fact, I think he had the sound good sense to believe me a genius, and I encouraged the belief by every means in my power.

George Harewood and I agreed to change the magazine's name to *Ballet and Opera*, and as such it continued for fifteen months. It was proposed that Philip Dossé's Sport-in-Print should buy two-thirds of the shares in Ballet Publications for a certain sum, retaining at stipulated salaries my services, those of Peggy Newman, our secretary, and Peter Williams, who had never been paid before. This arrangement was to have come into force in February 1949, but although we drew our salaries, the signing of the agreement was continually postponed. One pretext was that Sir Thomas Beecham was suing George Harewood and our firm for libel. Perhaps Philip never intended to sign the agreement and perhaps he never had the money to buy the shares. However, he had taken charge of our books and was supposed to be looking after our circulation and advertising.

Meanwhile the balletomanes were complaining that an increasing amount of space in the magazine was given to opera, while George's opera enthusiasts demanded even more. I suggested that George should assume the responsibility of a separate opera magazine, and that *Ballet* should revert to its maiden name. George made quick decisions. He agreed. *Opera* came into existence in January 1950; and because George said he knew no one with a room as big as mine – which struck me as quite funny – the launching party was held in my Red Room at Bloomfield Terrace on 9 February, and Benjamin Britten and Peter Pears crossed my threshold for the first time. Dossé was to handle *Opera* on a percentage basis, but the magazine was backed by Harewood.

Early in 1950 Philip told me that it was necessary to put up the cost of *Ballet* to half-a-crown (35c), reduce my salary and get rid of Peter and Miss Newman. A few days later he announced that he could take no further responsibility for *Ballet*, that we owed him nearly £3000 ($8400), and that he was starting a new cheaper magazine, *Dance and Dancers*, with Peter Williams as editor. Peter and I both thought each other treacherous: but Philip had a talent for making mischief between friends. This move had obviously been carefully planned, for Philip had stopped paying the blockmakers and contributors several months before. Ballet Publications was responsible for these debts. Meanwhile, Philip had made use of our mailing list to issue circular letters to our readers and subscribers with the news that a new shilling paper was on the way. I had the choice of raising money to pay our debts to Philip and carry on the magazine, or of putting it into liquidation. I craftily waited until the day before payment of the debt to Sport-in-Print was due, hoping that Philip would settle for a lesser sum in order to salvage something of his two thousand pounds-odd. He did telephone; and he accepted £500. Meanwhile I had raised £1000 from nine friends, my mother helped, and *Ballet* carried on for another two years.

Philip was planning to follow *Dance and Dancers* with a second magazine about classical music. George Harewood brought an injunction to prevent him from using the mailing list of *Opera*: this was granted, and *Music and Musicians*, the second of seven magazines Philip was to start, did not appear until September 1952.

Before long I had forgiven Philip and we were friends again. I even forgot so completely the boring details of his perfidious behaviour that if I had not written them down and published them in my book *The Adventures of a Ballet Critic* (1953) I should not be able to relate them now. George

Harewood, on the other hand, never forgave him. Fifteen years later, when Philip drove me up to Edinburgh for the Festival, we ran into George in the entrance hall of the North British Hotel, and although George talked to me he cut Philip dead. I begged him next day to make up the quarrel, but he was adamant. When Philip Dossé severed his connection with us, Andrew Sykes became not only the chief supporter of *Ballet*, but my unpaid assistant editor.

To pep up the seductive power of *Ballet* I decided to create new and more interesting critics. Elsa Brunnelleschi, London's foremost teacher of Spanish dancing, was well qualified to write on classical ballet, and this she did with gusto. My friend Nigel Gosling, features editor of the *Observer*, had been a painter, he wrote well and moreover he was married to Maude Lloyd, who had been Rambert's leading dancer up to the war: this accumulation of visual sense, literary expression and technical knowledge of dancing could surely be combined. It was: and from behind the mask of Alexander Bland, a new voice of authority rang out. The Goslings chose their pen-name from an off-stage character of Beatrix Potter's, a brother of Pigling Bland who was known to be 'hopelessly volatile'. Maude, South African-born, was fine-boned and beautiful. The gentle, whimsical Nigel, whom I admired for his courage to be a wartime pacifist, had been a friend of David Astor's (the *Observer*'s editor) since Eton days, and was descended from Charles II and Lucy Walter. I have never known a more devoted couple; but once, when I was staying with them, I heard Maude reproving Nigel for dusting the leaves of a plant instead of getting down to work at his desk, and it occurred to me that without her loving pressure he might not have carried through as many valuable books as he did.

Series, serials, I decided, were what was needed to keep the reader in a state of suspense and to increase circulation. Perhaps I also had the idea that, once launched, they might save me trouble: for I was getting increasingly bored with the business of producing a magazine every month. On the way to lunch at Overton's, opposite Victoria, I saw some skilful and very detailed architectural drawings propped up against the windowless brick wall of the station – a rampart which always made me think of the Vatican. The pavement artist was away for lunch, but in the cap left for pennies I dropped my telephone number. Rather disappointingly, he turned out to be not a Cockney youth of radiant beauty but a middle-aged and conventionally educated cousin of Field-Marshal Montgomery's, called David Thomas. I commissioned a series of drawings of London buildings which had played a part in the history of ballet – Taglioni's last home, Beaumont's bookshop, Pavlova's Ivy House at Golders Green, various theatres. For these John Betjeman consented to write the accompanying text. Then I persuaded Beryl de Zoete to put together her writings on Oriental dance in a long and, if necessary, endless serial, which I suggested calling 'The Million Mile Journey'. She demurred at the title, but Arthur Waley liked it. Next, I decided to write my own scandalous reminiscences, and the first instalment of 'The Adventures of a Ballet Critic' came out in May 1950. When Lincoln Kirstein was staying with me that spring I used to read him the early instalments of this, and enjoyed seeing him rock with laughter. When, however, I posted the proofs of what I wrote about *him* to America later in the year, these caused consternation. Lincoln did not mind being called eccentric, but I guess he was afraid my account might endanger the existence of his company and put off potential backers. I realized my mistake and Lincoln was allowed to censor my chapter on him before it appeared. Of all the living critics of ballet, the New Yorker Edwin Denby had the sharpest eye, keenest ear and most evocative pen. That he should contribute long reflective articles to *Ballet* became, in my opinion, the ultimate justification for the magazine's existence.

John Hayward, an *éminence grise* of the literary world, who had lost the use of his legs through poliomyelitis and shared with T. S. Eliot a flat in Cheyne Walk, Chelsea, overlooking the river, saw a hint of possibility in the instalments of my 'Adventures' which appeared in *Ballet*. He was adviser to the Cresset Press, and recommended them to publish my essays in book form. He had the perception to realize that I was trying to write about London and London life as much as about ballet, and he liked the hidden motive. If he also considered that this secondary plot might widen the audience for my work, he was wrong: for it has been proved that 'ballet writers' sell more books by staying strictly within their category. 'Ballet readers' are on the whole interested in nothing but ballet, just as most ballet dancers see little but their own reflections in the classroom mirror.

My prose in *The Adventures of a Ballet Critic* was too ornate. In those days (more, I think, than today) I was a chameleon and took on the colouring of what I had recently been reading – just as, after a few days in Edinburgh, I found myself speaking with a Scottish accent. In 1950 and 1951 it was Osbert Sitwell's autobiography that influenced me. I had always admired *Left Hand, Right Hand*, although my Granny had written to me during the war, when the first volume appeared, that she could see nothing in it; and perhaps the reason I re-read it in 1950 was that Kirstein had just introduced me to its author. Such baroque prose has been derided in recent years, but hearing passages about Osbert's father, Sir George, read aloud on the radio in 1981, I thought their pompous style enhanced the comedy of that fantastic personage, whom Osbert has certainly rendered immortal. Raymond Mortimer praised my use of words in *The Adventures of a Ballet Critic*, my first book since the childish *John Innocent at Oxford*, but when I dip into it today I observe a straining after effect.

My godmother, Dolly Sandford, was a little proud of my literary effort, for she chose to be photographed by me, holding it, both in the garden and in the drawing-room of my mother's house at Overstrand.

During the feckless forties and up to the closure of *Ballet* in 1952 my scribbled engagement books recorded impartially deaths and cocktail parties. In the course of ten days before I moved from Alexander Square to Bloomfield Terrace near Chelsea Barracks (on 29 January 1948) I had met at a Ballet Rambert party the young South African John Cranko, later the founder of Stuttgart State Theatre Ballet, and at the Vic-Wells Ball Peter Darrell, later director of the Scottish Ballet; I had also dined with Fred Ashton at the Jardin des Gourmets, had Ninette de Valois to lunch at the Dog and Duck (next door to the office of *Ballet* in Frith Street), and been fascinated by Mae West in *Diamond Lil* at the Prince of Wales's Theatre. I read my first piece published in the *Observer* on 15 February 1948 in the plane on my way to spend a holiday with Andrew Sykes in Malta, where I saw Caravaggio's 'Beheading of St John the Baptist'; and returned to attend a Baroque exhibition with Erich Alport, admire the Indian dancer Ram Gopal with Beryl de Zoete and lunch at Brooks's with Michael Wood. On 8 September 1948, two days before I went north on what would be my last visit to Granny Buckle, Boris Kochno came to dinner, along with Jean Babilée and his wife Nathalie, and the young couple met for the first time Mme Karsavina, who mimed to a gramophone record a passage from Massine's *Les Femmes de bonne humeur*: David Lichine and his wife Tatiana Riaboushinska were there too. During the few days before Granny died (on 14 January 1949) I entertained Doris Langley Moore, the costume collector and authority on Byron, took a ballet lesson from Vera Volkova, went with Michael Block to see Gertrude Lawrence in a poor play, had George Harewood to lunch at the Guards Club, which he was shy of entering, and took Roger Wood, the 'action photographer' of ballet, whose work I had been proud to promote, to see a female impersonator on a tight-rope at the Clapham Grand. I returned from

Granny's funeral to hear *Aïda* with Peter Williams, and to see John Gielgud in *The Lady's Not For Burning* with Andrew and my widowed aunt Violet Kinnaird.

I heard Callas and Stignani in *Norma* at Covent Garden with Erich's mother a few days before *Ballet* went into liquidation on 24 November 1952. That evening Philippe Jullian gave a party at my house, and I dined at Andrew's with Willie and Viva King and Lauretta. Four days later, while Cyril Beaumont was making me an offer for some of my ballet books – for I was broke as usual (and I was amused that Cyril deducted his taxi fare from the money he paid me) – I heard on the telephone that my grandfather was dying. On the last night of that year I went to four parties, of which Arnold Haskell's and Bunny Roger's were two.

What remains alive in my memory of those post-war years before my magazine bowed to the inevitable and went bust? Unforgettable was the moment in Roland Petit's *Les Forains* when, to a cue in Sauguet's score, the ragged curtain of the booth erected by the strolling players was suddenly lit up and flamed scarlet against the black night: it was like the waving of a banner, an assertion by Kochno and Bérard and Petit of the theatre's power to transform our drab lives. Another shining present from Paris was the frieze of gods and mortals in *Les Amours de Jupiter*, disporting in the clear colours of Jean Hugo – but particularly Nathalie Phillipart as Danaë reclining with tremulous legs to receive the shower of gold – another of Kochno's lighting effects. Then there was Babilée in *Le Jeune Homme et la mort*, dressed in paint-daubed overalls, yearning and hanging in the filthy attic Cocteau had devised, before being led by the White Lady of Death across the rooftops of Paris to Bach's 'Passacaglia', while an illuminated Eiffel Tower flashed the commercial message of CITROEN on and off.

After Kochno and Petit had parted company, the latter worked out for his Ballets de Paris that incredible *ratatouille* of a *Carmen*, shamelessly mixing Bizet's travestied tunes, the

long legs, wide smile and urchin haircut of Renée (not yet
Zizi) Jeanmaire, with the prosaic ladders, wheels, chairs and
flea-market bed of Antoni Clavé, turned to poetry by the
designer's blacks and purples, his whorish reds and his light
filtered through broken shutters on to a white wall. Then
Kochno engaged Lichine to fill the gap left by Petit; and his
last collaboration with Bérard, who died in 1949, was for
La Rencontre, ou Oedipe et le Sphynx. I marvelled at the idea
of the Sphinx's lair as a red velvet trapeze, trimmed with
gold fringe, suspended like an acrobat's platform in the
mother-of-pearl air. (John Taras did not agree with me, and
wrote of the riddles which Oedipus asked the Sphinx, 'What
is questioned and what is answered is never clear in spite of

John Taras. Photograph by the author, 28 October 1951.

the intense mouthings of both Babilée and Leslie Caron', and, of the set, 'The Sphinx having to go up and down a Jacob's ladder is too absurd.')

Taras's own *Designs with Strings*, to the second movement of Tchaikovsky's 'Trio in A Minor', a mournful delicate little work for six dancers originally devised for the short-lived Metropolitan Ballet, became one of the best-loved ballets of our time, and was revived in subsequent years for many companies.

In Jerome Robbins's *Fancy Free*, which Ballet Theatre brought us, the grotesque variations of the three sailors, John Kriza, Michael Kidd and Robbins himself, particularly Jerry's mock rhumba, were an earnest of the perfection to which Broadway musicals could and would soon attain in the hands of a choreographer with know-how.

At Covent Garden Margot Fonteyn inclined her sad neck in *Swan Lake*; and in *The Sleeping Beauty*, whose triumph in New York awoke Margot herself out of a spell of English reticence, she balanced serenely in that most perfect of dances, Petipa's 'Adage des roses', supported by her four cavaliers. A beautiful moment in Oliver Messel's production came when his clustered baroque columns and arches were seen in silhouette just before Aurora's awakening; and I thought the way in which Ashton, in his rearrangement of the Garland Dance, when he had formed the peasant girls into two concentric rings with wired floral festoons upraised, suddenly suspended their movement except for one girl who rotated clockwise in the middle while another passed on tiptoe anti-clockwise through the flowery arches, was one of those simple devices which only occur to true poets of the theatre.

Then came the revelation of Balanchine's *Ballet Imperial*. In the course of this formal ballet, whose slow middle movement struck a necessary note of sadness – like a coronation blighted by broken hearts – but which closed in exultation, Balanchine, without ever departing from the geometrical language of the classic dance (as second nature to him as prosody to Pope), seemed to me to throw off images which were essentially poetical: and the 'fine phrases' which I found to convey the similes and metaphors he had implied with dancers' bodies were no more, I believe, than their exact verbal equivalent. When in the second movement ten women swung 'into arrowheads', they really did suggest 'the aërial drill of birds'. When Michael Somes knelt, stage centre, with his back to the audience, and Fonteyn made her way towards him through a double file of the *corps de ballet* she really did seem to be 'parting the branches of an avenue of girls'. 'And with what pounding heart,' I wrote, 'we watch the whole company rise and flash in the air together in the final mazurka, like jewelled rockets shooting from an imperial crown!' The mass movements of girls in a finale such as that of *Ballet Imperial*, revived by Balanchine for Sadler's Wells, were seen again when New York City Ballet came to Covent Garden in July 1950: in the Mozart *Symphonie Concertante*, the Bizet *Symphony in C* and the Chabrier *Bourrée fantasque* the diagonal countercharging, the epic alignments and even the way a ballet would finish with the whole *corps* sinking neatly on one knee or with all the girls raised suddenly on their partners' shoulders with arms extended, gave me a new feeling of the exhilarating possibilities of the classic dance. I had learnt that the regularities of Racine could corset as much anguish as all the raving of Shakespeare. In one of Balanchine's slow movements, such as those of his Tchaikovsky *Serenade* or *Ballet Imperial*, when the choreographer formally parted two dancers whom the palpitating music had brought together, it was like the cry of Titus in *Bérénice*, who knew that a hundred kingdoms could not console the banished queen for the loss of his love. '*Faibles amusements d'une douleur si grande!*'

My off-stage memories are mainly of friends – of Andrew casually remarking, 'This must be the only magazine in the world whose assistant editor does up the editor's laundry,' of Iain Moncreiffe's kindness and exertions on my behalf, of the many evenings Lauretta Hope-Nicholson and I sat talking or watching ballet together, and of her bringing Jean Hugo into my life. After Iain's marriage he lived in Scotland and I saw less of him. Then Lauretta married Jean and lived in the south of France. Andrew soon sailed away with the RFA to the Caribbean or Singapore. Most of my dearest friends were destined to live at a distance from me. It was natural that my two new American friends, Taras and Kirstein, should be seldom in London; and I longed for their letters. 'I am surrounded by *corps de ballet* girls,' tapped out John Taras on his typewriter in the train between Paris and Monte Carlo, in October 1948, 'and constant giggles and chatter, and concentration comes hard. The landscape gets lovelier and lovelier as we skirt the coast line. This is my first viewing of the Mediterranean.' In March 1950 Lincoln Kirstein wrote, before he had even met me, 'You had better give up *Ballet*, as damn well done as it is, because you have done it long enough. You should be a novelist . . .' Two and a half years later, willy-nilly, I took his advice and *Ballet* closed down: it was not novels, however, but plays I tried to compose. In 1959 John Taras would write: 'I am on enforced liberty . . . I plan to go to New York to see if I can't find some sort of usefulness with Balanchine.' In this he was successful. Not only he, but Jerome Robbins, who had not yet become a friend of mine, would be enrolled in the cohorts of Lincoln Kirstein and George Balanchine.

Although Balanchine and I sometimes dined tête-à-tête in 1950, and I used to carry him off to dinner in Soho or with friends such as the Duke of San Lucar, Spanish *chargé d'affaires*, and Dick Addinsell, the composer of film music – at whose house I remember George improvising on the piano what he called a 'Russian Tea Roomba' – and although he sometimes took over my kitchen to make a Russian dinner, we never fell into the intimacy of total friendship. His absorption with his dancers was more engrossing (since they were human) than a sculptor's with his clay: and in New

York his rare 'evenings off' were spent in the company of a few Russian cronies. Nevertheless, he remained a hero of mine: I revered not only his genius but his imperturbability. I thought he had healing powers, and would have made a fine doctor.

One friend who lived in England was another George and another genius, George Lascelles, 7th Earl of Harewood: but his public duties, the running of his Yorkshire estate and, after 1951, his work at the Royal Opera House, prevented us from meeting for months at a stretch. This George was a few years younger than I, but his upbringing, education and worldly experience – which ranged from courts to prison camps – made him seem, and made me think of him as, rather older. I was aware that I could not claim a thorough knowledge of ballet, whereas George really knew music and his experience increased daily. It was said that he had in Colditz read through and memorized Grove's *Dictionary of Music* – but in fact George told me he had only got as far as 'S'. He was above all a connoisseur of the human voice. He was, however, interested in, and a good judge of, all the arts, as the Prince Consort had been. He was also an astute judge of people – even surer in his reactions than myself.

Because of my slightly impoverished upbringing, because I had not been at Eton, because I fell between the two stools of upper and middle class, because I did not shoot or hunt or even like horses, because of a strong streak of Granny Buckle in me – in fact, because I was 'not quite a gentleman' – I had an inferiority complex which made me, as my mother called it, 'show off'. Granny had observed this unattractive tendency in me, just as she recognized and deplored it in herself. In addition I was sometimes offhand and impatient and I did not suffer fools gladly. George Harewood was not only incapable of boasting but ready to overlook boastfulness in others, so that like Shakespeare's Theseus he could take a lenient view of rude mechanicals like myself and give 'thanks for nothing'.

I remember how once, in the 1930s, when I had arrived drunk at an Oxford party, Olivia Cooke, chuckling to herself, remarked, 'You're sometimes a hard storm for your friends to weather!' There was certainly a lot in my behaviour and patchy education which George too, later on, had to overlook or forgive, yet we grew closer. Perhaps I made him laugh. Like that of the easy-going Andrew, the chivalrous Iain and the loving Lauretta, his friendship was one I could rely on even after long absence to remain exactly the same. 'It is an ever fixèd mark/That looks on tempests and is never shaken.'

CHAPTER 3

A God Twice Buried

When Vaslav Nijinsky became a choreographer himself, in 1911 and 1912, he began to despise some of the ballets of Fokine which had made him famous in Western Europe. He thought Fokine's loose handling of the orgy in *Scheherazade* and the crowd in *Petrushka* was unforgivable, and he told Marie Rambert that 'choreography should be exact'; then, when Lady Ottoline Morrell complimented him on his performance in Fokine's *Le Spectre de la rose* he complained that it was '*trop joli*'. It was, however, as the Golden Slave in *Scheherazade*, glowing with lust, as the soulful puppet in *Petrushka* and as the embodiment of a rose's perfume in *Le Spectre* that he would go down in history.

Although the three Fokine ballets mentioned above are still performed today, it is my opinion that they are totally unacceptable, even ridiculous. How much they must have depended on the magic of their original interpreters! According to Nijinsky's sister, Bronislava, Fokine's method of blocking in the choreography left Vaslav free to fill in the detail of his roles – for instance, it was the manner in which he softened the classical geometry of *Le Spectre*, melting the clear curves of Fokine's *port de bras* into the convolvulus tendrils of *art nouveau* – that gave his long dance its special character. It might therefore be thought that he changed or developed his roles in order to render them more Nijinskian and to show his individual qualities to better advantage: but this was not the case. Every witness testifies how utterly different he was – how unrecognizable – in all his imperson-

77

ations. If his ability to disguise himself, to lose his identity – which was only partly due to skill in make-up – can be compared to that of the actor Laurence Olivier, born a generation later, Nijinsky's *cantabile* quality of movement, which caused his dancing to appear like music made visible, may be compared to the vocal modulations of another actor, John Gielgud, unparalleled in our time.

The donning of costume and make-up contributed mentally even more than physically to Nijinsky's process of becoming. We are told that when the male dancers of the South Indian dance drama called Kathakali lie on their backs on the floor to be made-up, a two-hour ordeal which involves not only the application of colour but the moulding of fantastic beards in rice paste – they undergo the experience of turning into gods. In her clever historical novel, *The Mask of Apollo*, Mary Renault showed insight into the minds of players when she described the performance of Greek tragedy in the language of the modern theatre. I wrote in an article: 'Her narrator, a tragic actor, sits quietly before an archaic mask of Apollo before "going on" . . . On lucky days this actor is conscious that the god takes over and speaks through him. I think this is a fine way of describing "inspiration" – a word we are no longer allowed to use.' Alexandre Benois gave an account of Nijinsky in his dressing-room:

> The final metamorphosis took place when he put on his costume, about which he was always very particular, demanding that it should be an exact copy of the sketch made by the artist. At these moments the usually apathetic Vaslav became nervous and capricious. Having put on his costume, he began gradually to change into another being, the one he saw in the mirror. He became re-incarnated and actually *entered* into his new existence . . . The fact that Nijinsky's metamorphosis was predominantly subconscious is, in my opinion, the very proof of his genius. Only a genius – that is to say, a phenomenon that has no adequate natural explanation – could incarnate the choreographic

essence of the *rococo* period, as did Nijinsky in *Le Pavillon d'Armide* – especially in the Paris version of my ballet. Only a genius could have given so authentic an image of a youth pining for his dead beloved in *Giselle*. His interpretations of the strange being who dances with the Sylphides, of the Ghost of the Rose, of the Negro in *Scheherazade* and of Petrushka were equally manifestations of genius.

Those who have handed down to us descriptions of Nijinsky as the Slave in *Scheherazade* seem to be tumbling over each other with breathless epithets to convey the uncanny nature of his incarnation. 'He was half-cat, half-snake, fiendishly agile, feminine and yet wholly terrifying,' wrote Benois, who had devised the scenario. Fokine, who came to resent Nijinsky's subsequent experiments in choreography and liked to imply that his famous interpreters owed everything to his guidance, wrote: 'The lack of masculinity which was peculiar to this remarkable dancer and which made him unfit for certain roles . . . suited very well the role of the Negro Slave.' That is an odd statement which at once arouses our curiosity, for what use as a lover to Queen Zobeïda would be a Negro Slave without virility? Fokine's following words hardly elucidate his meaning: 'Now he is a half-human, half-feline animal, softly leaping great distances, now a stallion, with distended nostrils, full of energy, overflowing with an abundance of power, his feet impatiently pawing the ground.' Geoffrey Whitworth, however, the author of the first English book on Nijinsky*, helps us to imagine in what way this passionate Slave was somehow more feminine than the cold imperious Queen of Ida Rubinstein. 'From the moment of his entrance the drama takes on to itself a new and terrible meaning. The dark youth flickers here and there among the mazy crowd of slaves,

---

* And whom I met in about 1937, at dinner with Clifford Bax in Albany. He was a tiny bent man, almost a hunchback; and he then edited a magazine called *Drama*. He paid me £1 to reproduce one of my puerile designs in it.

hungry for the faithless wife of the sultan . . . He finds her soon, and his lecherous hands play over and over her body with a purpose too subtle, it seems, to take and hold her once and for all. And presently he leaves her, threading his way in and out of the passionate dancers, to lie at last on a soft cushion, like a flame of lust that smoulders and sinks but never dies . . .' 'From his first bound on to the stage,' Nijinsky's sister, Bronislava, told me in later years, 'the whole characterization of the Negro Slave was present. He was first a snake, then a panther.' Of the Slave's death Francis de Miomandre, author of an essay which introduced a book of drawings by Georges Barbier, wrote, 'the transport of his movements, the encircling giddiness, the dominance of his passion reached such heights that when the executioner's sword pierced him in the final tumult we no longer really knew whether he had succumbed to the avenging steel or to the unbearable violence of his joy in those three fierce somersaults.' Of his death agonies Jean Cocteau wrote, 'He beat on the boards like a fish at the bottom of a boat.'

Nijinsky, visiting Stravinsky in Switzerland in the company of Diaghilev in September 1910, heard the piano composition which they all called 'Petrushka's Cry', which gave Diaghilev the idea for the fairground ballet, and which was to accompany the episode of the tragic puppet locked in his cell by the Magician, his creator. Because Nijinsky heard this music some months before Fokine, it occurred to me that he himself had probably devised the jerky breast-beating and stiff extended arm movements of Petrushka which later became the central motif of Fokine's choreography: and Bronislava Nijinska agreed with me that this was very likely. Yet, Diaghilev hesitated for a while before allowing the god-like *premier danseur* to take on the lineaments and angularity of Petrushka, the Russian Punch, who was to be given, at Benois' suggestion, the embryo of a soul. Alexandre Benois was surprised at Nijinsky's courage 'in appearing as a horrible half-doll, half-human grotesque'. He reflected that 'The great difficulty of Petrushka's part is to express his pitiful oppression and his hopeless efforts to attain personal dignity *without ceasing to be a puppet*. Both music and libretto are spasmodically interrupted by outbursts of illusive joy and frenzied despair. The artist is not given a single *pas* or *fioriture* to enable him to be attractive to the public . . .' After the Paris production of *Petrushka* in June 1911 Diaghilev delayed until February 1913 before he risked frightening the English with Stravinsky's discordant music. Then Cyril Beaumont noticed 'the startled expressions on the faces of the audience', but he himself was soon won over. He admired the way that Nijinsky, when he was first revealed inside the booth with the Moor and the Ballerina, supported under the arms by iron props, 'succeeded in investing the movements of his legs with a looseness suggesting that foot, leg and thigh were threaded on a string attached to the hip'. He recognized 'a curiously fitful quality in his movements, his limbs spasmodically leapt or twisted or stamped like the reflex actions of limbs whose muscles have been subjected to an electric current . . . His features were formed into a sad and unhappy mask, an expression which remained constant throughout the ballet.' Looking back in later years, Osbert Sitwell fancifully considered Nijinsky's Petrushka, victim of the heartless Magician, as the prototype of a whole generation of European youth sacrificed by their wicked elders on the altar of War, 'in the same way that the legend of the Minotaur had once summed up, though after the event and not before it, the fate of several generations of Greek youths and maidens'. Other interpreters of signs, taking their cue from Romola Nijinsky, found a parallel between the subjection of Petrushka to the Magician-Showman and the relationship of Nijinsky with Diaghilev in real life. Biographies, novels, a play, a film and even a long ballet were based on this facile comparison.

As for *Le Spectre de la rose*, its interpretation by Nijinsky and Karsavina seemed to make spectators drunk, so that when they came to write about it, they raved incoherently about

youth and love and summer nights. All agreed with Whitworth that Nijinsky was 'a spirit rather than a man, a fairy
thing and as light as a waft of perfume'. Cocteau wrote:
'He conveys – which one would have thought impossible –
the impression of some melancholy, imperious scent.'
Beaumont watched the ballet 'in a kind of trance. It seemed
too beautiful, too flawless, too intangible to be real . . . the
most perfect choreographic conception I have ever seen.'

An idea of how Nijinsky transformed his dance in Fokine's
Le Pavillon d'Armide into something more than a mere
classical *variation* in a would-be *rococo* style, is given by
Geoffrey Whitworth, whose description seems to me quite as
odd as something I might have written myself. Bear in mind
that the dancer was merely performing a series of difficult
steps: he was given no character to express. 'The vivid radiant
boy is also the hierophant of mysteries . . . The court of
Armide, one believes, is part of a definite and settled polity,
with its own laws, its own customs, and its own business
from day to day . . . The secret of this effect lies . . . partly in
the conviction of *aloofness* which Nijinsky brings to his
rendering of the part of Armide's Slave . . . The art of Nijinsky
has made one free of a strange country, where dancing and
simple melodies of music are the natural language of the
soul . . .'

Nobody wrote with more feeling about the pre-war
seasons of Diaghilev's ballet, and of Nijinsky in particular,
than Charles Ricketts, the English painter, printer, collector
and art historian, who had been a friend of Oscar Wilde's.
Here is an extract from a letter of 1912:

> All that the antique world thought and said about the
> famous male dancers who were seduced by Empresses etc.,
> is quite true. Nijinsky outclasses in passion, beauty and
> magnetism all that Karsavina can do, and she is a Muse, or
> several Muses in one, the Muse of Melancholy and of
> Caprice, capable of expressing tragedy and even volup-
> tuous innocence; the wildness of chastity and the sting of

desire; she is the perfect instrument upon which all emotion can be rendered. Nijinsky is a living flame, the son of Hermes, or of Logi perhaps. One cannot imagine his mother – probably some ancient ballerina was answerable: but I prefer to believe in some sort of spontaneous nativity, at the most a passing cloud may have attracted some fantastic and capricious god.

When Richard Capell, critic of London's *Daily Mail*, wrote in December 1911 'There is a compensation for some of the depressing conditions of modern life in the reflection that our epoch is alone, in the history of art, capable of producing such a stage spectacle,' he seemed to me to be unconsciously echoing poor Oscar's flippant lie that 'Yellow satin is a consolation for all the miseries of life.' Six months later Capell welcomed back Nijinsky, Karsavina and the Diaghilev Ballet with the words: 'The Russians are.back at Covent Garden. This means that the London of 1912 is offered a series of pantomimic and choreographic spectacles of a complete and luxurious beauty, such as was beyond the command of Nero and Sardanapalus.'

In the summer of 1946 Cyril Beaumont remarked to me in the back room of his tiny ballet bookshop in Charing Cross Road, 'I've got something here that I think you'll find rather interesting.' He always gave his favoured adjective four whole syllables, with a stress on the third, which used to send Peter Williams and myself into fits of giggles. (Peter and I were always taking him off behind his back; yet I can't deny that Beaumont's *Diaghilev Ballet in London*, full of almost domestic details, was one of my favourite books.) The interesting object was a letter from Romola Nijinsky, which Beaumont saw as a scoop for *Ballet*, and which he offered with the suppressed self-satisfaction of a provincial schoolmaster who has discovered life on Mars. 'Of course, I'd be delighted to publish it. Thank you very much.' 'I thought you'd find it interesting. Mind you, I wouldn't say

83

one can always be too sure of Madam Nijinsky's strict adherence to the truth.' Indeed, it had been clear to me for several years that much of what Romola Nijinsky had written in her husband's biography was exaggerated or untrue; and I was used to hearing Nijinsky's former colleagues speak of her as a wicked woman. Here is the gist of Romola Nijinsky's long letter to Beaumont, which.appeared in *Ballet* (Vol 2. No 4):

Castle of M [Mittersill], near Zell am See   20 July 1946
Dear Mr Beaumont

   Mrs Power informed me that during her stay in London she visited you and you expressed the desire to publish a statement about Mr Nijinsky's present state of health.

   As since 1940 I have nursed my husband constantly, I am the only person in a position to tell how Nijinsky is at present.

   You have heard without doubt that in 1939 he underwent several times the insulin shock treatment and was discharged from the nursing home as socially healed. No doubt you will have heard that we were confined in Hungary and were liberated through the Russian Army. Both Mr Nijinsky and myself were in great danger during the German occupation and escaped after much suffering and hardship quite miraculously.

   Mr Nijinsky is quite sociable and lives a very quiet life . . . For the last two weeks we have been at M., where my husband very much enjoys the country life. He takes long walks in the woods, is interested in music, all artistic matters, receives our guests and leads a normal life . . . My husband takes a very great interest in dancing and *dances* quite frequently for us, and sometimes for his countrymen . . . His dancing is quite as marvellous as it used to be. One would not think that he ceased dancing so many years ago. He is quite as graceful and light as ever . . . Our only difficulty is that he only dances when he is in the mood . . . This is the only reason he has not yet appeared in public . . .

We intend to go to Paris in the autumn and from there to the States, where we intend to settle and where Mr Nijinsky will undergo one more insulin shock treatment from his physician Dr Sackel, the discoverer of the said treatment. After that Dr Sackel feels my husband will be able to appear again . . . Nijinsky still is what he was in 1919 as an artist . . .

Both Mr Nijinsky and myself would be grateful to you if you would inform the public of the truth about us.

Romola Nijinskaya

How could I have been so foolish as to publish this letter? The idea that the fat, bald, fifty-seven-year-old Nijinsky, who had not appeared on a stage since 1917, could be 'quite as marvellous as he used to be' was too absurd to contemplate, setting aside his mental condition.

If Margaret Power had had any hand in the sending of this letter to Beaumont for publication, it was very naughty of her: but I cannot believe that she did.

Since the 1930s, when Arnold Haskell had suffered from balletomania in the stalls, Margaret had been the most ardent balletomane in the gallery. In 1945, while working for the Foreign Office in Vienna, she had discovered the Nijinskys living at the Hôtel Sacher, and had brought them supplies of food, sweets, soap and toothpaste from the British canteen. Margaret said that at first Romola had treated her in a condescending and offhand way, but as soon as she realized that Margaret sought nothing for herself they had become friends. Margaret used to give up her free evenings to sit with Vaslav when his wife wanted to go out; and when the Nijinskys moved to Schloss Mittersill she paid them visits.

She had a strident voice, which may have been what put the fastidious Romola off her in the first place, as it did me. In the course of time I grew very fond of her. When we became close friends in later years she told me that all Romola's lies were aimed at the single object of obtaining visas for America. The United States did not permit mentally sick people to enter their republic. Nijinsky never recovered his sanity, although he had ceased to be violent. During the five years that Margaret helped to look after him, although he obviously liked her – one evening she had been alone with

Vaslav Nijinsky in an hotel bedroom. Photograph by Igor Stravinsky, c. 1911. Copied by Gjon Mili, 1977.

him in Vienna when the lights failed, and he had patted her hand – and although she had a strong sense of his fundamental goodness and loved him dearly, he never once spoke a word to her. They used to play games of futile ping-pong – futile because Nijinsky was beyond understanding rules or scores. He liked throwing things about and would not always stop; and he liked piling things up and knocking them over. Margaret bought him some light, hollow, coloured bricks.

Duff Cooper facilitated the Nijinskys' move to England, and for a while they stayed in luxury at Great Fosters, an Elizabethan mansion turned into an hotel at Egham, near Windsor. Here Alexander Korda paid their bills. Then they moved to a house at Sunningdale overlooking Windsor Great Park.

On 15 June 1948 I was at the Prince's Theatre, Shaftesbury Avenue (now renamed the Shaftesbury) for the first night of Carmen Amaya and her Gypsy dancers. Leon Hepner, the impresario, approached me in the stalls during an interval and asked if I would like to meet Nijinsky. I looked up at the box to the left of the stage and saw a stout, bald man, smiling vaguely. I thanked Leon, but said no.

Romola Nijinsky came to see me in Bloomfield Terrace. She must have rung up and proposed herself, then driven straight round to tea or for a drink, because there is no note of her visit in my scribbled engagement books for 1948 or 1949. She wanted me to help raise money for her husband's care. She was always in debt, but so was I. The silver was in pawn. *Ballet* was jerking forward from crisis to crisis. I felt powerless. Mme Nijinsky sat on my sofa in the Red Room, looking wistful, talking in a low voice. I knew she had never been a beauty, but I was sensible of her charm. She was just such a *chic*, intelligent woman (I realized in later years) with whom Diaghilev would have got on well: and yet she had cast herself as his sworn enemy. Now she was landed with the job of breadwinner for a poor sick man. I pitied her.

In spring 1950 Lincoln Kirstein was staying with me and

we were getting to know each other, going to the ballet and visiting exhibitions; and the genius of Balanchine was dawning before me. On Easter Saturday, 8 April 1950, three days after the première of *Ballet Imperial* at Covent Garden, Lincoln and I were at a matinée of Sadler's Wells Theatre Ballet (the second company) at Sadler's Wells; we were sitting on the extreme right of the dress circle, in the second or third row. Lincoln was on the outside because of his long legs. As the curtain fell on the first ballet an attendant in uniform came down the steps to tell me that I was wanted urgently on the telephone by the *Observer*. My immediate boss, the Literary Editor, told me that Nijinsky had died that morning: an obituary notice was required for the next day's paper. I went backstage and asked if I could use an office to write in, and was given that of Ninette de Valois. I thought that neither Ninette, nor Lincoln, nor I would be where we were or doing what we were doing, had it not been for Nijinsky and Diaghilev. Lincoln had never told me – indeed in the ten days we had known each other he had hardly had a chance to tell me – about the part he played in helping Romola with her book: so when I returned to watch the last ballet and gave him the news, remarking that if it had not been for Romola's life of Nijinsky I might never have got interested in ballet, and he replied, 'I wrote it,' I was astounded. 'You *what*?' 'I ghosted it. I helped her write it down – the first part anyway. Haskell finished it.' I felt like Oedipus learning the fatal pattern of his life: it was as though Lincoln had revealed that he was my father.

Four days later I was at Covent Garden to see *Ballet Imperial* for a third time (counting the dress rehearsal). In the interval I was approached by Margaret Power. She had come to tell me that Romola was very upset because no member of the Royal Ballet had offered to be a pall-bearer at Nijinsky's funeral on Friday. Dolin had been invited, and Lifar was flying from Paris: why was there no one from Covent Garden? It was absurd of Romola to be offended because, as

I told Margaret to explain to her, no Englishman would dream of being so presumptuous as to *offer* himself as pall-bearer at a great man's funeral. I promised to arrange something. I went straight up to George Balanchine. When he heard Lifar was coming he refused outright. No doubt he remembered how Lifar, out-Hamleting Hamlet beside Diaghilev's open grave, had flung himself in a rage of jealousy, self-pity and self-dramatization on to the unfortunate Kochno. Boris had been obliged to fend off the vulgar assault and was condemned to bear thereafter the stigma of having brawled over Diaghilev's coffin. After George's refusal, I asked Frederick Ashton and Michael Somes, Britain's principal choreographer and chief male dancer, who both consented to carry the coffin. Lincoln had gone to Aldeburgh to visit Benjamin Britten. Next day I telephoned Cyril Beaumont, who also agreed; and I myself made up the six.

On the morning of Friday, 14 April I bought some lilies at Victoria Station, picked up Fred and made for St James's, Spanish Place, the gloomy Catholic church behind the Wallace Collection. It was just opposite my old art school, Heatherley's. When the Requiem Mass was over, the pall-bearers, forewarned by the undertakers, took their places according to height: Dolin and Lifar, the shortest, in front; then Ashton and myself; Beaumont and Somes in the rear. We carried Nijinsky's coffin to the waiting hearse. I did not go on to Marylebone Cemetery to see the burial of the dancer who had changed my life.

He was not long allowed to rest in peace. Lifar had bought a plot in the Cemetery of Montmartre, and he intended vaingloriously to share it with Nijinsky. In 1953 he obtained Romola's permission to transfer Nijinsky's body to Paris. According to British law, when a body is disinterred it has to be identified. It fell to Margaret Power to perform this gruesome task in a chapel in the Marylebone Road. The inner lead coffin was then placed in a new wooden one. Margaret accompanied the coffin to Victoria Station – where

Mme Legat, widow of one of Nijinsky's teachers, brought a group of her pupils to adorn it with flowers – and she sat beside it in the luggage van, crossed the Channel with it and arrived with it at the Gare du Nord, where Lifar had promised to meet her.

Twenty-four years later, in 1977, when Margaret was dying of cancer, she climbed my eighty-two stairs in Covent Garden to tell me a few things which would otherwise be forgotten. I will give my notes just as I jotted them down the moment she had left me.

> Funeral in Paris, 16 June 1953. Romola too poor to come from USA. Paul [Bohus, her cousin] was dealing in antiques in S. Francisco in a v. small way. R telegraphed would pay M's fares, hotel, red roses to be thrown *into* grave (but coffin never lowered [in Margaret's presence]). Trip cost M £70 or £80 [about $200], never repaid. M lost at Gare du Nord. Lifar never turned up. M, landed with big outer coffin w. handles, said it was *not* to go to church [having, I suppose, received instructions to that effect]. Trouble with formalities. Next day car came at 10 to her hotel for service [at the Russian church] rue Daru 10.30. Sat 2 away from Bronia, representing Romola. Lifar bossing about, organizing people. Endless service. She pee-ed at Russian restaurant opposite. Appalling scrum at cemetery – cameras, TV. Preobrajenska clung to her, horrified. Minister, clutching vast floral tribute, held forth, hoping for photo in papers. Lifar orated. Crush and fighting. Nightmare.

CHAPTER 4

Enter Three Ladies:
The Fading Ghost of a Fourth

It would be impossible to imagine three more different women – more different, that is, within the world of ballet and the arts – than Karsavina, Lopoukhova and Sokolova, who were among Diaghilev's most celebrated dancers, and each of whom became a close friend of mine in her old age.

Mme Karsavina, a lustrous beauty, was the only one of the three who could be designated a great classical ballerina, but her mimetic gift and her long association with Fokine had also turned her into a dramatic dancer of unusual power. She was the first I met, and my friendship with her continued longest, for by the time I attended her ninetieth birthday party, Lydia Sokolova was dead and Lydia Lopoukhova (who lived until 1981) had relapsed into a serene second childhood. Of the two Lydias, Sokolova was English and had been renamed by Diaghilev in 1915 when he promoted her to leading roles. Her real name was Hilda Munnings, and she told me that the Russians and Poles in Diaghilev's company persisted in calling her 'Eelda': but I never did – I always called her Lydia. To avoid confusing the reader I shall for the most part refer to the two Lydias by their surnames. These were great enough names for this not to appear disrespectful. Although after twenty years I came to write 'Dearest Madame Karsavina' in my letters, I never called her Tamara. To me she was a queen.

If I had to sum up these three friends – in a telegram, for instance – I should distinguish them as aristocrat, bohemian and old trouper: but what I am writing is not a telegram, so I shall try to give a slightly fuller impression here, where they make their first entry, of three characters who enriched my life.

In order to have me meet Mme Karsavina, the thoughtful Iain Moncreiffe contrived first to introduce me to Lady Kennet. The latter was born Kathleen Bruce, of a branch of the great Scottish family long settled in Northern Ireland, and latterly at Clifton in Nottinghamshire. Her first husband had been Scott of the Antarctic, by whom she was the mother of Peter Scott, the ornithologist; her second was Edward Hilton-Young, Lord Kennet. Mme Karsavina had married Kathleen Kennet's cousin, H. J. Bruce – always called Benjie – when he was *en poste* in St Petersburg during the First World War. It was at luncheon at St James's Palace on 20 February 1946 that I first met Lady Kennet, Iain being that day Captain of the King's Guard. She was a little woman, bursting with vitality, and an able academic sculptor. The next afternoon I took her to an exhibition of Constable's sketches at the Victoria and Albert Museum. On 25 March I went to tea with her to meet Tamara Platonovna Karsavina.

Lady Kennet lived at a house called Leinster Corner at the angle of Leinster Terrace and the Bayswater Road: a large front garden behind a wall on the Hyde Park side distinguished it from other houses in that busy thoroughfare, and in a garden at the back Lady Kennet had her studio. I did not know that J. M. Barrie had lived in this house between 1902 and 1909: but then, in 1946 I thought Barrie was beneath consideration. Mme Karsavina, on the other hand, remained proud all her life that he had written in 1919 a fantastic comedy, *The Truth about the Russian Dancers*, specially for her. In this she danced instead of speaking, replying to the spoken questions or observations of the other characters in mime or with a *pirouette*. I did not know that Barrie had been godfather to Peter Scott – or, for that matter, that Lady Kennet (who died the year after I met her) had in 1905 kept

Isadora Duncan company on the bleak seashore of Holland during her first pregnancy, and assisted at the birth of Deirdre, her child by Gordon Craig. There was a lot I did not know in 1946.

I wish my diary had recorded more about the tea-party. I was perhaps even shyer and more awkward than usual – like Peter Bezoukhov in *War and Peace* talking either too little or too much. When I found myself in the company of the ballerina whom Fokine had loved and for whom he had created his most celebrated ballets, the partner of Nijinsky in so many historic works, I felt like a very inferior mandarin received in audience on the steps of the Temple of Heaven. Tamara Karsavina was small, like most ballerinas of her period. She had big, dark, searching eyes which, while they subjugated lesser mortals, both male and female, were busy making amused observations. Her back, when she sat in a chair, was very straight, and she held her head, on its long neck, imperially. She had meticulous manners and rather a deep voice. Her slightest pronouncement in carefully phrased English was rendered prismatic by a rainbow Russian accent; her triple vowels – for her 'No' would contain an 'o', a 'u' and an 'e' – had clearly been set by Fabergé in rubies, rock-crystal and diamonds.

Karsavina's father had been a dancer: but her maternal grandmother was a Paleologue, believed to be descended – which I found easy to credit – from Emperors of Byzantium. In her youth this lady had attended balls in St Petersburg's Salle de la Noblesse where, like Pushkin's frivolous wife, she had flirted with the Emperor Nicolas I. After Tamara Karsavina's sensational success in Paris in May 1909 she had been plied with offers by theatres and music-halls from all over the world. (Such highly paid guest appearances were made possible by the four-month summer closure of the Russian Imperial Theatres, without which, indeed, Diaghilev could never have presented his first seasons of opera and ballet in the West.) She had accepted a London contract –

93

to dance as a 'turn' at the Coliseum – simply because, ever since childhood, she had loved the novels of Charles Dickens. (In this – but in little else – she resembled my Granny Buckle.)

When, in 1913, she met the tall handsome *attaché*, Benjie Bruce, it was on both sides *le coup de foudre*. In his memoirs Bruce omitted to mention that this lovely ballerina whom the British Ambassador invited to dine at his Embassy and on whom Bruce himself called shyly at her flat overlooking the Kriukov Canal – in the same building as that of Stravinsky's family and near to that of Benois – was married already. Mme Karsavina's first husband was disposed of, presumably by divorce. I never liked to mention him. In 1918 Benjie and Tamara Bruce escaped with their son to England. Thenceforward this Queen of Sheba set out to become as correctly English as possible. Her discovery of the English language must have been an adventure to her, for she came to write it with such wide-eyed relish that she might have been Chaucer. The boy Nik was sent, like his father, to Eton, and though he aspired in later years to be an actor, he settled for a career in business. Bruce's marriage to Karsavina may have shortened his diplomatic career, for in the 1920s it was presumably impossible for a British Minister to have a dancer as a wife; and because he sometimes found himself without a job in later years he was accused by ballet gossips of living on his famous wife's earnings. Certainly in the days when money flowed in, they were extravagant, and it soon flowed out again. In the twenties, when Karsavina was past her prime, and appeared only occasionally as a guest artist with Diaghilev, she was reduced to touring with a series of partners in Central Europe, and even made one disastrous excursion to America. At the time I met the Bruces they had been living for several years in a small flat overlooking Primrose Hill, north of Regent's Park, and they were certainly not well off. I recall, when they came for a drink at Alexander Square before going on with me to the theatre, how Mme Karsavina picked up Lauretta's coat by mistake and they were

Tamara Karsavina in Lady Ripon's garden at Coombe, Kingston Hill, Surrey, c. 1912. One of Baron de Meyer's only four known colour photographs, this was given to Lady Ripon. It was inherited by Lady Juliet Duff and then by Simon Fleet, who gave it to the author.

obliged to change over; and how Lauretta told me later that she felt embarrassed because her heavy astrakhan coat was real and Karsavina's was artificial. For the first year or two my meetings with Karsavina were intermittent: but I remember, after I had moved to Bloomfield Terrace in 1948, Karsavina embarking, at the end of dinner, on a fascinating reminiscence of her Grand-Ducal admirers in pre-war St Petersburg, of the bacchanalian suppers at Cubat or Mdved, and of one Grand Duke who was particularly tall and beautiful; and while I resolved at all costs to memorize the details of her discourse (which, naturally, wine effaced from my memory), I noticed that Andrew Sykes, seated beside her at the table, was fast asleep.

Even when she was a pupil at the Imperial School of Ballet, Karsavina's beauty and talent had attracted Grand-Ducal attention. In her book *Theatre Street* she told how during a school performance Grand Duke Vladimir Alexandrovitch – Tsar Nicolas II's eldest uncle, grandfather of Princess Marina, Duchess of Kent, and the only member of the Imperial family to help Diaghilev in his ventures – was heard above the music commenting in his booming voice 'Who's that? A sparrow, what? Jolly good!'; and when the girls had assembled to have supper with him, he had pointed her out and proclaimed, 'She will beat them all, in time.' Later Grand Duke Vladimir demanded her photograph from the Director of the School, and the headmistress, afraid of making Tamara Platonovna conspicuous or conceited, had decided that the only way out was to have photographs taken of every girl pupil. 'He was always drunk,' Mme Karsavina later confided in me, fondly.

Mme Karsavina consented to give (on Sunday, 5 March 1950) a lecture-demonstration on mime to the Oxford University Ballet Club, of which I was briefly President. When Margot Fonteyn heard what was afoot she wanted to come too. Luckily there was plenty of room in the hired car, for we were six besides the driver: Karsavina, Fonteyn, her mother, Dick Addinsell the composer – famous for his wartime 'Warsaw Concerto' – Andrew Sykes and myself.

Determined to share with my favourite ballerinas the pleasure I felt in contemplating my favourite Oxford buildings, I led Karsavina and Fonteyn an architectural dance from Broad Street, round the Sheldonian and the Radcliffe Camera, across the High to Oriel and the House. They submitted sweetly; but I think even the most intelligent dancers have a rooted dislike of sight-seeing on foot or of taking any form of exercise on Sundays. In Tom Quad I relented and we went back to the Randolph Hotel for tea. We were to dine in the Fellows' Dining Room at Balliol with John Bryson, who had encouraged me in my writing ever since Oxford days and who, in the recent crisis over *Ballet*, had been one of the friends who came to my rescue with a sum of money. Bryson had drawings by Degas and Modigliani as well as by Rossetti and Alfred Stevens, and it was among these, in his pretty rooms on the Library staircase, that we assembled before dinner. All the Balliol silver was produced and we had the best dinner – I might say the only good dinner – I had ever eaten within the walls of my old college.

I had been at some pains to ensure that Karsavina was received with proper honour. Philippe Jullian, who had been staying with me a few days before, had designed a special poster, printed on mauve paper, which was displayed in the porters' lodges of every college. It was in vain, however, that I had attempted to ensure a handsome setting for the great lady's appearance. The statelier lecture rooms and libraries were all in men's colleges, where the women members of our Ballet Club could not be admitted after dinner. Then there had to be a stage of sorts. In the end the lecture was given in a long Nissen hut in the grounds of Somerville – a depressing interior. The stage was very small, and if Karsavina got at all carried away in her miming she might fall over the edge: this danger restricted her performance. The Secretary of the Ballet Club was Clive Barnes; John

Percival and Clement Crisp were members. All these later became well-known critics. A bouquet of sagging tulips was produced. I felt that post-war Oxford lacked the grand manner. But Karsavina was magnificent. Calm as a queen, in her black-and-white flowered dress, her head held high and her eyes glowing with dark mysteries, she accepted the flowers, the little stage and the crowded hut as if she were Catherine the Great entertaining ambassadors from Barbary. Her miming was the revelation to me of an ancient art of whose existence I had only dimly been aware. With what potency, in passages from *Giselle*, from some of the old Petipa ballets we had never seen, and from the works of Fokine, who had abolished the conventional sign language in favour of a more naturalistic acting, she reinforced the gestures of her arms with the expressive passion of her eyes! She told me later that, while dance steps should always be perfected in front of a mirror, this was out of the question with mime.

The drive back to London was a little nerve-racking. The Spanish dancers Antonio and Rosario were on their first visit to England for an appearance on television; I had arranged a party in their honour at Bloomfield Terrace that very night (I was mad about Antonio), and Elsa Brunelleschi was to receive them in my absence. But a mist had come down; our old chauffeur was either tired or tight, and kept dropping off to sleep and waking with a jerk on the brakes; I wondered if Antonio and Rosario and my other guests were sitting tongue-tied in a circle, glaring angrily. I wanted to give pleasure to the Spaniards by bringing in Karsavina and Fonteyn to meet them, but it had been a long day for the ladies. Karsavina was exhausted and Fonteyn felt sick with the motion of the car. Suddenly, as we sat silent in the darkness, travelling along the damp Thames Valley, a girl's laugh tinkled – it was the sixty-five-year-old Karsavina's. Was she thinking of the tulips, comparing her performance for the eighty undergraduates with golden evenings at the Mariinsky

before the Tsar and all his court? Was she laughing at something silly one of us had said – probably myself? Was it god-
like laughter at the futility of human endeavour? Or was she
just wondering whatever chain of circumstances had brought
her to be hurtling with us in a horseless carriage through the
English mist on a cold Sunday night? At Bloomfield Terrace
the party were getting on very well without us. Both
Karsavina and Fonteyn came in to say a word to the 'Kids
from Seville'; and when I saw the divine dancer who had
inspired Fokine sitting in an armchair by the Red Room fire,
with Antonio, chattering merrily, on the floor at her feet, I
was happy.

I think Mme Karsavina got fond of me, for she used to say,
'You knuow Dyicky, you are my whuite-hyaired buoyy.'

Karsavina had been born in St Petersburg in 1885: Lydia
Lopoukhova was born there six years later. She had never
been a beauty like Karsavina, but her odd charm and exuber-
ance were irresistible. Vivacity combined with intelligence
and humour can be more winning than beauty. Although
she had taken her turn in the classical repertory – even
danced some performances of Aurora in Diaghilev's *Sleeping
Princess* – and interpreted certain romantic roles of Fokine,
she was by nature a *soubrette* and excelled in what are called
demi-caractère roles. Lopoukhova's private life had frequently
interrupted her career. She was a bit of a bolter. In 1910,
having danced Columbine in Fokine's *Carnaval* for the first
time in Berlin and Paris (only a year after graduating from
the Imperial School in St Petersburg), she had signed up with
an American impresario and left Diaghilev at the end of the
season. When the Russian Ballet went to New York in 1916
she rejoined them and toured with the company from coast
to coast. She was engaged to be married at the time to the
celebrated sporting and dramatic columnist Heywood
Broun, but she jilted him for Diaghilev's Italian secretary,
Barocchi. She returned to Europe with the Ballet and was

thus on the spot for the new wave of creativity under Massine. In 1919, and for several years afterwards, she and Idzikovsky, as mentioned earlier, were the most popular dancers in London. Randolfo Barocchi's multi-lingual wit is described by Beaumont, but his other charms, to judge from photographs, would seem to be hidden. I never asked Lopoukhova about Barocchi, knowing how ballerinas dislike reference to their first husbands. Already at the time of *La Boutique fantasque* in June 1919, Beaumont, who had made friends with them both, saw signs of Lydia's disillusion. 'When I went to greet Lopokova★ in her dressing-room, she would sometimes lean back in her chair, a wave of weariness would pass over her feautres, and she would murmur half plaintively, "*Kak yah oustala!*" (How tired I am!).' On 10 July, leaving a note for Diaghilev, she eloped – but no further, as it turned out, than to St John's Wood – with a Russian officer; and the hoardings announced 'Ballerina vanishes'. A few weeks later Diaghilev took her back, but she departed for the third time before the end of the year.

When Diaghilev brought his Ballet to the Prince's Theatre in 1921 Massine had left the company, but Lydia was welcomed back to dance her Can-Can in *La Boutique fantasque*, this time with Woizikovsky. She was one of four ballerinas to take the part of Aurora in *The Sleeping Princess* at the Alhambra Theatre that winter, and she also danced the Lilac Fairy. She must have made a charming fairy godmother; but since the famous solo for that character at the christening is designed, with its swooping leg movements, for a taller dancer, Diaghilev inserted for her the Sugar Plum Fairy's variation, to tinkling celesta, from *Casse-Noisette*. She also danced the Bluebird *pas de deux* with Idzikovsky. Lydia married Maynard Keynes in 1925. After that she returned to dance for Diaghilev only once, on the occasion of a gala for

★ Diaghilev had a habit of simplifying the spelling of his dancers' names, regardless of their Russian pronunciation; and 'Lopoukhova' was always printed 'Lopokova' in England.

the King of Spain at the Prince's Theatre in July 1927. (Boris Kochno told me that when King Alfonso asked Lopoukhova 'How is your husband?' she replied 'Very well, thank you. How is your wife?') But she created the role of the Milkmaid in Ashton's *Façade* for the Camargo Society in 1933, danced *Coppelia* for the new Vic-Wells in the same year, and played a part – as did her husband – in the establishment of ballet in England.

Lopoukhova and Massine in the Can-Can in *La Boutique fantasque*. Drawing by Pablo Picasso, London, 1919.

I was sure, though he never said so, that Cyril Beaumont had been a little in love with Lydia in 1919. His descriptions of old ballets were often long and lifeless, but he found phrases to bring Lopoukhova's interpretation of Mariuccia, the maid in Massine's *Les Femmes de bonne humeur*, to life. 'I shall always remember her becoming little white wig and panniered, ochre-coloured frock barred with red, and the violet bow at her breast; together with the little mannerism she had of tilting her head on one side and slightly arching her expressive eyebrows, while her lips perpetually trembled between a pout and a smile.'

There exists a sheet of blotting-paper, scribbled over by Picasso, inscribed to Massine and dated 'Londres 1919', which evoked the character of the Can-Can in *La Boutique fantasque*. Between three studies of Lopoukhova's rounded ballet hands, the artist has flicked in with a sharp hotel pen three impressions of the delirious duet. In one the ballerina is poised on point with drifting arms; in another she is supported by Massine holding her right arm above her head; in a third, as he kneels with one arm raised, Lopoukhova lies across his knee, hand cocked pertly under her chin, and it seems to me that in this image particularly the artist has perpetuated in a few scratchy strokes the charm of her chubby profile and her doll-like perfection of awkward grace.

The other (English) Lydia, whose memoirs I edited in the late 1950s, wrote:

> All choreographers must agree that there are certain dancers who excel in the particular type of movement they invent. Just as Karsavina and Tchernicheva were essentially Fokine dancers, so I am sure that Lopoukhova, Idzikovsky, Woizikovsky and myself were most suitable and adaptable to Massine's individual kind of ballet . . . I responded to his type of movement because the whole system of it seemed to be part of me . . . This applied also to Lydia in *Les Femmes de Bonne Humeur* and in the can-can from *Boutique*: nobody was ever able to give quite the same accent and flavour to the steps which Massine had invented for her. Leon Woizikovsky understood and danced some of Massine's own roles almost as well as their creator; and what Stas Idzikovsky did in the Scarlatti and Rossini ballets could never be repeated by anyone else. That is why these perfect ballets, although they are still done, are in a way *lost*, and when Massine ceased inventing his extraordinary movements for Lydia, Stas, Leon and myself we were lost too, and never did anything so great again.

It was in January 1950 that I was introduced to Lopoukhova.
An invitation to go to the ballet with her and to have supper
afterwards with her brother-in-law Geoffrey Keynes and his
wife at 46 Gordon Square, soon followed. We plunged into
intimacy. Lydia expressed herself in the oddest but most vivid
English, so that I treasured her brief letters.

King's College   28 February 1950
Dear Dicky (may I)
      You are *molto simpatico* as a private personality. I
was so glad you came and I will gladly come with you
again, only at the moment war damage is going on in
Gordon Square, the windows clothed with tarpaulin, and
I cannot live without light. Can you? How exciting it was
to read you in the *Observer* when you became a public
personality. The space was used wisely. Burra [the designer
of de Valois's *Don Quixote*] is much better in black and
white than on the stage, and your critique is only *one* worth
reading, yet not harsh . . .
                    With every best wish
                    Yours
                    Lydia Keynes

'Bloomsbury' had been shocked by Maynard Keynes's
marriage to Lydia. This cannot have been for the eminently
Victorian reason that she was a dancer. Was it because she was
a woman? If Lytton Strachey had had an *affaire* with Idzikovsky – a grotesque improbability – the Bloomsberries
would surely have been delighted. Would they have accepted
more readily the beautiful, intellectual Karsavina? Possibly:
but Karsavina, so aristocratic by instinct, so fastidious in the
conduct of her personal relationships, would probably not
have accepted *them*. Virginia Woolf wrote to her sister,
Vanessa Bell: 'I can foresee only too well Lydia stout, charming, and exacting; Maynard in the Cabinet; 46 Gordon
Square the resort of dukes and prime ministers. Maynard,
being a simple man, not as analytic as we are, would sink
beyond recall long before he realized his state. Then he would

103

awake, to find three children and his life entirely and forever controlled.' This sentence has for me the ring of a tirade by Mme Verdurin against the aristocracy she failed to lure to her *salon*: and we all know how *she* ended. I think Mrs Woolf would have enjoyed a duke or two, just as she took to Victoria Sackville-West and Knole. It was Vanessa Bell, however, who ruled the roost in WC1. She painted a large decoration, which was either the advertisement for or the commemoration of an entertainment given in Gordon Square: it depicts Lydia taking a call, curtseying, and Maynard looking round the curtain like a ridiculous stage-door Johnny. In 1954, studying this picture in my Diaghilev Exhibition, Cyril Connolly remarked to me that it was Vanessa's revenge. I think Lydia always remained a little afraid of Mrs Bell, whom I met once in her company; and when she said to me, obviously expressing a conviction born of long experience, 'I do *not* like *women in power*!', although she was referring to Ninette de Valois, perhaps she also had in mind the autocrat of the Bloomsbury tea-table.

When she was not at her flat in Cambridge or at Tilton in Sussex, Lydia camped out in the two ground-floor rooms of 46 Gordon Square. The fact that these constituted her regular London home in a mansion which belonged to her did not prevent her household arrangements from having an air of Polovtsian impermanence. In all her homes the furniture was perfunctory, as if borrowed from a friendly warehouse. She entertained, at a table normally covered in oilcloth, in the small high back-room, where, among the piles of books and tins of food, one was surprised to find a Cubist Picasso and a sketch by Delacroix. The upper part of the house was let to some society for Christian aid, and when the door-bell rang Lydia would dart to answer it and ask an astonished young man, 'Are you Christian?' The front room which, with its large mirror, had once been used for dancing practice, was Lydia's bedroom. I never set foot in it; but I was sure that when she fortified herself within her stronghold, transformed

on the stroke of midnight from a British peeress into a
Russian peasant, she slept in a cupboard on top of a stove,
under ten eiderdowns, with Pushkin and Dostoievsky.

Lydia was tiny, eager, a wren with a dodo nose. She was
totally uninterested in clothes, and usually had a scarf wound
tightly round her head, as if her whole day were taken up
with housework, which it wasn't. Her appetite for art,
nature, people and life was invigorating.

King's College   5 March 1950

Thanks for the information . . . I have seen Rosario
and Antonio on the films – real good Spanish earth! My
dry rut soon will be cured and then I shall turn up in
London . . .

46 Gordon Square, WC1   26 March 1950

After talking to you I went to Sadler's Wells Rosebery Avenue and was pleased. *Carnaval* has been a nightmare, but this young company [the Sadler's Wells Theatre
Ballet] has a kind of verve . . . I came away with a feeling
that trees do grow in every country. When can you sup
with me and bring Kirstein?

(With Lincoln Kirstein, George Balanchine and Frederick
Ashton I dined with Lydia at nine o'clock on 29 March.)

When Nijinsky died on 8 April 1950 and I wrote my short
piece about him in the *Observer*, I think I must have asked
Lydia to compose an obituary for *Ballet* – as I asked Karsavina,
Sokolova, Rambert and Beaumont – for I have a telegram
which reads: 'Forgive cannot do it not a born writer rather
talk with you when in London later Sunday article supreme
. . . love Lydia Keynes.'

Gordon Square   8 May 1950

It was handsome of you to escort me in such a
grand manner. Thank you. I felt like a lady, quite. Did I
behave?

King's College   24 May 1950

    I was pleased with the Ballet in the *Observer*. Your sense of humour! I laughed till my mouth split (hare lip). Please, let me know the address of L. Kirstein, to thank him for nylon. Admonition! Do not give up your paper. Economise, work harder, you mustn't lose 10,000 Everyman.

The summer of 1950 rises like steam from Lydia's next few letters.

King's College   8 June 1950

    . . . For the last days I have have been sweating like a dancer. I was so hot I wished for nothing but sea shells around my neck, but that would be the case for the Blue lamp. [I think she meant she would be arrested for indecency. Blue lamp = police station?] . . .

Tilton, Firle, near Lewes, Sussex   2 July 1950

    Where are you roaming? I am surrounded by broad beans, green peas and weeds, my skin almost rattles from the sun, so rewarding and sudorous.

7 July 1950

    . . . The hay smells good and English country is beautiful, I circulate, exist like a plant with two arms.

25 July 1950

    Where are you? . . . At the moment I am shelling broad beans, like a Tibetan monk with his beads. I find life a melody, away from Oxford Street.

27 July 1950

    Although I am keen to see the new ballets, I am so stuck, cannot move to city life: half-naked creeping like a lizzard (non poisonous) amongst cabbages and beans, I forget the world in 'contemplative idleness'. I was annoyed last Sunday when the *Observer* was not delivered, can you supply with a copy of last Sunday (23 July) please?

I was to visit Lydia at Cambridge before I stayed with her at Tilton.

> King's College   9 October 1950
>> I am away from London to reach warm walls with my cold in the chest. I am well again, as everyday I eat roast beef. We all want you to visit Cambridge . . .

'We all', I supposed, were the Provost and Fellows of King's, breathless for my visit.

I had a crowded, enjoyable visit to King's, where there was a Roger Fry on every wall, and was welcomed by Provost Sheppard, the Annans, Richard Kahn (Lydia's trustee) and other distinguished dons. Lydia made rather a fool of me by telling me to wear a dinner jacket for a dinner party in college, as I turned out to be the only person in evening dress. Playing up to the role of London gigolo, in which I seemed to have been cast, I announced in an affected voice, 'I bet I'm the only person at the table wearing cuff-links given him by a Fellow of King's.' This remark provoked various surmises, but nobody guessed that the donor was that austere sinologist Arthur Waley, who, admittedly, without the collaboration of Beryl de Zoete, would not have dreamt of giving me a Christmas present.

At Tilton I was allowed to breakfast and write throughout the morning in bed. This, I felt, would not have been encouraged without the precedent of Maynard, who was known to have made his fortune by lying late in bed to read the newspapers. Maynard's principles were strictly adhered to. Gin and whisky were therefore not provided, though a glass of sherry was permitted before meals and wine was plentiful. (Once, meeting Lydia at Covent Garden and attempting to salute her with the usual kiss, I had been repulsed with a firm 'Maynard say no kissing in public.') Tilton was a white box-like farmhouse under the South Downs. The hall was stacked with tins of food, tribute from America, and with innumerable pairs of shoes. Shoes held a sexual fascination for Lydia: she could not resist buying them, and on excursions to Lewes would stand spellbound outside a shoe-shop window. The furniture was as character-less as in the London flat – except for one piece painted by Duncan Grant, who lived with Vanessa Bell at Charleston, a field away; but the pictures were not only by these two stars of the Bloomsbury Pléiade, but by Sickert, Picasso, Braque, Cézanne, Renoir, Degas and Seurat. Sickert had told Lydia her head was like a pigeon's and I admired his profile of her in murky tones of green and purple. The Seurat study for 'La Grande Jatte' was particularly precious. Lydia and I would meet for a jolly lunch, tended by two rosy elves, her house-keeper's children; then I walked on the Downs while Lydia rested and learned the poems of Shakespeare and Eliot by heart. I would stand, breathless from climbing, on Firle Beacon and survey the iridescent landscape to the north; then, from a point only a few steps southward over the high ground I could see the Channel packet coming in to New-haven. After dinner with Lydia and Logan Thompson, who farmed her land, I would settle down by the log fire in the apple-green drawing-room to talk about ballet. Lydia, with a big box of cigarettes beside her, and wrapped in rugs and jackets against the 'curly winds', would tell me about her youth at the Imperial Ballet School before Diaghilev brought her to Paris in 1910; then, filled with nostalgia for her St Petersburg past, she would pounce on the upright piano and play a tinkling tune she had danced to in Theatre Street over forty years ago.

Tilton   7 October 1951

A beautiful letter. Thank you. I shall never go to the theatres any more if I get your critique . . . In spite of your opinion I must have a look at Tamburlaine, even if it is a 'female bishop' [my description of Donald Wolfit] makes me roar with laughter. Most of the day I am in the hills, learning poetry, bitten by invisible insects in the

lower parts of my body. Still I have the taps of water to
rinse me through and degrade the bites.

Best love,
Lydia Keynes

Next February Lydia was not well and wrote: 'One day I
hope I shall jump over the river like a fox, and then we shall
both jump together.' In August 1953 she was expecting me
'to eat raspberries'. In January 1954: 'I am taking things easy
this time of year, but the sun was full of mirth and that is why
I am writing to you, feeling gay.'

For years I was a regular visitor at Tilton; and I wrote the
first act of my first play there. Other friends who popped in
to amuse Lydia were Frederick Ashton, Robert Helpmann
and Vivien Leigh. Lydia used to say, 'I like to be alone, yes
I *do*! But I must have a man for Sunday Lunch.' There were
certain aspects of her early life which she never discussed,
and it is known that she neither helped Roy Harrod with his
biography of Lord Keynes, nor read it when it was published.
She must have been afraid that someone would bring up the
subject of Maynard's homosexuality, or perhaps her own
raffish past. Could she have foreseen the encyclopaedic
documentation of Bloomsbury by scholars during the 1960s
and 70s, when every infidelity was analysed and every
orgasm collated, how shocked she would have been! I
think that a slight fear of being betrayed and 'put into a book'
tinged her friendship for me with reserve. In her letter of
thanks for my *Adventures of a Ballet Critic*, she wrote 'I
should think most saleable with so much inside information',
implying that my material had been procured by stealth.

Although the English Lydia – Sokolova – had contributed
an article to *Ballet* before the war, I had never met her. I was
introduced to her by Frederick Ashton after Nijinsky's
funeral in 1950, and instead of going on to the cemetery we
all three went to a pub in Marylebone High Street. 'But that

wasn't him, dear. It wasn't *Vaslav* in the box. He wasn't there,' said Sokolova. I was startled for a second, expecting some revelation of body-snatching or substitution: then, as I looked into her pale, benevolent, optimistic eyes, I realized that she was expressing her belief in the soul's survival. Sokolova had danced with Nijinsky in *Le Spectre de la rose* during war-time tours of the United States, and in later years had taken over other roles in Fokine ballets, such as Columbine in *Carnaval*, the Ballerina in *Petrushka* and Chloë in *Daphnis et Chloë*, which had once been Karsavina's. Yet, although she could hold her own in classical and romantic ballets, dancing a Fairy's variation in *The Sleeping Princess* or the Mazurka in Fokine's *Les Sylphides*, she was by nature a character dancer, and excelled – as she described in the passage from her memoirs quoted earlier – in the kind of roles which Massine created between 1917 and 1921.

Over our gin in the pub I asked Sokolova to write a tribute to Nijinsky in my magazine: and her brief essay was published that June. In a letter of 24 April 1950 Sokolova wrote: 'You really must help me do something about my life story. You see, so many people have offered to write it, but I *will* have a good book or none, and I feel confident you understand enough of our life, have the sense of tragedy and comedy and above all write so well. I could trust the history to you.' It was not, though, until eight years later that we began to work on her memoirs together.

Sokolova had had a harder life than Karsavina or Lopoukhova. It is true that all three had shared the rigours of a dancer's routine: but though Karsavina had been obliged to make one loveless marriage, had undergone the privations of revolutionary Russia, and in her old age during the Second World War had had to adapt herself to straitened circumstances and learn to cook, she had been adored by princes and poets, she was happy in her second marriage and she had a son to dote on. Lopoukhova had never done anything she did not want to – not even dance, when it interfered with her

Lydia Sokolova and Leon Woizikovsky in *Le Tricorne*, c. 1921.

111

love life: in old age she was very comfortably off, and her walls were hung with works by the greatest modern painters. Sokolova, who ended her days in a tiny cottage near Sevenoaks in Kent, which became continually noisier and more suburban as buildings crowded in and traffic increased, had not, like the other two, had the good fortune and privilege of beginning life with a sound training at the Imperial Ballet School of St Petersburg: until she was able to join Cecchetti's classes in 1913, she had had to learn her dancing as best she could in the basements of Soho. At sixteen she had toured America with a second-rate troupe and been stranded penniless in New Orleans. Her men, until in 1934 she settled down at thirty-seven with the charming, thirteen-years-younger Ronnie Mahon, had been Russians or Poles of undependable character. Kremnev, the father of her daughter (born in ghastly circumstances in Sao Paulo), drank and beat her up. Woizikovsky gambled away every penny of both their earnings; and whenever he made off to stay in comfort with rich admirers Lydia had to fend for herself. When she was at the height of her fame her drunken father had begun to blackmail her and make scenes at stage doors. Abortions and other grave afflictions had laid her low, and she had more than once had to fight her way back from total prostration into a physical state which made dancing possible. She had never had any security but her loving heart and pride in her profession. She told the story of how, when the Diaghilev Ballet had been on its beam ends, stranded in Barcelona in 1918 without money or engagements, she and Kremnev found themselves alone in Madrid, with a sick baby and no money to pay the bill of their lodging house; and how relieved they had been to run into Diaghilev in the street. He was making desperate efforts through the Russian and French embassies and through King Alfonso to secure an engagement at an English music-hall and to obtain permits to take his company through France. His clothes were as shabby as Sokolova's; and he used to sit with her on a park bench, holding her baby.

One day, when the child Natasha was so ill that Lydia thought her last hour had come, Diaghilev took them to his hotel and emptied a bag of copper and silver coins on the bed; he gave Lydia all the silver to pay for a doctor and medicine. After the Ballet had been rescued by Oswald Stoll, and Sokolova was reunited with Diaghilev on the stage of the London Coliseum, she realized from his casual greeting that their shared experience of desperation was never to be referred to again. 'And I never spoke of it to anyone until his death,' she told me. The quality I admired most in Diaghilev, apart from his creative imagination, was the courage with which, again and again, he rose above disaster: even when he had no hope left, he presented an arrogant mask to the world. Lydia Sokolova possessed the same courage and the same determination to *fare bella figura*. Life had to be faced, with its hospitals and pawn-shops; its daily trudge round the market, cooking and cleaning; its insomnia, bronchitis and headaches: and with the help of God and a drop of gin it would be faced in the style she thought befitting a former member of Diaghilev's Ballet. Sokolova's eyesight was failing and she was obliged to wear a wig: but she was always spick-and-span, letters were answered promptly and properly, and she knew right behaviour from wrong.

I never saw my three friends – or even two of them – together, except once or twice when Tamara Karsavina and Lydia Sokolova were at the same party, though they must occasionally have been under the roof of the Royal Opera House at the same time as myself. The two Lydias held Mme Karsavina in awe. Lopoukhova, who was always fascinated by other people's private lives although she discouraged interest in her own, told me that she had once dared to ask Karsavina why she had not married Fokine. Everyone knew that in the early years of this century the budding choreographer and the not-yet ballerina had loved each other. Mme Karsavina replied: 'My mother did not think it would be a good idea.' The mother, brought up at the Smolny

Convent for well-born orphans, had married a dancer; and when Platon Karsavin retired from the stage she found it very difficult to make both ends meet. The struggle for existence, I guess, coloured all her thinking. So, while it was quite a good idea for Tamara to *become* a dancer – and it was indeed the mother's idea – for the stage would be as good a shop-window as the Salle de la Noblesse in which to display her to prospective husbands, she had no intention of letting her *marry* a dancer. Many years later, in Paris, I found that a Mme Souvtchinsky I was talking to, wife of the distinguished musicologist, was Karsavina's niece, daughter of Lev Kars-avin, the philosopher brother who was purged by the Com-munists. I asked if Moukhin, Karsavina's first husband, had been a businessman. 'Not at all,' exclaimed Pierre Souv-tchinsky in such a way that implied I was casting a slur on his friend. 'He worked in the Ministry of Finance. He played the violin.' The Souvtchinskys seemed to think that Kars-avina had treated Moukhin very badly by deserting him for Bruce. It was the only time I ever heard anyone say a word against her.

If it were possible to think so controlled a character as Karsavina capable of hatred, one object of her unlove must have been Anna Pavlova, who had actively resented her potential rivalry in early years and, in the twenties, had twice lured an essential partner away from her. Pavlova's trans-cendental other-worldly quality as a dancer, her indefinable element of genius, may have owed something to her Jewish blood: she obeyed no rules and the bad taste in music, design and choreography which Marie Rambert at least said she thought *necessary* for Pavlova to fulfil herself, made it illogical for her to remain long in Diaghilev's company. Even though Pavlova's image, exquisitely drawn by Serov and enlarged to become the first poster of the Russian Ballet, was plastered all over the walls of Paris, she had hesitated to join Diaghilev in 1909, so that Nijinsky and Karsavina had won the hearts of

Paris before she arrived to dance – in the second programme – the Mazurka in *Les Sylphides*, the ballet in which Serov had depicted her. In 1910 she disliked the music of Stravinsky's *Firebird*, which Diaghilev had commissioned for her, and took off to earn more money in easier ballets before an uncultivated audience at London's Palace Theatre music-hall. Pavlova was a sacred monster, a Sarah Bernhardt, a Maria Callas; and her playing-down to the immense public she reached with her world-wide tours brought her a fame such as Karsavina had never enjoyed. Karsavina was not only a beautiful but a highly intelligent woman: whereas, Benois reported, 'with Pavlova it was only possible to converse in a flirtatious ballet kind of way'.

In early days at the Mariinsky Theatre, soon after she had passed out of the school, Karsavina found she was getting fewer parts than she had the right to expect. 'A prominent ballerina,' she wrote, 'not, I fear, among my well-wishers, had shown an unexpected anxiety for my health, and begged the director not to overwork me, as I was consumptive.'

In 1906 Karsavina began to be paired with the phenomenal Nijinsky, who was three years younger than herself.

The first time we danced before the whole company was at a theatre rehearsal; I was aware of the intense interest of all the artists; I felt a scrutiny, not unkind, round us both, and was more nervous than at a performance. We finished; the company clapped. From a group in the first wing, a sanctum reserved only for primas, an infuriated figure rushed up to me. 'Enough of your brazen impudence. Where do you think you are, to dance quite naked? . . .' I couldn't realize what had happened. It appeared that the strap of my bodice had slipped off and my shoulder had become uncovered, which I was not conscious of during my dance. I stood in the middle of the stage dumbfounded, helpless against volleys of coarse words hurled at me from the same cruel mouth. The *régisseur* came on and led off the Puritan. By this time a dense crowd of sympathisers had surrounded me; my chronic want of handkerchiefs necessitated the use of my tarlatan skirt to wipe away the tears. Preobrajenskaya stroked my hand, repeating: 'Sneeze on the viper, sweetheart. Forget her, and think only of those beautiful pirouettes of yours.' The scandal spread rapidly, and an ovation met me at the next performance.

It was my duty as an historian to check up with Mme Karsavina, as I did, that the villainess of both these episodes was the divine Pavlova.

The ballet *Giselle* had been brought back into the Mariinsky repertory because the role of the carefree village maiden, whose heart was won by a prince in peasant's clothing, who went mad and died, then appeared as an ethereal spirit in the second act to prove her love had survived the grave, brought out all Pavlova's extraordinary powers of interpretation. When in 1910 Diaghilev decided to present Pavlova in her great role in Paris, he found that the ballerina had fled from him and from the music of Stravinsky, so that he was obliged, somewhat doubtfully, to allow Karsavina to dance the old romantic ballet with Nijinsky. 'Did Pavlova help you learn *Giselle*?' I asked Mme Karsavina. 'Not her!' The critic Svetlov, one of Pavlova's former protectors ('One for every day of the week,' said Diaghilev), wrote that Karsavina took the part 'in another key'. 'In her interpretation there enters no deep tragedy. It is the lyrical song of a woman's grief, sad and poetic . . .' Benois thought Karsavina 'almost outshone Pavlova'. I knew, however, from the accounts of friends such as Viva King, that Pavlova had a quality that made her in some way insurpassable. I could not prove this but, much as I loved Tamara Karsavina, I *had* to believe it. Marie Rambert, in her collection of old ballet films, had a fragment of Pavlova in a number called *Christmas*, in which the *seated* ballerina, whose legs never appeared, received compliments, flowers and gifts. I could recognize in this a jewel of artistry. Because of her rich admirers Pavlova always had a great many pairs of beautifully made ballet shoes from Niccolini in Milan, and Lopoukhova told me that in 1909 she used occasionally to steal a pair from her dressing-room.

Lydia Sokolova described so well in a letter to me her own timid visits in 1912 to Pavlova at Ivy House, a mansion newly acquired in a northern suburb of London, that I think I had almost no hand at all in the following account, published in her book *Dancing for Diaghilev*.

Golders Green was lovely in those days. From the station you walked up the hill, which had huge trees on both sides. There was no traffic: it was a country lane. When I entered Ivy House that hot summer day, everything seemed so cool, white and shady. The French windows were wide open with sun-blinds pulled down over them. There were big vases of flowers, and perfume everywhere. The studio was awe-inspiring and seemed to me almost sacred. It was the centre of the house: not quite square, two storeys high, and with a gallery running round it. Off this gallery with its pretty ceiling, white doors led to Madame's bedroom, boudoir and bathroom. Below was the *barre*. On the opposite side to the front door, windows opened onto the garden, and round the room there hung several life-size paintings of Pavlova in her most famous roles. Although the sun poured in at the upper windows, down below there was a sense of coolness which I shall always associate with Pavlova.

On that first day when we went to her house she gave us a wonderful welcome, and had iced fruit drinks brought to us in her drawing-room. [Sokolova had come with one or two other English aspirants in hope of joining Pavlova's company.] I am afraid we were quite speechless, over-whelmed by the beauty of the house and by the glamour of Pavlova.

It was impossible when one met Pavlova like this in her own environment to believe the stories one had heard of her tantrums and hysteria, yet some of them must have been true. Perhaps even her scenes were part of an act, because in my limited acquaintance with this remarkable woman I could see that the only time she wasn't acting was when she was asleep. I never saw her asleep. I wish I had.

There was always a swain in attendance to kiss her hand and tell her how beautiful she was, or to drape her silks and chiffons as she sat down. One of these admirers would enter, approach her with the utmost reverence, click his heels together, accept her outstretched hand, linger as long as possible over kissing it, then, with deep devotion in his eyes, bring a bunch of her favourite flowers from behind his back and whisper 'Anna Pavlova'. She then would kiss the gentleman on each cheek, fondle the flowers and thank him with such ecstasy that you would think she had never been given flowers before.

Pavlova had a profound understanding of the value of receiving graciously. She brought this to a fine art. Being the wonderful dancer that she was, it was rare for her to give anything less than a perfect performance. However, on an evening when she had danced less well than usual I have seen her work the audience up into tumultuous appreciation merely by the way she behaved with her bouquets. Accepting them with a charm which is rarely seen on any stage, she would press the flowers to her body, moving first one hand and then the other as she almost cuddled them. She would bend deeply from the waist, bowing to various parts of the house, give a brilliant turn of the head and shoulders, then run off, with head thrown back to reveal the line of her neck, taking the longest possible route to the wings. This picture she gave of herself, moving so delicately and swiftly with the flowers, was only the beginning. Before she had taken two curtain calls people had entirely forgotten her earlier performance in watching another important and exquisite aspect of Pavlova's art. They loved every movement she made during those curtain calls, and applauded accordingly. I've seen several dancers try to copy this amazing feat of Pavlova's, but they have never succeeded. She was the only one who has been able to build up applause from nothing.

So much for Lydia Sokolova's memories of that strange dancer. It was Fred Ashton who described to me Pavlova's departure from a theatre. He said she was the only artist, apart from Dorothy Dickson, whom he had hung about to watch at a stage door. I tried to give the essence of what he had told me in an article in the *Sunday Times*.

> Pavlova's car would be drawn up in front of the stage door, and a crowd surrounded it, patiently waiting till she had held court in her dressing-room and changed her make-up and clothes. The first sign of life would be that the chauffeur would light up the interior of her car: this produced a buzz of anticipation. Then came a procession bearing flowers, and the car was lined with Pavlova's bouquets. Next, the people who were going to sup with her came out and took their places in the car. Lastly, Pavlova appeared.
>
> Exquisite and bird-like creature, she would be draped in a wide stole of ermine or sable which fell right to the ground. She wore no jewels, but always carried one superb bouquet. Nobody dreamed of daring to ask for her autograph, any more than he would ask Royalty. She paused for a moment on the doorstep, then, amid a murmur of admiration, got into the car.
>
> Now the windows were lowered, and everyone had a final picture of the goddess, shining among flowers. She broke roses and carnations off her bouquet and threw them out to the happy crowd; and continued to do so as, gently, almost imperceptibly, the perfumed and illuminated shrine moved off into the night.

CHAPTER 5

◆—◆—◆

The Diaghilev Exhibition:
The Search

My old school-friend Derek Hill had travelled far and wide
in Europe, Russia and Asia since he left me imitating Van
Gogh with a palette knife in the art classroom at Marlborough
in 1933. He had not yet achieved fame as a portrait painter,
being known chiefly for his landscapes, but he already had
a dazzling cast of friends. He had lived in Ireland and Florence
and sat at the feet of Berenson. Derek loved opera – he had
designed *Il Trovatore* at Covent Garden in 1947 – and he
never missed an Edinburgh Festival. For Ian Hunter, who
succeeded Rudolf Bing as director of the Festival in 1951,
Derek organized a Degas exhibition in the following year;
and when Hunter, casting around for subjects for future
exhibitions, realized that 1954 would mark the twenty-fifth
anniversary of Diaghilev's death, he asked Derek to think
of someone he could get to arrange a show of designs for the
Diaghilev Ballet. Derek suggested me. Ian Hunter discussed
the idea with me over lunch on 13 October 1953.

As I was a stage designer *manqué* it may seem odd that the
only reason I had for hesitating to accept Hunter's invitation
was that I thought there was something depressing about an
exhibition of stage designs. Few artists took the trouble to
make their costume sketches into a picture – and they were
quite right not to do so, for the purpose of these should be
to guide the dressmaker; while their designs for décors
tended to be pictures without foregrounds. But I did not
hesitate for long. I was delighted to have been asked; it was
a new departure; and I thought I could supplement the

designs I assembled with portraits of Diaghilev's friends and collaborators.

It was the French painter and stage designer Jean Hugo, not I, who had married my dear Lauretta Hope-Nicholson; and as there was to be an exhibition of Jean's pictures at the Hanover Gallery in November 1953 they arrived to stay with me at Bloomfield Terrace. While his pictures were being hung, Jean, Lauretta and I set out on a series of exploring walks, and Jean made notes for paintings. In Lower Thames Street, at Rotherhithe, among the West India Docks or on the Isle of Dogs, Jean stood motionless and monumental, formally dressed for the other London in dark-blue overcoat and black Homburg hat, with his dominant nose and green eyes switching from architecture to sketch-book, impervious of the passers-by whom he would omit from his finished pictures; while Lauretta, who was now the mother of three, hovered in a huge cloak, shivering patiently, and I studied the map, looked forward to lunch at 'The Tiger' on Tower Hill or at a Chinese restaurant in Penny Fields, and considered the possibilities of the Diaghilev Exhibition.

Over Christmas, which Jean and Lauretta spent with my mother and me at Overstrand, I continued to hatch schemes for the Exhibition. I wanted to supply some of the theatre's excitement, so music would be necessary. I did not yet know in which Edinburgh building the show was to be held, but I dreamed of a large space transformed into a baroque theatre where visitors could sit listening to the scores commissioned by Diaghilev; and I thought the designs and portraits might hang in smaller rooms opening off this atrium. The little collection of designs which Hunter had envisaged was already becoming something else. Diaghilev himself, in the nineties and in the early years of our century, had thought out ways of making exhibitions more sensational. For his huge display of Russian Historical Portraits at the Tavrichevsky Palace in St Petersburg in 1905 he had ordered Bakst to create a trellised Winter Garden, full of green plants, to contain the marble busts of emperors; in 1906, in Paris, Bakst had made a variation on this theme at the Salon d'Automne, when Diaghilev presented for the first time a retrospective panorama of Russian art in the West; and Benois had then criticized his former 'pupil' for the ostentatious idea of hanging ikons on cloth-of-gold.

'31 December. 3.30 Edinburgh [Festival London] office.' '1 January 1954. Dine Rosoman French Club.' '14 January. Lunch Lady Juliet Duff Hyde Park Hotel.' '18 January. To Edinburgh on night train.' '19 January. Walk. Call for Hunter 11. To College of Art. Leonard Rosoman and Lyon. Lunch there . . . Hunter Caledonian at 6. Dine with Ponsonby. Train back to London 10.40.' '20 January. Ring Karsavina. Lunch James Laver, V & A.' '21 January. I. K. Fletcher lunches. Call for him 11, Stafford Street at 1. Beaumont. Redfern. Browse.' '22 January. George Harewood lunches Rule's. Sup Rambert 10.15.' '23 January. To Lydia [Lopoukhova-Keynes] at Tilton.' '27 January. Festival office 10.30. Arnold Haskell lunches. Juliet Duff and Simon Fleet drink.' '3 February. Karsavina 4.' '5 February. To Juliet Duff at Wilton.' '10 February. 12, Kenneth Clark at Arts Council.'

These stark notes may be interpreted as follows. I had already begun to write letters to people who might be helpful. Juliet Duff had been Diaghilev's staunchest English friend and supporter in latter days, just as her mother Lady Ripon had been from 1911 to 1914. I had met her briefly, introduced by Sacheverell Sitwell at George Harewood's wedding reception at St James's Palace. She was rather too tall, with a pampered voice, and lived with (that is, under the same roof as) Simon Fleet, who was thirty years younger. The tall dandyish Simon, a would-be actor, would-be playwright and would-be designer (rather like myself), was kept too busy driving Juliet around and making her happy, to achieve any of his ambitions. These two friends would change my life, though their influence took effect gradually. When I stayed with Juliet at Bulbridge, across the road from Wilton House (Juliet's mother had been a Herbert), Simon took me for a walk in the Pembrokes' park, which was under snow, and I saw the Palladian Bridge for the first time. I did an awful drawing of this glorious edifice, with two tracks of footsteps converging on it. This was for Juliet's birthday-book, in which I found that Diaghilev had signed himself (in 1911) '*L'ami des dieux*'.

The Wadsworth Atheneum, Hartford, Connecticut, had one of the world's most important collections of Diaghilev designs, and I had telegraphed to them before finally agreeing to plan the exhibition. The Victoria and Albert Museum's Department of Prints and Drawings, of which James Laver was curator, had another. Naturally I needed his help as well as that of the Arts Council, of which Kenneth Clark was chairman; and I combed the West End art galleries such as Rex Nan Kivell's Redfern and Lilian Browse's Roland, Browse and Delbanco, for clues to the whereabouts of certain works of art. Mme Karsavina, Lydia Lopoukhova and Cyril Beaumont were all persuaded to lend their treasures. George Harewood agreed to plan programmes of music, for which EMI (Electrical and Mechanical Industries) were induced to supply facilities. Ifan Kyrle Fletcher, an antiquarian book-seller who specialized in music, ballet and the theatre, and from whom I had bought first editions of Firbank during the war, undertook to borrow musical scores, letters, program-mes, photographs and all the books written about – or illustrating – the Diaghilev Ballet. By a remarkable chance, Leonard Rosoman, whom I admired as a painter of distinction and liked as a friend, was teaching at the Edinburgh College of Art. When, on my lightning trip to Edinburgh in mid-January, Ian Hunter showed me the College of Art, and the Principal, Robert Lyon, proved willing to lend part of it to house the exhibition, it seemed too good to be true that Leonard might be on the spot to design and supervise the transformation I envisaged, and that some of his students might, as a holiday task, execute his plans. Robert Ponsonby, Hunter's assistant, with whom I dined before catching the night train back to London, later became Artistic Director of the Edinburgh Festival in turn, then Controller of Music at the BBC.

It was with a sense of breathless anticipation that I climbed the steps from Edinburgh's Waverley Station to Prince's Street on the early morning of Tuesday, 19 January, for I was about to see the building in which my exhibition would take place. Not even Hercules-Diaghilev, on his way to examine the stage of the shabby old Châtelet Theatre, which he would transform into a fit setting for the triumphs of Nijinsky, Karsavina and Pavlova in 1909, can have looked forward more eagerly to appraising the scene of his future labours. I would soon know to what extent, and by what means, I could make my winter dreams come true. But I was early for my appointment with Ian Hunter at 11 o'clock, so I walked around. I had known a little of Edinburgh during and even before the war, but had attended only two Festivals. During that of 1950, when Antonio and Rosario had danced for the first time on a British stage, I had stayed in Iain Moncreiffe's absence at his house on Calton Hill and breakfasted daily in solitary state among Diana's ancestors. Black as Edinburgh was in the 1950s before a beginning had been made to clean the stone, I already knew it was Britain's most splendid city. It was also to me the most Romantic, not because of Walter Scott, whom I had hardly read and whose monument, canopied with as soaring a Gothic ciborium as that of Prince Albert in Kensington Gardens, dominated Prince's Street, but because of the three steep hills among which and on which it was built. Arthur's Seat, with its sensational outline, was bare of buildings and lay outside the city, with Holyroodhouse at its foot. Calton Hill, though its lower slopes were crossed by grandiose terraces, had a bare rounded grassy top (dangerous at night), adorned with strange classical shrines and a Greek temple which was the more interesting for having been left roofless and incomplete. The Castle Rock, precipitous on three sides, was the heart of the Old Town, and on its gently graded fourth side the Canongate or Royal Mile led down to the gates of Holyroodhouse. From Prince's Street, and from the two vast station hotels at either end of it, the North British and the Caledonian, could be enjoyed famous views of the Castle's silhouette – which, truth to tell, comprised no medieval towers, but only a conglomeration of later buildings; and this street, Edinburgh's 'Piccadilly', had houses only on its north side, to leave the view open. Below the Castle's northern precipice there had once been a lake, since drained to allow for the railway to be built. This was discreetly sunken and screened by the trees of Prince's Street Gardens, where my Granny Buckle had taken my father to play and listen to the band in the early 1890s, and where the band could still be heard on summer afternoons, wet or fine – for the Scots ignored a drizzle. North of Prince's Street lay the squares, terraces and crescents of the Georgian New Town, nobler than any in London because built of stone; but even this classical lay-out bore a romantic scar, for it was cleft by a plunging chasm, wooded among its crags, through which flowed towards distant docks the Water of Leith. Then, how thrilling to stand on the ridge of George Street and look north, down Castle Street or Frederick Street, over the slope of the modern Athens, across the Firth of Forth – blue in clear weather – to the opalescent hills of Fife!

But that Tuesday morning was cold and grey. I picked up Hunter at his office and we walked to the College of Art, which I had never seen before. This red sandstone building stood next to the Fire Station in Lauriston Place on yet another hill, which was separated from the Castle Rock by the Grassmarket. The College had all that I hoped for. There was a huge arcaded hall, the Sculpture Court, with an upper gallery above the arcade, whose pairs of columns supported the coved and sky-lit roof. Because the hall was due for redecoration (what luck!) certain liberties were to be permitted us. I planned to show the designs and portraits in the screened-off upper gallery and in large rooms leading from it and from the arcade below. As I hoped to conduct the visitor from surprise to surprise, one-way traffic was essential, so it was convenient that a monumental main staircase could take him straight from the entrance to the upper floor and, when he had gone round three sides of the gallery above the Sculpture Court (hidden from him by partitions), there was a smaller back staircase to bring him down to the 'portrait gallery' on the south side of the building. This was the only room whose windows I would leave uncovered because it had a fine view of the Castle Rock. Last of all, the unsuspecting visitor would walk into the gloom of the blacked-out and transformed Sculpture Court, where there would be chairs, and where he could hear Harewood's programmes of music, if he liked, for hours at a stretch. For the first of many times I paced up and down to take in the possibilities of a building, and began unconsciously to learn the lesson that the source of all inspiration must be the site.

Shortly after my return to London I walked on an impulse into Cole's wallpaper shop in Mortimer Street. I had the idea of hanging all the smaller rooms of the exhibition with wallpaper, and I asked the director of the firm, Douglas Robertson, if, in return for publicity, he would give the Edinburgh Festival all the wallpaper I needed. The amazing coincidence that he turned out to be a native of Edinburgh, schooled at the College of Art, predisposed him in our favour. He agreed to make us a present of all we wanted, and to print the papers in colours chosen by me. We dug out some old wood-blocks which had not been used for years.

I was writing letters all the time (in longhand, but making carbon copies), for I was determined to collect every single surviving Diaghilev design in the world. The English loans had mostly been bespoken, the chief American collection had been guaranteed: there remained France. On the suggestion of Arnold Haskell I had taken on Georges Reymond a former underling of René Blum, as liaison officer for France, and he acted as intermediary and arranged a number of interviews. On my first visit to Paris 'in search of Diaghilev' I lodged at the Hôtel Quai Voltaire, where Wagner had written the libretto of *Die Meistersinger*.

I was aware that because of Diaghilev's impatience with the familiar and thirst for the new, the friends with whom he surrounded himself and the climate of his artistic court had changed drastically between 1900 and 1929. During the first years of the Russian Ballet in the West, Benois, the wise 'elder brother', had had bitter scenes with the high-handed Sergei Pavlovitch, who did not always give him the credit he deserved and who realized that the more sensational designs of Bakst, which astounded Paris as much as did Nijinsky or the music of Borodin and Stravinsky, held more publicity value; and if Benois, the inveterate St Petersburgher, was suspicious of the more experimental Moscow painters, Larionov and Gontcharova, he was downright disgusted by Diaghilev's later essays in Surrealism or Constructivism in the 1920s. Likewise, Diaghilev came to think of Benois that he had 'lost every atom of colour and taste' and was 'exactly where he was thirty years ago'; and Larionov derided both the delicate pastiche of Benois and the lush 1890-ish exoticism of Bakst (who had died in 1924). I was careful not to mention Benois to Larionov or Larionov to Benois. Boris Kochno, on the other hand, who came into Diaghilev's life only in 1921, was interested above all in painters of the school of Paris.

Benois and I sat chatting in his studio on a little seat, which just contained us, drinking tea. The old boy was by then eighty-four. He was neatly dressed in a dark double-breasted suit, the front of which hung down, unbuttoned; he wore the rosette of an Officier de la Légion d'Honneur and a knitted skull cap. I looked affectionately at his big expressive features, white hair and moustache, and shrewd, twinkling eyes. While he expressed interest and willingness to help over my Exhibition, I suppose he was thinking something like this: 'Only the other day, it seems, Serioja arrived, uncouth, ignorant and provincial in St Petersburg, and what a job we all had civilizing him! And what a job I had persuading him that ballet was a serious art like opera! Certainly one can't deny that, wrong-headed as he was over so many things, he had the push and drive to put on our ballets in Paris and London, to make us world-famous. Although he lorded it over Western Europe for two decades, the only years that were worth anything were the early ones, and then it was as much *my* ballet as his! Clearly, one should die young to become immortal. Now the whole of Europe is to glorify the twenty-fifth anniversary of his death. And I suppose my young friend here will be hanging all those awful daubs by Larionov, Picasso and Matisse alongside the work of our group – Bakst, Doboujinsky and myself – who really loved the theatre and didn't just want to draw attention to ourselves. Poor old Serioja! He always liked to be talked about, and now his legend has taken root with a vengeance!'

Benois was encouraging to my plans, but I detected an underlying amusement. He was perfectly willing to lend designs. He taught me how to spot a fake Bakst. (Fakers used gold paint, whereas Bakst applied gold leaf to raised lumps of gesso. With a few exceptions – mostly designs for *The Sleeping Princess*, which were done in haste – sketches covered with instructions to the dressmaker were all copies by Bakst's assistants. The artist kept his original designs to exhibit and sell.) Benois complied, protesting mildly, with my demand that he should design a frontispiece for our catalogue; and the arrival in London a few months later of this enchanting and exactly appropriate wash-drawing, rolled up in a magazine, was one of the most exciting moments of my year. It was done in sepia and blue-grey

Frontispiece for the catalogue of the Diaghilev Exhibition. Watercolour by Alexandre Benois, 1954.

wash; and represented the Magician from *Petrushka*, lifting the curtain of a little rococo theatre to reveal, in the formal garden of Armida, Rinaldo courting the Doll from *Petrushka*, watched by the crowned and sceptred Boris Godounov.

Petrushka himself looks under the curtain (like the cherub in Beardsley's prospectus for *The Savoy*), finger to lips, hushing the audience, while above the marbled proscenium a male and female harlequin support an admirable *tondo* head of Diaghilev in top hat and white tie, flanked by smoking censers. It was in the excessive adulation which the censers seemed to imply that I again suspected a hint of mockery. Was not Shura, two years senior but still alive, pulling young Serioja's immortal leg?

When I called at the old house in the rue Jacques Callot where Larionov and Gontcharova lived, I climbed four spiral flights and knocked at an impenetrable-looking door. After a mysterious pause I heard movement and sounds of a discussion. Then the door opened a little, and I was scrutinized by the calm eyes of Nathalie Gontcharova. The interior of the apartment was unique. No walls and almost no ceilings or floors were visible: the three rooms and the little vestibule were crammed from top to bottom with piles of books, parcels of drawings, pictures, portfolios. I felt like a robber in the tomb of an Egyptian king. But a narrow path had been left for me through the dusty stores of treasure, and this led to the bed of Pharaoh-Larionov.

The big man, with his round child-like face, was recovering from an illness and received me lying down: but he was so eager and enthusiastic, and any talk of painting or the theatre excited him so much, that he was continually sitting up, propping himself on one hand in the most uncomfortable way, and throwing a leg off the bed.

No one was more devoted than Michel Larionov to the memory of Diaghilev; and he revered him for exactly what Benois disapproved – his determination to be contemporary and up-to-date. From the way Larionov talked I could see that he had remained, as Diaghilev did all his life, a youthful open-minded anarchist. (When I told him about the pillared hall Leonard Rosoman was decorating for the Edinburgh Exhibition, I said it would be a contemporary interpretation

Alexandre Benois. Drawing by George George, made for *Ballet*, 1949.

of baroque, and he exclaimed, 'Contemporary! That's the important thing.') But even so, I found, there were limits and one had to be careful. Looking round my hotel room, before setting off on a subsequent visit to him, I could find nothing but the colour-print of a recent Picasso landscape to take him as a present. This was handed back to me by Larionov, without ceremony or comment: I had made a grave mistake. I suppose Michel thought that Picasso had sold his soul for money.

Gontcharova had the enclosed air of a nun. Her grey hair, parted in the middle and dragged back in the humblest way, her anonymous black dress, her folded hands, her silent entries and exits – everything about her conveyed an impression of reticence and withdrawal. Perhaps she guessed what I was thinking, as she came and went, fetching paintings and portfolios at the behest of Larionov, for she gave me a secret smile, and said, 'I am invisible, like the servants in Chinese plays.'

On my first visit I had planned to spend an hour or two with this dear couple: but I soon realized that time does not exist in a hermitage. First, although I had just eaten an enormous luncheon, I had to be plied with cakes, and – because I was coughing – with sweet wines and syrups mixed with warm water. We talked; and it was four hours before I could bring them to look out the designs I needed for the Exhibition. Then, the question was to find them! Which room? Which stack? Which bundle? Some of the works of which I made notes on my first visit could not be found on my second. Pharaoh-Larionov was so lavish with his own work and that of Gontcharova that I ceased, after a while, to express admiration for the pictures they showed me, for fear of being showered with more gifts.

It was because of Michel's impassioned remark about the importance of the new that I decided not to have a design by Benois, Bakst, Picasso or Larionov himself on the cover of my catalogue, but something by Leonard Rosoman. I had already conceived the idea that an exhibition of old work should give employment to young artists. Partly because of Larionov's aged youthfulness and because he had reminded me that to follow in the steps of Diaghilev one must keep an open mind and create opportunities for the young, I maintained this principle, whenever possible, throughout my new career (as it turned out to be) of exhibition designer. I was thus able to give rein to Medician impulses at other people's expense.

Boris Kochno, who was not a painter himself, had amassed with thought, cunning and will-power, a very individual magpie hoard of other people's work; and his reputation as a miser was so widespread that I thought it quite likely, though he was well disposed towards me, that he might lend me nothing. Although Boris and I saw eye to eye on many matters, his unpredictability at that time made me a little nervous. Since the death in 1949 of Christian Bérard, Boris had moved into a new flat in the ninth *arrondissement*. It was a noisy, commercial quarter; but the small flat was chosen because it had all its *Directoire* cornices, chimney-pieces and door-handles intact. Here Kochno's personal museum had been arranged. Only three rooms were open to the public, that is to say, me: a hall, a sitting-room and a bedroom in which it was quite clear that nobody slept. In these were disposed, with careful negligence, the magpie's precious and heterogeneous spoils. A portrait by Géricault, metal fruits from Persia, ikons, late eighteenth-century mechanical furniture, jewelled boxes, curious sculptures, portraits by Bérard, a diminutive 'Picasso museum' (containing nine mock Salon pictures drawn on the fragments of a match-box) and designs for the ballet. There were sketches by Matisse for *Le Chant du rossignol* on the wall, by Marie Laurencin for *Les Biches* and by Braque for *Les Fâcheux*; but I knew that there must be a great number of other Diaghilev relics hidden away, which no one had seen for years. Kochno had lent nothing to Lifar's Paris exhibition in 1939.

Amid all these rarities stood Boris Kochno, like a bull tamed by a china-shop. He was balder, thicker and unhealthier-looking than when I had seen him last, a few years before. I had a theory that his carouses and his collecting were equally forms of compensation for his disappointment at not having been able to carry on the Diaghilev Ballet after 1929. It must have been a bitter ordeal to remain obscure and inactive while Lifar postured all over Paris. He was the one man whose devotion for Diaghilev had been as great as Diaghilev's for Nijinsky, Massine, Dolin, Lifar and Markevitch. He had fetched and carried for Diaghilev. Now the imagination and taste which had initiated such works as *Les Fâcheux*, *Ode* and *Le Fils prodigue* for the Diaghilev Ballet, *Cotillon* for Blum, and *Les Forains* for the Ballets des Champs-Elysées, were concentrated on the arrangement of this flat. Tchelitchev had written to me, 'Boris Kochno has a Muse, of which the name is Dipsomania, hélas!'

Kochno had let no scrap of paper slip through his fingers. Besides important designs by a number of painters, there were the hieroglyphic scribbles with which Joan Mirò indicated that the costumes for *Romeo and Juliet* should be bought at a common bazaar; the diagrams in a letter to Diaghilev of Yakulov's intentions for the setting and choreography of *Le Pas d'acier*; a caricature of Diaghilev by Igor Stravinsky on a sheet torn out of a pocket note-book; some of Bakst's first ideas for scenes or dresses for *The Sleeping Princess*, on writing-paper of the Savoy Hotel; and little pencil portraits of Dolin and Prince Schervashidze, the scene-painter, by Pruna. Kochno himself had been drawn or painted by Picasso, Juan Gris, Tchelitchev and Bérard.* To my delight I found he was going to lend me everything I wanted.

In my visits to Benois, to Larionov and Gontcharova, and to Kochno, I had followed within a few days the whole artistic trajectory of Diaghilev – from nostalgic St Petersburg to experimental Moscow; through the works of French painters who had once been *Fauves*, through Cubism to Surrealism and Soviet Constructivism and beyond. None of

---

* Also – for he gave me a list twenty years later – by Soudeikine, Maliavine, Delaunay, Larionov, Pruna, Derain, Berman, Balthus, Drian, Hugo, Masson, Freud, Dubreil and Costi.

these Russians, who lent me so many designs and portraits, had had any contact with each other for nearly a quarter of a century.

Then I also went to see Jean-Louis Vaudoyer of the Académie Française, who received me seated at a southern window, with a rug over his knees, as he was just recovering from an operation: he had adored Karsavina and had suggested the theme of *Le Spectre de la rose*. I called on the director of the Musée de l'Opéra, who showed me the opera-glasses Diaghilev had stolen as a souvenir of his opening night at the 'Palais Garnier'; on the director of the Musée des Arts Décoratifs, a department of the Louvre, who lent me the huge famous design by Bakst for the décor of *Scheherazade*, which had changed the appearance of drawing-rooms and the style of women's dresses throughout Europe, and which was in a very ugly dark oak frame; and on the director of the Musée d'Art Moderne, who lent me the painting of Stravinsky by Blanche and the drawing of Anna de Noailles by Vuillard, but could not lend me Picasso's front curtain for *Parade* because it was too big. Another Picasso curtain, that for *Mercure*, was in the ballroom of Etienne de Beaumont's great house, where Douglas Cooper, a keen supporter of mine at that time, took me to call on him. Cooper, the unchallenged authority on the Impressionists and Cubism, also led me to Picasso's dealer, Daniel Kahnweiler, who showed me maquettes by Juan Gris for *Les Tentations de la bergère*. I had tea with Mme de Forceville, the niece of Reynaldo Hahn, who lent me a portrait of Cocteau by Madrazo. I called on Lucienne Astruc, daughter of Gabriel Astruc, the impresario who had made Diaghilev's early Paris seasons possible; and she unrolled for me the immense poster of Pavlova by Serov for the season of 1909, and Cocteau's two of Nijinsky and Karsavina for later seasons. These I took away to be laid down on canvas. With introductions from Juliet Duff, I called, at his palace off the Boulevard Saint-Germain, on François de Ganay, son of an early supporter of Diaghilev, who lent me many Baksts; I lunched with Marie-Blanche de Polignac, Lanvin's daughter, beneath the frescoes painted by Bérard; and in the mansion of Marie-Laure de Noailles, whose grandmother Mme de Chevigné had been transformed by Proust into the Duchesse de Guermantes, I was shocked that throughout the delicious lunch for twenty, during which the vintages of precious wines were murmured in one's ear by a butler, people smoked incessantly. The habitually love-lorn Marie-Laure, whom I liked very much, screamed her head off with the rest, but a sadness seemed to come over her as they began to leave and, when at last she led me, sighing, into a little low-ceilinged ante-room to see a caricature by Cocteau of Diaghilev, Sert, Misia and the artist himself in an opera box, I guessed that she would spend the afternoon dying of a broken heart until people came in for cocktails at six. I also went to lunch with Diana Cooper at Chantilly, during which meal Enid Bagnold exclaimed, when I told her about the huge novel I was even then beginning to plan, 'You can never marry.' Lady Diana helped me to borrow designs by Bakst from the Rothschild family.

The time had come to move my headquarters south. I would continue my correspondence while staying with Jean and Lauretta at Fourques. I also wanted to meet Cocteau, who was adjudicating at the Cannes Film Festival and, with luck, Picasso, whose villa at Vallauris was considered impregnable.

With joy, and with only about five francs in my pocket, I got into the night train at the Gare de Lyon. It was only the second time I had gone to stay with the Hugos among their vines near Lunel, between Nîmes and Montpellier. I dropped off to sleep, book in hand; shifted into a better position at Dijon; woke in the echoing void of Avignon station; got up to watch the day dawn on a classical red-gold landscape; saw the southern sun strike the towers of Tarascon, which made me think of troubadours and crusades; decided not to shave at Nîmes; then hauled down the luggage and prepared to be born into a different world. The symbol of this southern world which had so long haunted my imagination was Corot's little blue and gold painting of the Palace of the Popes at Avignon, seen from Villeneuve across the Rhône, a paradise of classic calm. This hung in 1954 in the Tate Gallery: later, after the settlement of a long dispute between Ireland and England over the will of Sir Hugh Lane (who was drowned in the sinking of the *Lusitania*), it came to stay in Trafalgar Square.

Basking in the sun, surrounded by children and peacocks, walking through a maze of curving paths lined with lilacs, seated at the oval table in the vaulted dining-room, or beside the library fire after dinner, I discussed with Jean and Lauretta my alternative strategies.

I had written to Cocteau asking him to be on the Committee of Honour and had received a message of assent. With Picasso I had made no attempt to communicate, as I was told he seldom read and never answered letters: he would have to be taken by surprise. The austere, forbidding Kahnweiler might, however, have passed on to him the news that I was planning an exhibition. Cocteau was an old friend of Hugo's – indeed Jean had designed his adaptation of *Romeo and Juliet* in 1925 and his *Orphée* in 1927 – yet they had seen little of each other in recent years: and it is always awkward to re-open old friendships. Still, Lauretta had persuaded Jean to invite Cocteau for Easter, by which time the Film Festival would be over. Of course, he might not come. Picasso, on the other hand, whom the Hugos knew, and who had lunched more than once at Fourques – leaving traces of his visit in the form of animals torn out of coloured paper for my godson Charles – would very likely be coming our way, because he usually attended the bullfights which began after Easter in Arles, Nîmes and even Lunel. I might wait, but how long could I afford to wait? If I went to find Cocteau in Cannes would he spare time to see me during the Film Festival? Should I ever gain admittance to Picasso's house, even with introductions? Jean Hugo was doubtful.

One day I packed a bag and left for Cannes. It was much hotter on the Riviera, and two British warships were riding at anchor in the blue bay. I took a room in a cheap, noisy hotel beyond the railway, surrounded by main roads, trains, pneumatic drills and a children's playground. I was introduced to Cocteau by Georges Reymond in a passage at the Palais du Festival, and presented my letter from Jean Hugo. Cocteau was smaller than I had expected. He asked me to luncheon next day.

The entrance hall of the Carlton Hotel was full of awful-looking film people. Cocteau was surrounded. I stood apart for a few minutes, then saw him raising his elbow at me as a signal that we should go to the bar for a drink.

He had done a drawing of Diaghilev for me, a simple but grotesque caricature. 'This is for you, it is yours,' he emphasized – very thoughtfully, I considered – so that there should be no mistake. In Paris Mlle Astruc had produced for me, among other letters, one from Bakst to her father, in which he recommended that Cocteau should design the poster of Nijinsky for the season of 1911. Now Cocteau had made a drawing for me!

It was natural that at luncheon, which we ate in a dark corner of the hotel dining-room, we should begin by talking about films. The gist of Cocteau's argument was that the artist was helpless in a world of business.

'Do you know that my film *Le Sang d'un poète* was given at one cinema in New York every night for eighteen years? And do you know what I got out of that? Nothing! When *Orphée* was to have its first performance in a certain European country, the boss of the circuit of cinemas wrote to our "producer" asking him to be present. At the end of his letter he extended the invitation to Marie Dea and Jean Marais. Then, after the signature there was a postscript. "If M. Cocteau would like to come too he will be welcome."'

'If working in films is so awful,' I said, 'I wonder why you do it.'

'We do it because we have an idea – something we want passionately to see as a film. And because we want to do it so much, the gangsters know they can safely offer us twenty francs and we shall have to accept it. But I shall never make another film.'

I asked if there was no subject that might prove irresistible.

'I should like to make a film about Duse and d'Annunzio; and if I could get Garbo and Charlie Chaplin to play the two parts I might direct it. I once told Garbo she ought to do *Phèdre*, but she had never heard of the play.

'In the days of Diaghilev we did what we did for almost nothing: but then one could live for five francs a day. Why are there no longer great rows over works of art? On the first night of *Parade* there was such a noise in the audience that Diaghilev, who was behind the scenes, thought the chandelier had fallen. That was when a woman nearly poked my eye out with her fan, and another exclaimed, "If I had known it would be like this, I should have brought the children!" – which I took as a compliment.'

Cocteau talked about the independent life a work of art takes on when it leaves the hands of its creator. 'One day Georges Auric was with me in my flat in Paris. A film for which he had written a tune had just been released. As we sat talking I heard some men, who were working on a scaffolding outside the house, whistling this tune. I opened the window and said to them, "*Messieurs, je vous présente votre compositeur!*" And to Georges I said, "*Voici tes interprètes!*"'

He promised that when he went north he would look out his old drawings of Diaghilev, Nijinsky and their friends and lend them to the Exhibition. (Marie-Laure de Noailles, as I have mentioned, had already promised me one of this famous series, and Igor Markevitch was to produce another.) One objective of my campaign seemed to have been attained! But what about the second? I asked Cocteau how I could gain admittance to see Picasso. He beckoned to a waiter and took from him two small sheets of paper. On one of these he wrote a note, which began, I remember, 'I never send anyone to you, but –' and went on to tell Picasso that I was very shy and that he must be kind and see me. On the other piece of paper he drew me a little map showing how I must turn off the main road at the beginning of Vallauris, climb the Route des Ecoliers and find Picasso's villa, La Galloise, on the side of the hill. At last! I could have kissed him.

Next day the taxi deposited me at the beginning of the little town in the hills. It was very hot. I found my way, and saw the house; but I had taken the wrong path up the slope and arrived above and at the back of it. I saw a little girl in red in the garden, and heard a boy's voice calling 'Paloma!' So these were Picasso's children by Françoise Gilot, whom he had painted so marvellously! There was no other human being in sight, but I imagined the surrounding vineyards and olives to be populated with peasants who were paid to give warning of a stranger's approach; and it occurred to me that I might be spotted and mistaken for a snooping journalist. I hurried back down the path and approached La Galloise from the front. There was a garage, with a flat over it, beside the gate. The little house itself stood back from the road, fifty yards up the hill.

As I advanced, a shaggy old lady in a straw hat came out on the balcony of the flat above the garage, and shook her head at me. A good-looking young man with an insolent expression got out of a huge Hispano-Suiza which he was cleaning and asked me what I wanted.

'I have come to see M. Picasso about an exhibition I am organizing in Edinburgh.'

'He is not here.'

'When will he be back, then? Here is a letter from Jean Cocteau, introducing me.'

The name of Cocteau appeared to mean nothing to him. 'He won't be here all this week.'

'Well, I can't stay on in Cannes indefinitely on the chance

of being able to see him. Couldn't you take in this note, and I will wait?'

'What is the use of my taking in the letter if he's not there? There is no point in your waiting, as you won't be able to see him.'

I turned away and went sadly down the hill.

Failure! I felt a hundred years older. After I had walked about Vallauris, which was full of incredibly vulgar pottery, taken a taxi to Antibes, gone twice round the Picasso Museum in the Château Grimaldi, and wandered for a while in the market, I thought it must be well on in the afternoon: nevertheless I entered a restaurant and asked for luncheon. I was greeted by surprised looks. It was only just after eleven.

By midday I was in a bar at Cannes watching Cocteau and Orson Welles giving imitations of Sacha Guitry saying 'Good morning'; and at three I was on the train back to Lunel.

Licking my sores among the lilacs, I wondered whether to admit defeat. Lauretta said that the young man who had turned me away was undoubtedly Picasso's elder son, Paulo, who spoke perfect English. His mother had been Olga Khokhlova, Picasso's first wife, one of Diaghilev's dancers: and it was Paulo who stared out so innocently, a pretty child Pierrot, from famous canvases of thirty years ago. After an adventurous youth, he had settled down as chauffeur-bodyguard to his father. Paulo-Pierrot seemed to me a kind of bogy – an enemy of art, of Edinburgh and of the Queen!

On the Sunday after Easter we drove into Nîmes, and I went to the bullfight with Vyvyan Holland, the son of Oscar Wilde. Looking across the oval Roman arena I caught my first sight of Picasso. A great white embroidered cape was spread out over the barrier in front of him; men in gold and silver swung their scarlet *muletas* below him; and bulls were dying at his feet.

Lauretta had stayed away from the bullfight as she was pregnant, but she met us in the street outside. Suddenly, there was Picasso, advancing towards us, beaming. He put his arms round Lauretta's belly and listened for a message from the child within. Lauretta towered over him. He was tiny, dressed in a shapeless suit of mole-coloured corduroy. On his head he wore a large, flat, red and black dog-tooth-checked Harlequin cap, which he later pointed out was English, with a Bond Street label inside. He had the most mischievous eyes I had ever seen. He was a goblin.

Twenty minutes later we were in a white-tiled laboratory, drinking wine out of medical-looking beakers. Our host, M. Castel, was a wine-doctor. I heard Picasso saying to Castel's daughter, 'If I were a woman I should certainly be a barrister. You wear nice clothes; you go to the law courts; you make up your face; and you say to some poor devil [pointing] "Condemned to death!"'

Picasso and Paulo were to dine with Douglas Cooper and John Richardson at the Château de Castille, half an hour's drive away; and although this was something long-hoped-for and carefully planned by Douglas, who had never managed to lure Picasso to his house before, he was kind enough to invite me too. Lauretta and Vyvyan went back to Fourques.

It was Lauretta who had found Castille for Douglas. Standing in an austere landscape near the Pont du Gard, this neo-classical madhouse, girdled by a colonnade, approached by an avenue of columns, and with its stables and, yes, theatre surrounded by a circle of forty more columns, had been in a state of dilapidation until Douglas restored it to hold his collection of Cubist pictures. Douglas himself was a curiosity, pink, portly and preposterous. He had pigeon-holed the School of Paris – his catalogue of the Courtauld Collection alone was a masterpiece of scholarship: yet his character or behaviour had excluded him from such posts as Director of the Tate Gallery, and everything English was anathema to him. He had evolved the absurd doctrine that art criticism was an exact science; and he carried on like a spoilt child who had been allowed to play King for a day, but refused to resign his paper crown. When he spat out his high-pitched denunciations he expected heads to roll.

Picasso had to be shown the famous collection, so we moved off in a body. I tagged along in the rear with Hispano-Paulo, who had meanwhile become quite friendly, and even lit my cigarette.

The painter seemed pleased to rediscover certain of his own works. He exclaimed admiringly, in front of one painting, as if it were by someone else; then, turning to me, he said, 'Painting is a wonderful thing. It's not useless. One is right to paint.' I agreed feebly. He said that one of the worst deeds he had ever perpetrated was to paint, when too poor to buy canvas, a still-life over a fine picture by Modigliani. Looking at some watercolours by Paul Klee he said, 'You'd think there was a light inside them.' Our host compared a Cubist Gris to Zurbaran. 'That's just what I was thinking,' said Picasso. 'It's like Zurbaran, only better. Yes, that's better than Zurbaran.' Was he being polite? I had a feeling that he was oppressed by our deference, by the luxury of the house and the omniscience of our host.

Having penetrated into the presence of the master, I was already overwhelmed with guilt at the thought that I was hoping to turn this simple social occasion to use. I did *not* want to spoil the evening by bothering him about his old designs. At the moment I was a harmless Englishman without much to say for himself, wearing a brown suit. Once I spoke about the Exhibition, I should be transformed into a Harpy.

To complicate the situation, though not perhaps deliberately – for no one could have known for certain that Picasso would come to dinner – Douglas Cooper had invited for the night a lady who had some years before been the painter's mistress and model. If the evening turned into a great sentimental reunion my importunities were going to be more than ever *de trop*. Dora Maar arrived, a sturdy, brave, intelligent and attractive little figure. She was accompanied by a young American, who seemed as eager as I was to miss no word of the master's, though he was less self-effacing, and

143

called Picasso '*tu*'. Picasso was obviously delighted to see his old girlfriend, and Paulo's face lit up in an amused and anticipatory way. When we sat down to dinner in a small candle-lit Parthenon, I was on one side of Picasso, who refused everything except grated carrots and hot milk. But all his attention was taken up with Douglas and Mme Maar.

The question arose whether Picasso and Paulo should stay the night or drive back to Vallauris. The painter put forward a third alternative. Could we not all go to Perpignan? I was quite ready. Paulo, however, appeared to have reasons for returning home. In the drawing-room after dinner I was alone for a moment with Picasso, his son and his former mistress, and I heard him ask them, 'What are we doing here?' I saw his point.

But I at least was there for a purpose. Buoyed up by brandy, I got Picasso on a sofa and told him what I wanted. 'Yes, I have all the *Tricorne* designs, and a lot of different versions of the set for *Pulcinella*. Diaghilev couldn't make up his mind which he preferred. He liked them all so much, he wanted to use them all. I will look them out for you when I come to Paris in May. Keep in touch with Paulo.'

In fact, I knew from Kochno and Markevitch that Picasso had been mortally offended when Diaghilev had rejected design after design for *Pulcinella* and thrown his work on the floor. What Diaghilev finally succeeded in getting, nevertheless, was a masterpiece.

If promises were pictures I had done well for the Exhibition. At least I had done what I could.

The next day I returned to Lunel and caught the night train for Paris.

'When I come to Paris in May!' Picasso had said. In June I returned there myself and even went with Boris Kochno to knock on Picasso's door in the rue des Grands-Augustins. He never came north. In the early summer Jean Cocteau had a heart attack which nearly proved fatal, and was too ill to think of going to Milly-la-Forêt and finding his old drawings for the Exhibition. Except for the caricature of Diaghilev which Cocteau had done for me, my southern excursion had proved fruitless. No, it had had one other happy result. I found in Jean Hugo's studio some little drawings he had made, during seaside holidays in 1922 and 1923, of Cocteau, Georges Auric and Raymond Radiguet. There was one, which I thought specially historic, of Radiguet dictating *Le Bal du Comte d'Orgel* to Auric, who was typing it, while Cocteau lay reading in a deck-chair. (I considered Radiguet's novel one of the most perfect ever written in French.) The two dozen works of Picasso and Cocteau I eventually included in the Exhibition all came from other sources.

On this trip to Paris in June I visited the three nieces of Bakst, two of whom were far from comfortably off. All were devoted to the memory of their affectionate uncle, whose fame at that time was in eclipse. (So, for that matter, was Beardsley's; and he had been a potent influence on Bakst.) The youngest sister was married to the producer and designer André Barsacq, who succeeded Dullin as director of the Théâtre de l'Atelier at Montmartre; and it was in his office, across the courtyard from where Dullin had stabled his horse, that I was shown designs by Bakst for *The Sleeping Princess* and sketches for the dressing-table, sofa, table and birdcage for *Le Spectre de la rose*. The eldest sister, who lived in a less attractive neighbourhood, emptied whole portfolios. Among many designs for ballets I found scraps of paper with caricatures of Diaghilev by Chaliapine and of Bakst by Stravinsky. Although at that time designs by Bakst were not highly valued, Mme Nicolas was solicitous for her uncle's glory. I found a large, slightly damaged project for the original décor of *Les Femmes de bonne humeur*. 'This ought to be laid down on canvas,' I said. Sighing, Mme Nicolas agreed; then added: 'If you promise not to tell anybody, I will sell it to you for [the equivalent of] £10 [$28], and you can take steps to preserve it. But you must undertake, if you ever have to sell it, not to let it go for less than £100.' (I kept my promise, and a few years later, when I was in debt, sold it to Peter Daubeny for the sum mentioned.) A few tiny scraps of paper fell out of the portfolio. They were pencil drawings for hats, evidently made about 1910. Mme Nicolas gave them to me. That afternoon (19 June), adventure-bound, I went to the Piscine Deligny, the swimming-pool surrounded by a floating stockade of cabins and restaurants which is moored to the south bank of the Seine. I left my clothes in a hanging wire cage in the changing-room. The little Bakst drawings, tucked into the catalogue of an exhibition, were hidden between my trousers. When I returned in the evening to my hotel and opened the catalogue the drawings were not there. What thief in search of money could possibly have been interested in them? In Paris perhaps even thieves have good taste. I rang up the manager of the Baths and offered to pay a certain sum if the drawings were restored to me. Next morning I got them back.

When I dined with Colonel de Basil's widow, the former dancer Olga Morosova, I found her in the company of an older man, Anthony Diamantidi, whom I wrongly supposed to be her lover. He was in the process of taking over from her the Diaghilev scenery and wardrobe which she had inherited; and he sent me out to the *dépot* at Pantin where most of these were stored. I borrowed Utrillo's back-drop for *Barabau*, the first ballet Balanchine arranged for Diaghilev, and some constructions in wood and metal created by Picasso for *Mercure*.

I had attended the *vernissage* (on 18 June) of Tchelitchev's exhibition at the Galerie de la Rive Gauche, in the rue de Fleurus where, as he had written to me, 'at No. 27 used to live Gertrude Stein in 1927 . . . It was there that all my carrière had started . . . Sometimes life seems to go in spirals.' And spirals, circles and ovals of the most amazing kind outlined the featureless and luminous heads, drawn in paint and pastel, which I gazed on in this exhibition. I cannot say I 'understood' these visionary drawings at the time, but I was dazzled by their radiance and recognized their transcendent technique, which no living painter could rival. Tchelitchev wrote to me, 'The strange thing is that my actual [present] work is very much like the realized dream of 1928 – *Ode* – 25 years of investigation is really not so much time.' Although we met very seldom, the witty, malicious worldling who had become, in his own words, 'a monk', made friends with me by letter over the Diaghilev Exhibition, and within a year was signing himself 'Best love, Pavlik.' He had revolutionized stage design, and knew it.

Of my 4 ballets I did, *Ode* [1928], *Errante* for 1933, *Saint Francis (Nobilissima Visione)* [1938] and *Balustrade* (Stravinsky 1941, New York), I have done more for establishing a new principle of light on stage from [than] any of my contemporaries . . . *Errante* created sensation in Champs-Elysées, Paris 1933 – 32 curtain calls! And it gave me immediately an important position in N.Y. where it aroused an equal sensation. All stage designers will admit that their ideas about light come to a great change. As in my principle like in my work of today light come from the stage like out of a precious stone . . . Light creates space, mood, form and emotional states. People react immediately upon change of colour . . . Even without colour people understand psychologically light better than painted sentimental ragg-decors. *Balustrade* was like a vision, in starless night . . . When there is someone that looks and finds a door to open, not one of the contemporarys has eyes to see it and always they fail to notice to ask about the details . . . very important . . . and the door slowly closes.

CHAPTER 6

The Diaghilev Exhibition:
The Settings

The Diaghilev Exhibition was to open on 22 August 1954, and I had decided that I should spend at least the six weeks before that in Edinburgh, supervising the building of the décor. Work in London, however, mounted to a crescendo in July. I kept trying to get more and more exhibits right up to the last moment; there was correspondence about insurance and transport; pictures had to be photographed for the catalogue; the prefaces of Benois and Kochno had to be translated; and I had to write my own Notes on the Diaghilev ballets. Luckily Ronald Crichton undertook to compile for me a Biographical Index of Diaghilev's circle, the painters who were represented in the Exhibition and their sitters. It was no mean task to compress the essential information about, say, Ravel or Derain into three or four lines: and these miniature biographies were a necessary part of the catalogue. Mary Clarke, later editor of the *Dancing Times*, rushed round London collecting pictures, and sometimes slept with Picasso self-portraits on her wall. It is significant of how little value was placed in those days on the designs as works of art that it occurred to none of us to give their measurements. The letters and photographs, which were to go in showcases, were not even listed individually. It was during these hectic weeks that an old friend, Philip Dyer, came to my assistance. I took advantage of a vague offer to help, and soon had him slaving day and night. When he gave up jobs of his own to come north and work for nothing in Edinburgh, his practical experience as a decorator made him an invaluable interpreter of my ideas to carpenters, painters and electricians. He called on prospective lenders for me, ran errands, bought material, sorted exhibits, helped to hang pictures and pacified the offended. All this was done for love of art and for the glory of Diaghilev – who had once, when Pip was a stage-struck child, patted him on the head behind the scenes at the Prince's Theatre. The date of my final departure for Edinburgh was put off from day to day. At last, for the fifth time that year, I left by the night train, on 26 July.

The whole idea of spending a few weeks in a provincial town and probing its secrets had always held a fascination for me. Not that Edinburgh could be dismissed as a provincial town: it was a capital city, an ancient seat of kings. But it was still mysterious to me. I counted on it to provide me with varied adventures – not only topographical ones.

My host in Edinburgh was to be a solicitor friend, Ian MacGillivray, tall, gaunt, gentle, white-haired and rather prim. He had a typical Edinburgh fear of what the neighbours might be thinking, so I was no doubt an embarrassing as well as an exotic lodger. Yet time would prove that this careful bachelor, with his regulated life, could die of a broken heart. Ian lived in George Square, which seemed to belong – to judge from its classical architecture – in the New Town north of Prince's Street, but which stood in fact on the same southern ridge as the site of my exhibition, between the Meadows and the valley where lay the Grassmarket. Sir Walter Scott had grown up in this 'parallelogram', as it was first called (and which in the 1970s would be taken over completely by the University).

For weeks I followed a regular timetable. After breakfast at eight I wrote letters and telephoned – often to London or Paris. About ten I walked along the north side of George Square into Upper Meadow Walk, down Lauriston Place between the Royal Infirmary and George Heriot's School to the College of Art: this took five minutes. At half-past twelve I had lunch in the canteen with Leonard Rosoman

The Hall of Giants at Edinburgh, designed by Leonard Rosoman. Photograph by Hans Wild.

and the students; and at four, tea. Between five and six I walked back to George Square, where I dined and went to bed before midnight.

Rosoman had made a dramatic design for the great hall, and a dozen students were painting canvas and paper. The pairs of columns above were alternately black and vermilion; on the fourteen panels between them, which screened off the gallery, greenish and tawny painted statues gesticulated beneath orange canopies. The columns, once they had been covered in canvas, had to be garlanded with spirals of yellow and dark green leaves, nearly two thousand of which were to be stuck on by someone hanging from a tower of scaffolding. Below, the piers from which the arches sprang and the spandrels between the latter were covered with canvas and paper painted to simulate malachite. We were allowed to paint the cove of the ceiling a yellowish green: the panes of the skylight were filled in with gold paper to reflect the light of two great lamps contrived by Rosoman in wire and *papier-mâché*. When two immovable plaster casts of tombs had been boxed in and decorated, I suggested that we should make a virtue of necessity and construct two giant plaster negroes to lean upon them. These twelve-foot statues designed by Rosoman and modelled in six weeks by two of the sculpture students, Henry Clyne and Daphne Dyce-Sharp, were made by a method which was then new to me: round a wooden skeleton the shape was roughly enclosed in chicken-wire before being covered in scrim, plastered, given a smooth finish and painted. The negroes' turbans were then topped by plumes of stiffened paper feathers. These statues proved to be one of the most popular and publicized features of the show not only in Edinburgh but when it was transferred to London.

Lady Rosebery, a member of our Committee of Honour, one of the founders and certainly the queen of the Festival, introduced me to her son Neil Primrose, then at Oxford, who was an expert on stage lighting and had very big feet. Undeterred by difficulty or danger, he would take on any task, no matter how hazardous; and when he fell from a great height and damaged an artist's work, the labour of weeks, he would walk away without apology, as impervious to the miracle of his own survival as to the feelings of the frustrated painter.

As I watched the Hall of Giants taking shape – the first patch of malachite going up, the blue-grey grotto with its creepers, ruins and distant village beginning to emerge and to be lit beneath the arches at the southern end, the gilding of the columns' capitals and bases, and the first still unpainted negro being carried in by eight men from the sculpture studio and raised aloft – I was as happy as a child with a sequence of birthdays. Everyone in our team threw himself with a kind of passion into the work. Some of the students had shown such zeal and talent in carrying out Rosoman's designs that I contrived to give them little corners of their own to decorate. One day I found a man staring aghast at our work in progress. 'What on *earth* is going on here?' It was Robert Matthew, Professor of Architecture, one of the two creators of London's Royal Festival Hall. Such a profusion of ornament dismayed him. He walked away without another word.

Our group of regular workers, who met for meals in the canteen, with its view over the Castle Rock, was joined by a stream of volunteers from the outside world, which we had almost forgotten. Philip Dyer came close on my heels from the south. Hazel Armour, a gifted sculptress, married to a director of Jenner's, a big Edinburgh store, was working on some great golden cockerels which were to be erected at key points in the city to advertise our Exhibition. Up from London had come my loyal friend Viva King, to create, out of scraps bought in the Edinburgh shops, the 'Poiret' and 'Chanel' dresses for the *tableaux* which were to illustrate the influence of Diaghilev's Ballet on fashion. Juliet Duff and Simon Fleet were cutting out tough canvas leaves, gilding the cockerels and searching the town for chandeliers. Ifan Kyrle Fletcher had brought his wife to help him arrange the books and programmes. Finally, John Bryson came from Oxford to hang the pictures.

Because I had foreseen the difficulty of travelling up and down between Edinburgh and London, I had given the printing of the catalogue to the Edinburgh firm of McLagan and Cumming. Unknown to me, they farmed the work out to a London printer. Catalogues are always corrected, printed and delivered at the last moment. When the proofs were flown up to me in Edinburgh I was asked to correct and return them in time for the morning plane. There were several problems to be solved during the night. Many items promised had not been forthcoming: others came unexpectedly. For instance, Gontcharova and Larionov had not been able to find, in the chaos of their flat, many of the designs I had chosen and catalogued. They were sending others instead. Renumbering was a nightmare. Then there was the Committee of Honour, a list of distinguished people, including many surviving collaborators of Diaghilev, who had extended their patronage to our venture. I was worried about their order of precedence. Lord Rosebery said: 'Put ambassadors first, then people with titles in correct precedence, the rest in alphabetical order.' That was all very well, but who would confirm my instinct that La Vicomtesse de Noailles came before Comtesse Jean de Polignac? I had appealed for help to Iain Moncreiffe, who was now a Herald. On the Day of Wrath, his twelve-page letter arrived, explaining everything. Diaghilev's principal scene-painter in the 1920s, who was one of those I had invited to be on our Committee, was a Georgian prince and artist, Alexander Schervashidze. Now, I had always been told that you were a prince in Georgia if you owned three cows. Unicorn Pursuivant's letter began: 'The Schervashidzes were ruling princes in Georgia long before England was united under a single monarch . . .'

As the day of the opening drew near, our tempo accelerated and my problems increased. What had happened to a package of wallpaper which had left London nearly a week ago? Only the paper we were *not* ready for had arrived. This could not be hung till the canvas ceiling had been distempered; and the canvas could not be distempered until there was some light to do it by. But the electricians had gone away, saying they could not fix the lights until the ceiling was up . . . Which rooms could we afford to carpet? Could women sew standing on ladders? Where were we to get chairs? About three hundred of the exhibits would arrive at the last moment unframed. Who would frame them in two days? Where could X, Y and Z stay when they came up for the opening? There were people who had to be shown round, and journalists who wanted interviews. Desperate cries echoed throughout the building: 'Mr Buckle! You're wanted on the telephone!'

Leonard Rosoman sat drawing at his desk, and the students swarmed up and down scaffolding. The painters and paper-hangers were spell-bound by the beauty and novelty of the wallpapers Cole's had made for me – particularly by the gold flock paper for the portrait gallery, which gave an effect of silk damask. 'If ye're going to keep doing jobs like this all yeer life,' they said, 'we'd like to bide along wi' ye.'

It was a great day when Bourlet's van arrived at the College of Art and deposited the Diaghilev Exhibition in neat crates at our feet. I imagined the young driver coming by night impassively through the Midlands, up the Great North Road. He brought us the former Lifar collection, comprising works by Derain, Gris, de Chirico and Tchelitchev, from Connecticut; the treasures of Bakst, Larionov and Gontcharova from Paris; the Braque sketches for *Les Fâcheux* from the Victoria and Albert; the Benois designs for *Le Rossignol* and Roerich's little setting for *Prince Igor* from Oxford; costumes that Nijinsky and Karsavina had worn nearly half a century before; the manuscript scores of Stravinsky's *Firebird* and Falla's *Le Tricorne*. Another triumphant morning was that on which the music was suddenly switched on: the whole building was flooded with sound, and the exhibition came to life.

Like Diaghilev, who had worked almost as hard at the composition of his first-night audiences as over the perfection of his programmes, I had tried to bring together as many of his old friends as possible to bless my baby's christening. Karsavina, Lopoukhova and Sokolova could not be lured. Massine was far away. (I had even had trouble in getting him to answer my letters about possible loans; and it was only when I protested 'You must admit that it will be absurd to have six portraits of Lifar and none of you' that he wrote authorizing the disinterment from a warehouse in Manhattan of his portraits by Bakst, Picasso, Derain and Matisse.) Balanchine was not interested in commemorating the past. ('The only souvenirs I have of Diaghilev,' he wrote

to me, not meaning it, 'are some pornographic drawings I
made for him.') Boris Kochno, however, flew in to Edinburgh a few days before the opening, loaded with brandy
and jewelled boxes. Ian MacGillivray kindly put him up,
but Boris was so drunk on the first evening that I thought it
diplomatic to move him to an hotel. The next day I received
a flamboyant telegram from Serge Lifar: 'Today Venice has
celebrated the twenty-fifth anniversary of the death of Serge
Diaghilev. I arrive at Edinburgh tomorrow with his death-
mask at 11.15.' Although Lifar had promised me in Paris
that he would come I had not really expected him. He and
Boris were not on speaking terms, and I had warned each
of them that the other might appear in Edinburgh. Each
said that there was nothing to worry about: at a large party
there would be no need for them to speak. It was not at a
party, however, that they met. On the afternoon before our
opening I went to greet Alicia Markova at the airport and
brought her directly (on her insistence) to have a preview of
the exhibition. We found Serge Lifar alone with my French
'liaison officer', Georges Reymond, in the Portrait Gallery;
and within a few minutes Boris Kochno had come in out of
the rain. Pip Dyer's devoted friend, the photographer Hans
Wild, was busy recording the results of our labours (before
being swept off to the Royal Infirmary with appendicitis
two days later). Bold as brass, he asked Kochno and Lifar to
pose for a photograph together, which they were obliged to
do, with Reymond grinning like a mad witch between
them. In revenge, Boris pointed out to me that a Bonnard
portrait said to be of Diaghilev's best friend Misia Sert was
not of her at all.

That night neither Leonard, nor Fred Macdonald, his
chief assistant, nor any of the students, nor Pip Dyer went to
bed. Nothing seemed ready. Everyone was exhausted and
nearing despair. I realized for the first time in my exhibition-
designing career that in the final frantic stages of preparation
artists and craftsmen tend to turn against their director, and

that I had to be very careful what I said (in my anxiety to perfect every detail) if I were not to provoke mutiny. Tea was served at regular intervals, as if there were a war in progress. I deserted my friends at half-past three, as I knew I had to compose a speech in the morning. When I left them – in the early hours of what should have been such a happy day – I could think of nothing but that half the sets for the model theatres had not yet been painted. I even forgot I had just heard from a London solicitor that he had a warrant to seize all my possessions. All my correspondence, except what was relevant to the exhibition, had been neglected; and I was being pressed by creditors. Even the pages of my Diary, from 6 August, my thirty-eighth birthday, up to 22 August, are completely blank except for four words on the 20th: 'Press view. Mama dines.'

Ian MacGillivray and I had a luncheon for thirty people, including Grigoriev and Tchernicheva, Rambert, Kochno, Lifar, Markova, Juliet Duff and Simon Fleet, Iain Moncreiffe and Diana Erroll, Lord and Lady Crawford, Sir Robert Bruce Lockhart and my mother. Diana had been asked to be on our Committee of Honour because she was Hereditary High Constable of Scotland; Lord Crawford (a Trustee of the National Gallery) and Sir Robert (an expert on Russia, formerly imprisoned in the Kremlin) because they were friends of Juliet Duff.

There were two things Lifar could never resist: posing for photographers and speechmaking. We had no press cameras at our lunch, but when it was over Serge rose to orate. His rhetoric was boring beyond belief. At the end of his speech he awarded me 'the Diaghilev Prize for 1954' and handed me an envelope. As I haltingly replied – *'Je me sens très humble, moi qui n'ai pas connu Diaghilev . . .'* – I was remembering the solicitor's letter threatening to seize my goods and chattels, and I hoped the envelope contained a cheque. No such luck! There was nothing inside but a sheet of paper inscribed 'Prix Diaghilev, 1954'.

By half-past-two we were all seated on the platform of the Hall of Giants – well, most of us, for I find the *Sunday Despatch* reported next day that 'Something went wrong at the opening of the Diaghilev Exhibition. Distinguished guests arrived ... and were left ignored in a corner ... There were far too few seats, and no one quite knew what to do.' As I spoke, naming the illustrious colleagues of Diaghilev who had come to grace the occasion, I was conscious of Oliver Messel's face looking up at me from among the small crowd of visitors. I introduced Alicia Markova. Upstairs there was a basket of dead lilies-of-the-valley that Diaghilev had given her on 1 May 1924, when she danced the Nightingale in Balanchine's *Le Chant du rossignol* for the first time, with Diaghilev's card still attached to the ribbon by a rusty pin. As she ended her speech with the words 'I declare this Exhibition open for your instruction, inspiration and wonder' the music of the Prelude from *Les Sylphides* began to play.

Within seconds the Princess Royal arrived with George and Marion Harewood and Lady Rosebery. I remember how Ifan Kyrle Fletcher, our collector of documents, thrust himself forward uninvited and did the honours like a gushing mayor, and what a dirty look Princess Mary gave Lifar when, conscious of an approaching camera, he held her mesmerized by his oratory over the death-mask of Diaghilev. Juliet Duff had asked me what my mother's maiden name was, and when I told her, she recalled 'There were some rather dull Miss Sandfords who used to stay at Crichel.' Of course there were: so when I had introduced Mama to her I said, 'This is one of the dull Miss Sandfords.' It was Rose's elder sisters, however, Eva and Cynthia, who had stayed so often in Dorset in their youth with Féo Alington and her bewitching son Napier: so Mama escaped the slur. She said to me afterwards, 'I could see Lady Juliet summing me up, and noticing the way my scarf was pinned – you know, one can tell – and deciding I was a lady.' I recall how kind Oliver Messel was about our work; and how when I said to Lord

Crawford, 'Don't you think Rosoman has done well?' he insisted, '*You* have done well. It's magnificent.'

When the excitement was over I found myself sitting in the drawing-room at George Square with Leonard Rosoman, Kochno and Lifar. Boris and Serge nagged at each other like a couple of schoolboys. 'Why do you wave your hands about when you talk?' grumbled Boris. 'Put them in your pockets. Hide them!' 'But I have good hands. Why shouldn't I show them?' 'Hide them. Nobody wants to see them. I have good things too' – producing a heavy gold box – 'but I keep it in my pocket.' 'Well, I'm not a miser like you.'

As for my longed-for explorations of Edinburgh and my getting to know more about its inhabitants, I had seen nothing but the houses on either side of Lauriston Place as I walked daily to the Exhibition and back again. Nevertheless the same columnist of the *Sunday Despatch* who had criticized the exhibition's opening arrangements, made the most of a 'human story' about me which was hardly sensational. 'We are trusting people in Edinburgh. Dickie Buckle, who has made such a superb job of the Diaghilev exhibition, mentioned it yesterday. He dashed out one evening last week to post a letter at the post office beside the Art College. The post office was closed, and he found he had no change for the stamp machine. The postmistress happened to be standing outside talking to friends, and she saw his trouble. She opened the stamp machine and gave him stamps. "But I've no change," said Mr Buckle. "You can come in with it to-morrow" was the reply.' I remember that this kind lady of Lauriston Place gave her name as 'Mistress Mary Stewart'.

The press was generous; Kenneth Clark praised the exhibition; 'I think Sergei Pavlovitch would have marvelled,' wrote Beaumont in the *Sunday Times*; and we even made Monday's *New York Times*. Looking over the old press cuttings, it strikes me as remarkable, in the light of after events, that both the *New Statesman and Nation* in an article and Margot Fonteyn in an interview with the *Scotsman* expressed the hope that part of the exhibition might form the base of a permanent collection in London. (I also notice that, under the influence of Dior's 'new look', women's hats

Margot Fonteyn and the author in the Benois room in Edinburgh, with designs for *Petrushka*. Photograph by *The Scotsman*.

were very small.) It would be an exaggeration to say that crowds flocked to see the show, for the College of Art was off the beaten track: but we had twenty-five thousand visitors in the three weeks which the Festival lasted. We must have cost Edinburgh a pretty penny, all the same.

It had not occurred to me that the *Observer*, for which I worked, should put on the Diaghilev Exhibition in London. The week before our opening, however, I had sent the editor some snapshots taken by Daphne Dyce-Sharp of her Negro statue and of work in progress on the Hall of Giants, asking if he could not get a photographer to take a picture for the paper. On 22 August, the Sunday of our opening, a large photograph of Leonard pretending to paint one of the giant negroes was duly published. This may have been a crucial factor in the fate of the exhibition – and in my subsequent career. I was told that a very business-like lady was arriving to sum up the situation and report on the possibility of transferring the show to London. Diana Petry (later well-known for her travel articles) turned out to be a dear: she loved the exhibition on sight and typed a long summary of pros and cons. Of course, if we took the show south we should have to ask lenders to extend their loans – and find a suitable building in London. This had to be somewhere central. I began to think in terms of swimming baths and disused chapels. Were there any great mansions that had not been turned into offices? What about handsome Spencer House, overlooking Green Park, which Christie's had recently vacated? Or Bath House in Piccadilly? Then, I remembered that I had often passed, but never entered, a long dingy brick and stone mansion standing in a garden behind a high wall between St George's Hospital and Belgrave Square. I had no idea of its name. On 8 September I took the night train, and on arrival went straight with Nigel Gosling to examine these houses.

The state rooms of Spencer House, with their delicate plaster-work, were connected by a rabbit warren of passages with rotten floor boards: it was not practical. The former home of Lord Bath was hopeless. The mystery mansion in Belgravia, which had come into my head in Edinburgh, turned out once to have been Lord Granard's, and was called Forbes House. Although it belonged to the Grosvenor Estate a club had leased it, but left it empty and unused. It seemed to me to have 'capabilities'. I had lunch with my editor, David Astor, attended a conference, wrote an article and flew back to Edinburgh. Because of bad weather the plane was diverted to Glasgow, and I had to complete my journey in a freezing bus. The next day, a Saturday, the exhibition closed. 'Sunday 12 September. Ian away. Packing up. Lunch Diana Petry. Wet through and no fire. Bed early.' When it was learnt that Forbes House was available, and when Diana Petry, Nigel and others at the *Observer* had worked out a few sums, it was decided that the exhibition should be transferred. This was settled almost overnight. The *Observer* would employ Leonard Rosoman and myself to devise another décor suited to the new site. The Edinburgh students, who had done so well, were to travel south and do even better: the *Observer* would pay and house them. Cole's agreed to give us more wallpaper. Lord Primrose again undertook the lighting.

Because I wanted to keep the entrance hall of Forbes House, with its grand marble staircase and *faux Louis-Quatorze* ironwork as a final climax for the exhibition, I decided to build a tented exterior staircase to lead the visitor from the box office straight to the easternmost room of the first (or as Americans would say 'second') floor. Thence he would cross the 'Poster Room' and climb a narrow side staircase to the bedroom floor. In its six southern rooms we could hang our designs; and it was only necessary to knock holes in two walls to make a continuous route. Descending another narrow staircase the visitor would come to the loftier rooms of the *piano nobile*. The first was to contain three fashion *tableaux*; the second and biggest a portrait gallery; the third a 'haunted theatre' for the display of original old costumes, most of which were lent me by Grigoriev; the fourth, which I determined to make octagonal with a domed ceiling, a small library for books on the Diaghilev Ballet; the fifth a room for caricatures. Here the Diaghilev part of the exhibition would finish. The visitor would then emerge in a gallery where two branches of the main staircase descended to a landing and became one, which led down to the entrance hall. I wanted this last part to be the Palace of the Sleeping Beauty. To fill four arched recesses above, and several areas of blank wall below, Rosoman was to design painted canvases which would have the double meaning of 'vistas' and 'tapestries'. We took our cue from the pseudo-eighteenth-century columns and plaster-work of the house. On the

The Portrait Gallery at Forbes House. (*In the arched recesses to left and right*):
Romaine Brooks's portrait of Cocteau and Vanessa Bell's 'poster' of
Lydia Lopoukhova and Maynard Keynes; (*in between*): self-portrait by
André Bauchant, self-portrait by Rouault, 'Massine seated' by Picasso,
self-portrait by Tchelitchev, drawings of Massine by Matisse and Bakst,
Frank Dobson's bust of Lopoukhova, drawings of Massine by Picasso
and Derain, self-portrait by Matisse, self-portrait by Picasso, drawing of
Lopoukhova by Picasso and 'Lopoukhova and Massine in *La Boutique
fantasque*' by Picasso. Photograph by Manor Studio, Southall.

Massine seated. Drawing by Pablo Picasso, Rome, February 1917. This
drawing, which can be seen in the centre of the photograph opposite, is
now in the Theatre Museum, London.

landing would be a sculptured group of the sleeping princess on her canopied bed, about to be woken by the prince. Two twice-lifesize sentinels with spears would be sleeping on their feet on either side of the foot of the stairs. By removing the front door, the windows on either side of it and an ugly iron *porte cochère,* and by building a wooden pavilion extending into the garden, I planned to enable Rosoman to hang outside the palace a décor representing a tangled forest, with sleeping huntsmen on horseback in the distance. All this was duly carried out: but although two big log fires were kept burning on either side of the hall, my blue-grey forest tended to let in a draught.

The *Observer* decided that it would be a good idea to serve light meals; and that nightly lectures would give the paper a pretext for keeping the exhibition in the news. The two big rooms to left and right of the entrance hall, once a dining-room and library, were therefore to be a restaurant and a lecture-room. The meals were well arranged by Fortnum and Mason: but the lectures, though some of them were first-rate, proved an awful nuisance, for I had to introduce the lecturers, and for the rest of the winter would often find myself at nine in the evening stranded, too late for a theatre and without a dinner companion.

Naturally, I was anxious to make the exhibition more complete, so letters and telegrams started to flow once more, and I reopened my one-sided correspondence with Picasso.

One new exhibit turned up in an unexpected way. On the pavement outside a junk-shop in Cecil Court, off Charing Cross Road, Lydia Sokolova found a plaster head the subject of which she recognized. There had been much in the papers recently about the discovery of a Mithraeum under a demolished building in the City of London; and the head was jokingly labelled 'Straight from the Temple of Mithras. Ten

Opposite: The Sleeping Soldier. Design for one of four fifteen-feet-high panels at the top of the staircase at Forbes House. Drawing by Leonard Rosoman, 1954.

shillings'. It was Nijinsky in his horned wig and make-up for *L'Après-midi d'un faune*. We were both thrilled by the discovery; but who was the sculptor? I held a press conference on 6 October, and the finding of the portrait made a good story. Next morning, before I had even seen a newspaper, John Gielgud rang me up to say he had read in the *Manchester Guardian* about the head, and he thought he knew what it was. He came straight round to Forbes House. Yes, he had seen its replica in marble, when staying with the sculptor Lady Troubridge in Florence the year before; and he gave me her address. Una Troubridge, wife of Lauretta's cousin, Admiral Sir Ernest Troubridge, had been the close friend of Radclyffe Hall, author of *The Well of Loneliness*. She wrote:

Palazzo Guicciardini   13 October 1954
15 via Guicciardini, Firenze

> I can tell you all about the Nijinsky bust. The one that Lydia Sokolova found is the long-missing *original* plaster cast from the wax I modelled from life. I believe it to be the only portrait from life (in sculpture) that exists of him – as you probably know Diaghilev *hated* him to sit & made Rodin destroy a portrait he had begun, as soon as he heard of it. I was lucky (and clever?!). I made friends with old Maestro Cecchetti & he arranged for Nijinsky to sit to me during his lesson hours at the Drill Hall in Goodge Street [actually Chenies Street, opposite Goodge Street Station]. Karsavina would remember – & also when Diaghilev was away I worked in the wings of the theatre. Once Nijinsky posed for me in 'Spectre de la Rose' costume & make up. The first Diaghilev ever knew of it was when the marble was exhibited. The marble – done from the plaster you have – was in my possession until I gave it to my great friend, the writer Radclyffe Hall; at her death it returned to me and a few months ago – at the suggestion of my friend the Russian-Italian basso, Nicola Rossi-Lemeni, I presented it to the Theatrical Museum of the Scala, where it is on view in the Ballet

section on second floor. The plaster (yours) I gave to an old dilettante music-lover, Frank Schuster (for many years always in Lady Ripon's box – also had a much renowned music room in Queen Anne's Gate. Kept the Nijinsky with flowers always before it. He is now dead and forgotten).

We had six weeks to transform Forbes House. I was able to concentrate on artistic problems, as David Astor had appointed Nigel Gosling general administrator to take the burden of finance off my irresponsible shoulders. Several of the young artists, as well as Pip Dyer, were given individual opportunities to express their ideas or mine. The restaurant was decorated by six tall panels of scenes in a modern ballet classroom by Tom Deas, son of a miner from Fife, whom I found particularly congenial. These were all done, on my suggestion, in shades of grey and orange: and I recall that Clive Bell was deeply impressed by their gusto. Our London décor was more elaborate and more finished than that in Edinburgh: we only missed the immensity of the Hall of Giants. Gifts of materials for the Sleeping Beauty's canopy from Miki Sekers of West Cumberland Silk Mills, who had seen and liked the exhibition in Edinburgh, of carpeting in various colours, and of Diaghilev's favourite scent, 'Mitsouko' of Guerlain, to spray the 'Haunted Theatre' several times a day, were luxurious embellishments; and the many fine chandeliers, large and small, which were lent by Mrs Crick of Kensington Old Church Street, put a final touch of glamour to an unrecognizable Forbes House.

While carpenters hammered around him and students interrupted him with continual requests for advice about their painted enlargements of his work, Leonard Rosoman sat at a table by a window in what was to become the lecture room, drawing as imperturbably as if he were alone in his studio. My admiration for him was boundless: and I never, throughout the next twenty years, had a less temperamental artist to work with.

167

Our last-minute rush was worse than before: the weather was worse, too. The two negroes, which I intended to place out-of-doors on either side of the entrance, arrived from the north smashed to pieces a day or two before we opened, and it was incredible to me that they were stood upright, restored and repainted, not only out of doors, but at night and in the pouring rain. Volunteer helpers sprang out of the ground, as they had in Edinburgh. *There*, on the fatal eve, I had been surprised to find a dancer friend, who I knew should have been in his musical show in London, up a ladder, hammering away for dear life: and in London, when the last night came, he was at Forbes House from dusk till dawn sewing the gathered turquoise silk which lined the wire dome of Gerald Rickard's red library. That night we drank not only tea but champagne, for Robin Howard had sent me the biggest bottle I had ever seen. (This was the first sign I had of Robin's devotion to the dance. He had lost both his legs in the war. Later he fell under the spell of Martha Graham, founded the London School of Contemporary Dance and the London Contemporary Dance Theatre and installed them at The Place.) I walked home to Bloomfield Terrace between six and seven in the morning across an empty Belgravia.

David and Bridget Astor gave a dinner at the Hyde Park Hotel before the evening party. My mother was invited to this. She thought the world of David, who was charming to her. I could not find any buttons for my white waistcoat and had to borrow some of Fred Ashton's.

Cards for the evening party, which constituted the private view, were sent out in the names of Juliet Duff, David Astor and myself. Half the Diplomatic Corps had been invited, and there was such a bottle-neck as the five hundred guests piled up at the foot of the stairs that I think the butler gave up announcing them. I have only a few cuttings from the *Tatler* and other papers to remind me who was present. Derek Hill, the instigator of my exhibition-designing career, had evi-

The view down the main staircase at Forbes House, with Rosoman's 'Enchanted Forest' seen through the arches in the distance. Photograph by Manor Studio, Southall.

dently been dining at the French Embassy, as he was photographed coming downstairs with Mme Massigli. The *Evening Standard* recorded 'queues for champagne': but 'Mr Randolph Churchill went behind the bar and poured out a drink for choreographer Serge Lifar, who had come from Paris.' The *Evening Standard* had a photograph of the Duke of Wellington covering his face with his hands, possibly in embarrassment at my speech. Juliet, David and I stood receiving in the hall, with our backs to Rosoman's draughty forest, and as David's mother, Lady Astor ('in parma violet and diamonds'), came to shake our hands she greeted David with the remark, 'You seem to have got into bad company.' Since she cannot possibly have known who I was, I think she must have been referring to Juliet or Diaghilev.

Marion Harewood opened the exhibition. Then I led Mme Karsavina down the stairs. I had calculated that she would be most visible and audible from three steps below the landing where the Sleeping Beauty slept under her canopy of blue velvet and silver cloth. She ended:

I had the chance to see this exhibition a week or so before the opening day. It was hard to believe it would, in a short time, become what you see it now. Over precarious planks, under scaffolding with artists at work, dodging step-ladders and paint-pots, I found my way at last to the office. To see this chaos put me in a happy frame of mind; it reminded me of the preparations for the first season of the Ballets Russes in the Châtelet in Paris. With this difference – that we made far, far more noise.

Diaghilev, who never stooped to compromise where artistic values were at stake, had ordered several rows of seats to be taken away to enlarge the orchestra pit. We rehearsed on the stage, the carpenters hammered in the auditorium, at the back the stage-hands noisily shifted the scenery. The piano faintly but valiantly tinkled through all this. Diaghilev shouted orders to the carpenters and carried on a press conference in between. Suddenly all became quiet, the auditorium emptied, the stage-hands had left, the artists remained on the stage. Diaghilev looked at his watch, said: "Oh, it is noon", or, if you will forgive the slang, what he said was: "*Tout Paris bouffe à midi – allons bouffer!*" Don't think for a moment he went to lunch leaving his company starving – in a few minutes waiters appeared carrying trestles, and an excellent meal was served.

Looking at this exhibition I find a links with Diaghilev's method of arranging one – not a mere presentation of catalogued exhibits, but the effect as a whole. To have made it so representative of his influence on the arts, so comprehensive of its progressive development, was in itself no mean task. But to have transformed this house into a décor was imaginative and bold. I think he would have approved of it.

Sir John Rothenstein, who was Director of the Tate Gallery, and Douglas Cooper, who thought he ought not to be, were both on our Committee of Honour, and both were present. I was not in the room when their collision occurred, but it was reported to me by Lucian Freud and George Harewood. When Rothenstein passed him, Douglas spat out in his venomous way, 'That's the little man who's going to lose his job at the Tate Gallery!' He then followed 'the little man' around, repeating the remark, until suddenly the little man turned and gave big Douglas a punch on the chin. 'The critic went down, recovered, then groped along the floor searching for his glasses' (*Daily Mail*). 'He didn't touch my face . . . I'm still waiting for an apology . . .' (*Daily Mirror*). 'Undoubtedly Sir John did hit me . . . I said at the time "I'm bleeding from every corner", but I was being facetious' (*Daily Express*). The *Express* gave nearly two columns to the incident on its front page, mentioning that the film actress Ingrid Bergman, Dame Edith Evans and Lady Megan Lloyd George were present, and printed a cartoon by Osbert Lancaster with recognizable likenesses of the two combatants; but Lord Beaverbrook's paper confined its comment on our exhibition to an explanatory note at the foot: 'Diaghilev, subject of the new art exhibition, was the impresario who founded modern Russian ballet. He died in Venice in 1929, aged fifty-seven.' As Diaghilev would undoubtedly have agreed, any publicity was better than none.

That winter the Diaghilev Exhibition became a kind of club where balletomanes met for a snack, listened to music or a lecture and had another look at their favourite exhibits. Diana Petry sat behind the scenes, beaming at her typewriter in the little office with its *rococo* panelling. Here Major Bavin, a kindly gnome, lent us by EMI to play the records – and who sometimes gave afternoon lectures to children about the appreciation of music – fed his machine. Here Andrew Sykes, whom I had recommended as an organizer, prepared his rosters of part-time helpers who patrolled the rooms to keep an eye on the visitors. Here Pip would appear with the news that Joyce Grenfell or Audrey Hepburn had been seen coming in; or Juliet would bring Mrs Churchill or Somerset Maugham to sign the shabby improvised Visitors' Book. Princess Margaret took us by surprise on the afternoon of 15 November, and I was tracked down to another exhibition at the Victoria and Albert, to arrive breathless when she was already on the second floor. In later years the Princess was often kind to me, but on this occasion I sensed an air of caution, as if she were inspecting a homosexual brothel. Staring at Diaghilev's portrait by Elizabeth Polunin, she exclaimed 'What an awful-looking man! Was he a dancer?' Next day came Noël Coward. As I was going round with him, a friend rushed up to ask him to dinner: but Noël said he was just off to Jamaica. When would he be back? 'In the spring,' he replied. 'With the swallows. You'll recognize me easily among them.' On the seventeenth Vivien Leigh arrived; to be followed a few days later by Rex Harrison. There was a popular soap opera series on radio at the time called *Mrs Dale's Diary*. It had been running for years, and my mother and I teased my great-aunt Dolly Sandford because she and her old maid Parsons listened in to it religiously twice a week. When the cast of this programme were brought – presumably as a publicity stunt – to visit Forbes House, I gave them a drink and got Ellis Powell, the friendly protagonist,* to speak to Dolly on the telephone. Dolly, who was accustomed to hear the familiar voice coming from a different instrument, seemed slightly dazed, as if Christ had rung the doorbell in Tedworth Square. That morning, 24 November, I found Lydia Lopoukhova queueing up at the gates, before opening time, among a lot of boy-scouts; and the same afternoon E. M. Forster stole in. He wrote me a very kind letter afterwards.

The *Observer* announced: 'Ninety-thousand people see Diaghilev Exhibition.' Our run was extended until 1 January;

* Later replaced by Jessie Matthews.

then again till the sixteenth. On 20 December, when Lifar
came over from Paris to lecture, we had a dinner-party,
presided over by Mme Karsavina, of all the Diaghilev friends
we could assemble: Grigoriev, Tchernicheva, Sokolova,
Rambert, Idzikovsky, Evina, Savina (Massine's first wife), de
Valois, Markova, Malcolm Sargent and Juliet Duff. Cyril
Beaumont, Arnold Haskell, Fred Ashton, Diana (Gould)
Menuhin, Nigel and Maude Gosling and myself were the
only guests who did not belong, though Cyril, Arnold and
Fred had been witnesses of the Diaghilev Ballet, and Diana,
a pupil of Rambert, had been accepted by Diaghilev just
before his death, but was disappointed in her hope of joining

A 'family group' in the Portrait Gallery at Forbes House beneath
Elizabeth Polunin's portrait of Diaghilev. Wanda Evina, Serge Grigoriev,
Lubov Tchernicheva (*seated*), Anton Dolin, Tamara Karsavina (*seated*),
Alicia Markova (*on the floor*), Serge Lifar, Lydia Sokolova (*seated*),
Stanislas Idzikovsky, Lady Juliet Duff (*half hidden*), Vera Savina (*seated*)
and Marie Rambert. Photograph by G. B. L. Wilson.

his company. Somehow or other Lifar was prevented from making a speech.

One day when I had stayed in bed all morning for a change, Diana Petry telephoned to say that Pip had reported the appearance of Francis Poulenc at the box-office. I saw my way to performing a 'miracle'. Poulenc's ballet, *Les Biches*, written for Diaghilev's 1924 season, and one of my favourite scores, had recently been recorded, along with other half-forgotten works, by Igor Markevitch. I told Diana, 'Wait till the end of the record you are playing now, then put on *Les Biches*.' The effect was all that I had hoped. When Poulenc came with Pierre Bernac for a drink a few days later he said, 'I had the most moving experience. I entered a beautiful room and was greeted by a burst of my own music. I had not heard it for years, and it had never been so well played!' I said, 'How lovely!'

By the time the show closed a hundred and forty thousand people had seen it in London and forty thousand catalogues had been sold at three shillings. Alicia Markova spoke at the closing of the exhibition as she had at its Edinburgh opening. Sitting beside her on the platform, I watched her three sisters in the front row, weeping in unison.

The Diaghilev Exhibition came at a time when Britain, backward in everything, was still slowly recovering from the mess and shortages of war, and it seemed to light up the lives of Londoners. People remembered long afterwards the impression it made on them, and although I later planned shows which were more carefully constructed and more numerously attended, I was doomed for decades to find that the only spark of interest I aroused in strangers was when they were told I had arranged the Diaghilev Exhibition. Until 1954 exhibition design in Britain had tended to mean utilitarian displays in buildings such as Olympia and Earls Court, which had been built expressly to hold exhibitions. Half the charm of the 'tunnels of love' I devised at the Edinburgh College of Art and at Forbes House lay in my adaptation of an unlikely site. After the Diaghilev Exhibition I guess that the art of display began to appear more important to museum directors and more attractive as a possible career for imaginative young people. Today (1982) there are many delightful exhibition designers in this country alone. I had hoped that Leonard Rosoman's boundless imagination and resource would win him the recognition of Covent Garden and that he would be asked to design operas and ballets. However, there was no reaction from David Webster, nor from Fred or Ninette.

In fact, Ninette de Valois disapproved of the whole affair. In her book *Come Dance With Me*, published in 1957, she wrote: 'In spite of the superb examples of his life's work, I feel that the presentation would have irritated Diaghilev; the exhibition, in its visual decorations did not present the man as the autocrat of taste that he was to those who knew him . . . I feel that he would have preferred his exhibition to have been held in one of our National Galleries, without the kind of Madame Tussaud's effect to which it was subjected.'

CHAPTER 7

My Dear Old College Chum

Tamara Karsavina's *Theatre Street*, published in 1930, had at once been acclaimed as the best picture of a dancer's life ever written: it became a classic. Romola Nijinsky's lurid biography of her husband, published in 1933, had made Dicky Buckle aware of the existence of ballet, and had informed the world at large that homosexuality had not died with Oscar and Bosie. (Not that Bosie was dead in 1933. Evan Tredegar was going to introduce me to him in 1945, but he expired on the eve of our confrontation.) Cyril Beaumont's *The Diaghilev Ballet in London* of 1940 combined gossip, comment and chronicle: this and *Reminiscences of the Russian Ballet* by Alexandre Benois, published in 1941, which provided a detailed account of the beginnings of the great enterprise, had helped me while away at the war. In 1954, to coincide, like my exhibition, with the twenty-fifth anniversary of Diaghilev's death, Grigoriev brought out his *The Diaghilev Ballet 1909–29* and this extremely useful year-by-year record, containing the minimum of commentary, was widely regarded as gospel.

It was between 1957 and 1959 that I worked with Lydia Sokolova on her memoirs. She had wanted 'a good book or none'; so, prompted partly by my state of penury and John Murray's advance of £300, which we shared fifty-fifty, and partly by the conviction that there was an important book to be written, I set out to do the best I could for her. At first, with the aid of a friend who was living with me, I used to tape-record our conversations, question and answer:

Gino would type the results, I would edit them and Lydia would correct and modify. This led to her writing me long letters, and I soon realized that, once she had got into her stride, she wrote so vividly, with a touch of Cockney slang, that I ought to include as many of her own words as possible. Sometimes, however, I would describe a ballet in my own words, and she would say she couldn't do better and I would leave in the passage. In conversation she found it hard to stick to the point: she had so much to say (luckily) that she was always going off at a tangent into some fascinating anecdote irrelevant to our 'task for the day'. When all else failed, I resorted to a trick: I got Gino to type out a purely imaginary account of some event, such as the first night of *Le Tricorne*, which she had avoided describing. Then Sokolova would be on the telephone in a flash, protesting, 'Darling, could I have said that? It wasn't like that at all! What really happened . . .' Our collaboration was good training for me and proved useful when I came to interview so many people for my lives of Nijinsky and Diaghilev.

I also believe that working with Lydia taught me to write more simply, to cut out perorations and get down to brass tacks. My first shot at an opening paragraph for the book was an aria about the art of dance, with ruminations on the double meaning of the Latin verb *saltare*; my second, inspired by interest in local history, was all about the river Lea north of London, near which Sokolova was born, and 'on whose secret islands a hundred years ago there dwelt an isolated inbred tribe of robbers'. Thank God, I saw the light, and the book in its final version began with Lydia's own words: 'Mother's parents lived at the Manor House, Leyton, Essex . . .'

The sessions with Lydia Sokolova took place in my fourth-floor flat over the Westminster Bank (my landlords) in Henrietta Street, Covent Garden. Through the windows there came a perpetual *musique d'ameublement* of hooting vehicles, whose drivers had grown desperate in hour-long traffic-blocks, of the iron-wheeled trolleys of the market porters, of cussing and swearing. In February 1913, before I was born, Lydia, who was then appearing in a potted version of *Scheherazade* with the Kosloff troupe in music hall at the Coliseum, had walked past the house in Henrietta Street to her audition for the Diaghilev Ballet at Covent Garden 'at the awful hour of ten o'clock on a Monday morning'. During her terrifying ordeal of dancing before Diaghilev, Nijinsky, the old teacher Maestro Cecchetti and his wife, and Grigoriev, her new shoes caused her to fall down three times. But she was accepted, and when she joined the company at Monte Carlo she was given the repulsive (luckily short-lived) name of Muningsova. She worked hard, and before the Diaghilev Ballet broke up for the summer holidays she had her reward.

In pre-war years, when the Diaghilev Ballet were in London they rehearsed in the drill-hall in Chenies Street, off Tottenham Court Road, where Una Troubridge had made her sketches for the head of Nijinsky which Sokolova found in Cecil Court forty years later: and there the following episode took place in July 1913.

> For the final class before we broke up for the holidays, we were ordered by Cecchetti to wear our best clothes . . . The whole company was assembled, and Cecchetti gave us a terrific class, with lots of lovely jumping . . . At the end Maestro went up on the stage and said, in his own special mixture of Italian, French and Russian, 'I will now tell you who in my opinion has made the most progress during the year. I am going to give her a prize.' There was a dead silence.
>
> All the soloists had gathered near the stage and I was standing at the back. When Cecchetti said, 'Eeda', [sic] I thought I was being reprimanded for mopping my purple, sweaty face. But once again he called, 'Eeda!' and added, 'Come up here and receive your first prize for good work.' My legs trembled as I moved through the crowd

and up the steps. All those Russians and Poles had been working like blacks for nine months and it was the English girl who walked off with the coveted prize – a signed photograph of the Maestro in a silver frame. I think even Diaghilev and Grigoriev had a shock.

At that time Nicolas Kremnev, one of the company's chief character dancers, became Lydia's boy-friend; and when the 1914 war found the Russian Ballet scattered and on holiday, Kremnev was in London lodgings with Lydia in Bedford Place, Bloomsbury. They did their exercises every morning in a basement room in Maiden Lane (parallel with Henrietta Street), and it was there they met Stanislas Idzikovsky, whom they thought a remarkable dancer. In 1915, when the summons came from Diaghilev, who was with Massine in Switzerland reassembling a company to tour America, Sokolova and Kremnev were able to recommend Idzikovsky. Grigoriev, on his way from Russia to Switzerland, gave him an audition and he was signed up too. When the Ballet returned to London to perform at the Coliseum in 1918 it was in a first-floor club room in Shaftesbury Avenue that they had their classes; and when, in 1919, *Le Tricorne* was first given at the Alhambra in Leicester Square, Sokolova and Kremnev, whose daughter Natasha had been born in Brazil, were living in Burleigh Mansions between Charing Cross Road and St Martin's Lane. Kremnev had begun to maltreat her, and she was in love with Woizikovsky. Although Lydia described to me how cravenly Woizikovsky behaved to her at this time – and indeed at every other time – she only let fall in a letter *after* our book was published that she had become pregnant by him in 1919 while still living with Kremnev, and had a necessary abortion at the Charing Cross Hospital. By 1920, when Massine began working out with Lydia her role of the Chosen Virgin in the new version of *The Rite of Spring*, the company's rehearsal room was the one in the basement of Chandos House, Maiden Lane, where she had practised with Kremnev in 1914. It was shortly after this that she left Kremnev for Woizikovsky. The whole neighbourhood, north, south, east and west of my flat in Henrietta Street, was crammed with memories for Lydia Sokolova.

Shortly after Sokolova and I began work in 1957, Leon Woizikovsky arrived in London from Poland. She had seen little of him since 1934, when she had married Ronnie Mahon; and he had been in Poland during the war. She was determined to make it clear that she had kept her end up. Probably, like Bertha and Hilda Hughes, the dressmaker friends of my youth at Cromer, she held the belief that to appear well dressed, with a good bag and shoes, and with immaculate make-up to show that life had not got you down, was one way of keeping men in their place. Lydia described in a letter to me, how she and Natasha went to confront her unreliable ex-lover over lunch in Soho.

46 Chipstead Lane, Riverhead,   27 July 1958
Sevenoaks, Kent

Dorogoi Dicky

My writing today consists of a letter (all about Leon) to be read in a time of privacy, say in the bathroom. Tash and I were determined not to let the side down. I looked $\frac{1}{2}$ a million in a white suit with a cornflower-coloured hat. She walked into the restaurant worth a million in a tight-fitting pencil [-slim] black suit with a hat covered all over with multi-coloured flowers – 4 inch heels and Grannie's long-handled ivory umbrella. After the first shock of Leon's face, I began to see something of the previous Leon. He speaks Russian badly and sounds like Idzikovski. I speak Russian haltingly and to myself sound flipping awful. The experience of the war has left him peculiar. It took about an hour for the conversation to even start to be a normal one. One thing, Dicky, that struck me forcibly yesterday more than ever [about] all those excepting Karsavina and Lydia of my old colleagues is that this Diaghilev business has made a strange impression on them, and each has dwelt on it so intensely

that they take it individually as if no one else shared it with
them . . . He has in his possession here with him the famous
Chinese costume [by Picasso] from *Parade* [and other
items] . . . Vassili [Diaghilev's servant, later wardrobe
master] gave him these things after D. died. He has worn
the Chinese dress very much and is going to Paris to try
to sell them. Your guess is as good as mine to whom. He
kept this so secret from me [in the 1930s]. Where did he
hide them? He hinted that he has baggage at the hôtel in
Paris, 42 rue de Moscou where we always stayed and where
I nearly died. Can I bring him to lunch on Wednesday?
He speaks English almost better than Russian. His hatred
of Grigoriev is unbelievable . . . when I told him about
G's book, making a boxing gesture, he said I'd give him
this. Who does Spanish *Tricorne* in Spain? Only we. That
was something to do. I agreed. He is spending the weekend at Wilbury with Florrie [St Just]. He got a labour
permit yesterday to work for Festival Ballet & starts
rehearsing *Petrushka* today.

Please, Dicky, if you ever catch me out talking or thinking the Diaghilev Ballet was run for my own special
benefit give me a crack on the forehead with one end of a
ladies' shoe tree . . .

I didn't like him. I certainly didn't love him . . . Dreadful
chap, really.

He buried the costumes and other things in the ground
in Poland. His home was burnt down, but he found the
things intact.

All my love . . .
Lydia

Woizikovsky, short, with smooth black hair, a blobby nose
and crafty eyes, came to lunch. I did not get much out of him.
Ten years later, Lifar lent the Chinese Conjuror's costume
from *Parade* to an exhibition in Strasbourg: but it took me
another ten years to put the story together, because I had
forgotten the contents of this letter of Lydia's. Her many
letters to me lay dormant in bulging files, waiting for the

moment when her loving voice was needed to give me information and encouragement from beyond the grave.

Over the delicate question of the creation of Le Tricorne I had to weigh the evidence between Sokolova and Karsavina. This ballet, Massine's masterpiece, with music by Manuel de Falla and décor by Picasso, had been the fruit of the company's difficult war-time exile in Spain. To give an authentic tang to their performance of Le Tricorne, the company – and in particular Massine and Sokolova, who were to play the Miller and his Wife – had studied Flamenco dancing under Felix Fernandez, a brilliant boy, picked up by Diaghilev in a Madrid café, who later went mad in London. Shortly before Massine's ballet was due to be presented at the Alhambra Theatre in Leicester Square, Diaghilev discovered that Karsavina had escaped from Russia and was in Tangier, where her husband was First Secretary; and he decided that his beloved dark-eyed Tamara must be cajoled to appear in the ballet of his beloved dark-eyed Leonide Massine. Lured back to London, Mme Karsavina had to be taught the Spanish idiom of dancing in a hurry. Sokolova must have been disappointed, after all she had gone through, to have this plum snatched from her by Karsavina: but, as she wrote, 'I had the pleasure of helping Massine teach her the role.' Karsavina, in her book *Theatre Street*, described the twenty-two-year-old Massine as 'a very exacting master', but did not mention Sokolova. When I asked her if Lydia Sokolova had not helped to teach her the part of the Miller's Wife, she looked at me in her most Sibylline way and stated: 'Lyydia has vairy guood myemory: but she tyends to relyye upon it too muarch.'

It is impossible, as I look at all the papers spread out before me, to divide the material Sokolova provided for the book from her personal letters to me, for she mixed everything up in the most delightful way, business with pleasure. In fact she must have enjoyed reliving her past, for one day she wrote, 'Thank God we can get some fun out of it.' A batch of notes would begin 'Back to the old grind.' Then, she would wake in the night to recall a detail which might be either useful or irrelevant, but which she would jot down, anyway, just in case. For instance, she might suddenly recall how Woizikovsky's fat, grasping old mother arrived with one small suitcase to stay with Leon and herself in Monte Carlo, but left, two months later, with an immensely heavy trunk of loot. Having got Mme Woizikovskaya off her chest (and I could imagine her sighing when the task was accomplished) she wrote, 'That deals with *that* thieving old so-and-so.'

She got a crick in her neck as she burned the midnight oil. She arrived breathless at the top of my eighty-two steps in Covent Garden. She missed trains at Charing Cross and caught cold from waiting about in the draughty station. Then she would find an old photograph, invitation or newspaper cutting in 'Pandora's chest' which reminded her of 'moving accidents in flood and field' – of the look on Diaghilev's face when he caught Massine flirting with Tchernicheva at the Russian Embassy in Washington in 1916; of the special way Pavlova cut and stitched her ballet shoes, inserting strips of cork or leather near the toes to help her balance and sustain an *arabesque* so long that she held up the music; of a ludicrous performance of *Scheherazade* in the hill town of Logroño in Spain, when there had been no swords for the Shah's soldiers to slaughter the unfaithful wives, so that they had to strangle or smother them as best they could; of how the whole company plus the orchestra had been lined up – in Denver, Colorado, was it? – for the taking of a wide panoramic photograph; of the death of the company's former wig-maker Markovetsky, who became a drunken derelict, in a fire in Paris. Then the creative fury would possess her, and she would scribble away, snatching details from oblivion. Sometimes Lydia's literary labours, on top of all her housework, seemed to overwhelm her. 'I wish I had a quiet hut in a monastery garden': but she could still foresee that when our task was finished life might be rather empty.

'What shall we do when we've given birth to The Truth At Last?' Because of some joke I have forgotten Lydia sometimes addressed me as her 'Dear Old College Chum'.

To a letter of August 1958, in which she wrote of buying a birthday present for Natasha, Lydia added an afterthought: 'By the way I've always forgotten to tell you Picasso is Leon's daughter's godfather. [This was Woizikovsky's child by his early mistress Antonova.] He's been no more use to her than Grigoriev has been to Tash.' So Grigoriev was Natasha's godfather! Yet Sokolova considered that he had done his best to ignore her in his book on the Diaghilev Ballet, and she felt bitter about it.

I had first met Grigoriev and Tchernicheva lunching with the Russian-born Vera Bowen at her house in York Terrace, Regent's Park, in 1953. Grigoriev had been Diaghilev's Regimental Sergeant-Major, and, as Juliet Duff told me, if anything went wrong, it was he who got the blame and the abuse. He and Tchernicheva had been with Diaghilev almost continually from 1909 until his death; and he knew all the secrets. Few of these, however, found their way into his book, which Vera Bowen had translated and edited. Grigoriev was a big burly polite man, who spoke no English. It was clear to me that he had not been a maker of policy, but one who carried out orders. Regarded merely as a steward, he had seldom been admitted to Diaghilev's inner councils, and he had no comprehension of the new artistic movements his master sponsored. On the other hand, there was a certain nobility in his steady devotion to the memory of Diaghilev after the latter's death, and in his suppression of scandal. He scorned Romola Nijinsky and her revelations. Yet, although he greatly admired Nijinsky's dancing, it appeared from his book that he cared little for him as a person – and nothing for him as a choreographer.

Grigoriev had cause to fear scandal nearer home, for his wife Lubov Tchernicheva, a former beauty, had been a *grande amoureuse*, not only free with her favours among the dancers of the company but hotly pursued by such gallants as King Alfonso of Spain. Since her legs and feet were imperfect by ballet standards, she had specialized in character parts, rather than purely classical ones. During the First World War, when Karsavina was in Russia, Tchernicheva had been allotted the latter's more exotic Fokine roles of Zobeïda and Thamar; then Massine had created for her the Princesse Cygne in *Contes russes* and the melancholy Constanza with huge hooped red dress in *Les Femmes de bonne humeur*; and in the late 1920s she shared with Lydia Sokolova the role of the Miller's Wife in *Le Tricorne*, which Karsavina had been the first to dance. Possibly because of the comparisons involved by such a sharing of roles, the names of Karsavina and Sokolova were mentioned rather less in Grigoriev's book than either would have wished. The book could hardly diminish the glory of Karsavina but, even so, she complained of its bias. I noticed, on the other hand, that Karsavina had not had occasion to refer to Grigoriev in *Theatre Street*. Although it might have been questioned whether Tchernicheva or Sokolova was Diaghilev's principal female character dancer in later years, Lubov would never have had the stamina or ability to perform, as the six-year-younger Lydia did, the dance of the Chosen Virgin in Massine's version of *The Rite of Spring*. Grigoriev omitted to write that Sokolova was good in this, or as the Miller's Wife in *Le Tricorne*; and when Lydia came to compose her own book with my help, she took care to describe how Diaghilev only allowed her to relinquish a role she disliked in *Zéphire et Flore* on condition that she taught the Spanish style and steps of the Miller's Wife in *Le Tricorne* to Tchernicheva, who had always wanted to dance it.

Although Tchernicheva had announced her retirement from the stage during Diaghilev's last season, and (as Sokolova recorded in her memoirs) the company had clubbed together to give her a topaz ring 'the colour of her eyes', she had made a come-back in the days of de Basil. She was the first Zobeïda in *Scheherazade* I ever saw, and the only Thamar. In these Fokine ballets her noble profile, her dramatic pallor and her flickering false eye-lashes, loaded with black mascara, seemed to me thrilling beyond belief; and when Lichine created *Francesca da Rimini* for her in 1937, she looked magnificent in Oliver Messel's trailing Renaissance costumes, the first pink, the second vermilion, and it never struck me as incongruous that the passionate heroine who sat beside Paul Petroff reading about Launcelot and Guinevere, then finally, with a wrenching gesture, bared her bosom for the long sword of Malatesta, was nearing fifty. Grigoriev and Tchernicheva may in time past have been a schemer and a vamp: with the loss of his authority and her beauty they had become a mild and rather lost old couple, grateful that their former glories should be remembered. Ninette de Valois asked their help in revivals of *Firebird*, *Les Sylphides* and *Petrushka*. I saw them occasionally at the Royal Opera House. Tchernicheva had grown witch-like, with lank white hair.

Sokolova's book, which I suggested we should call *Dancing for Diaghilev*, was to be published in May 1960. Shortly before this Lydia wrote to me about an encounter with Tamara Karsavina at the Royal Academy of Dancing, where they both judged examinations.

46 Chipstead Lane, Riverhead,   25 March 1960
Sevenoaks, Kent

Dearest Dicky

    We talked a little of G[rigoriev]'s book. And she was most emphatic . . . that the whole of his bitter attitude towards both of us . . . was all Luba's doing. That I was a thorn in her side all the time, and he has not been allowed to say anything really nice about me because 'his wife wouldn't let him'. [Reference to the refrain of a music-hall song, 'My wife won't let me.'] I said 'But he states so openly I was *un*suitable for roles that Diaghilev approved and never once . . . corrected me [in]. She then said 'I *know* Grigoriev was a sincere admirer of your work until

186

you became a danger to Luba's position, because he called me out of my dressing-room to watch you dance the Bacchanale in *Narcisse*. [This must have been in 1914.] Knowing how difficult the role [originally Nijinska's] was, he was full of praise for your strength, musical and rhythmical understanding and big elevation.' . . . I could hardly believe it . . .

So there, chum. And Luba was my girl friend!

It happened that a Penguin paperback edition of Grigoriev's *The Diaghilev Ballet 1909–29* was to be published in 1960, the same year as Sokolova's book. The publishers asked if they might reproduce my Cocteau caricature of Diaghilev on the cover, and I consented. I took advantage of the occasion to prepare some notes for Vera Bowen about inaccuracies in Grigoriev's text (I was to discover many more later), and instances of how, in my opinion, he had been unfair to Sokolova. Giving page references, I pointed out how Grigoriev described King Alfonso sending Tchernicheva a bouquet for a ballet in which she did not dance (Lydia had told me how Grigoriev had tried to divert *her* bouquet to his wife, and how she had to fight to keep it); how it seemed churlish of Grigoriev to restrict his comment on Lydia's famous solo in *The Rite of Spring* to the statement that 'few dances can ever have been longer or more strenuous'; how the Spaniards' acclaim in 1921 for 'our mastery of their national dancing' was recorded without reference to Sokolova and Woizikovsky, and how Diaghilev's comment on the London triumph of *The Rite* in 1929 – that it had taken sixteen years to persuade the public to accept Stravinsky's ballet – was mentioned, but not the name of the one dancer without whom the ballet could not be given. I concluded, 'If you think I am being tiresome or partisan look at the Index. Tchernicheva – 21 lines. Lopoukhova – 15 lines. Sokolova – 8 lines. I have made these notes without consulting Lydia Sokolova.' However, the new edition of Grigoriev's book was published without any changes.

Lydia and Massine had been sent off from Liverpool and excused the last week of an English provincial tour in 1920 so that they should work together on that long solo dance in the gloomy basement rehearsal room in Maiden Lane. I never hear the music of the second scene of *The Rite* without thinking of Lydia's dance of death. Once she had been 'chosen' from among the other virgins as a sacrifice to the harvest god, she had to stand still for a long time, twisted into an awkward position, and the only way she could stop from blinking, which Massine had forbidden, was to fix her eyes on a red EXIT light at the back of the auditorium. Her terrible dance was preceded by twenty ominous chords, during which the forty other performers moved to the back of the stage and crouched in a semi-circle, hands curved over eyes, to observe her ordeal. At the end, two men lifted her and supported her under the arms during the curtain calls. 'I was very tired,' she wrote, 'but very happy. Also Stravinsky had kissed my hand before the audience. I was twenty-four years old.'

In only one particular did I come to suspect in later years that Sokolova had distorted her story in the light of hindsight: this was the matter of Nijinsky's mental deterioration. She claimed (as did Grigoriev) that during the wartime tours of the USA and South America in 1916 and 1917 Nijinsky already showed signs of madness, and that his last ballet, *Till Eulenspiegel*, in which she played an Apple Woman, was a shambles. During my researches in the sixties and seventies I found that the American press had acclaimed *Till* (the only ballet presented by Diaghilev's company that he never saw – because he had stayed in Europe with Massine), that it was often repeated, and that the company under Nijinsky's direction had enjoyed more artistic success on their long second tour of the United States, than on the first when Diaghilev was present. Romola Nijinska fiercely maintained that her husband's madness had only begun in Switzerland in 1918 when he was isolated from the ballet: and, following my hard-trained instincts, I was for once inclined to believe the inveterate liar Romola, rather than the persistently truthful Sokolova.

Dancing for Diaghilev appeared shortly after I began writing for the *Sunday Times*, and extracts from it were published in that paper. Lydia felt happy that she had brought it off. She wrote to me that she was sticking her newspaper cuttings in a book. 'I have never been proud of anything in the press before [impossible, surely], but I am of this. Ronnie is so thrilled. He remembers how, when phoning, you said, "Ronnie, I believe we have a good book".' Our work was well received (though it made very little money); and in 1962, the American choreographer Agnes de Mille (herself a talented writer) told me at a dinner-party in Winnipeg that she thought it was the best book on the Diaghilev Ballet since Karsavina's. That was something.

In summer 1962 Ninette de Valois summoned Massine to resurrect his *Good-Humoured Ladies* (*Les Femmes de bonne humeur*) for the Royal Ballet at Covent Garden. This elaborate work based on a play of Goldoni, with Scarlatti's harpsichord sonatas orchestrated by Tommasini and Venetian décor by Bakst, had been the young Massine's first big success in 1917; and, as mentioned above, it was in this ballet that Lopoukhova as the mischievous maid had won the heart of London. While Massine, Idzikovsky, Novak and Woizikovsky had been the principal men, Tchernicheva, Antonova, Shabelska and Khokhlova had been (after Lopoukhova) the chief women and old Mme Cecchetti had mimed the grotesque role of the aged Marchesa with delusions of irresistibility. Then Khokhlova married Picasso, and Sokolova had taken over her part and danced it at the Coliseum in 1918. It was the first time a Massine ballet had ever been seen in London. When Massine and Ninette invited Lydia Sokolova to make a return to the stage in Mme Cecchetti's role as the Marchesa, it was with some trepidation that she agreed.

I loved this revival, which plunged me into a dream of eighteenth-century Venice, but most of the critics got

Lydia Sokolova, Anton Dolin, Bronislava Nijinska and Leon Woizi-kovsky in Cocteau's ballet, *Le Train bleu*, for which Nijinska did the choreography. Sokolova's pink bathing costume by Chanel is now in the Theatre Museum, London. Photograph by Sasha, December 1924.

together and damned it. When I say 'got together' I should explain that my amiable old friend Clive Barnes, who wrote anonymously in *The Times*, also wrote signed pieces in the *Daily Express*. He and a clique of other critics could usually

190

be seen hobnobbing in the interval and I imagined them (perhaps erroneously – but the results often justified my assumption) 'arriving at a unanimous verdict'. I thoroughly disapproved of this, and often thought them wrong about everything. Yet, in the case of the Massine revival, it is possible that my opinion, being that of an older man – and one in love with the Diaghilev period – was too favourable. The complicated intrigue was perhaps no longer valid in the 1960s; and it was a high-handed action of Diaghilev's to allow the orchestration and inevitable slowing down of Scarlatti's sonatas. I myself usually disliked ballets with too much story. At any rate, Sokolova showed us that she could rise above age and physical disabilities to give a finished performance. I wrote:

> Lydia Sokolova as the vain and pompous Marchesa was outstanding. Every look and gesture told. There was an extraordinary moment during the slow number. Constanza [Anya Linden, with 'languishing melancholy arms'] laments; a street musician plays a violin; then the Marchesa, on the arms of Rinaldo and Captain Faloppa, crosses the stage. These three stare at Constanza, and as they go off Rinaldo throws a coin to the busker. Nothing and everything happened. Diaghilev lived again.

It turned out that I was not the only one to appreciate Lydia's miming. Punctual in her politeness, she wrote to me on the evening after my article appeared.

46 Chipstead Lane, Riverhead,   16 July 1962
Sevenoaks, Kent
Dicky darling,
   I must write and tell you how happy you made me
. . . Massine has been so very kind, sweet and gentle, coaching every artist. They have learnt so much in the last six weeks, stagecraft which none of them will ever forget. I hope I have also been a help. You do now see why I have always said what a demonstration of pure dancing artistry that ballet is. He was only 21 when he created the

work. He has improved it tremendously. Our dancers [of the Diaghilev Ballet] could not have performed the technical work with the ability that these youngsters most certainly have . . . The difficult movements he has put into the ballet they take in their stride. They are very sweet people and lovely to work with.

I would like you to know what Leonide said to me – when he came with Ninette on to the stage after our very first costume rehearsal, which was pretty ropey. In English he said: 'Do you know who was in front just now?' Of course I answered no. 'Diaghilev . . . And he said "It's alright. She can still do it!"' . . . He has so completely changed, and the company really loves him. Ninette amazes me more & more each day . . . Ability unbelievable in a dancer. Still has a terrific sense of humour. Like Massine, who said, as he came on to the balcony to me on Friday 'You missed a beat. Ninette never misses a beat' . . .

Thank you again, my dear old college chum, for the nice things you thought and said, because my secret was: *You* were the one person of whom I was really nervous.

Much love

Lydia

It was delightful to me that Sokolova's admiration for the company which Ninette de Valois had built up was soon focussed on one dancer in particular; and it was typical of Lydia that she took the trouble, three months after the above letter was written, to express this admiration in words. Ashton's *The Two Pigeons*, with its Messager music, was too sentimental for my taste, though the choreographer had succeeded, as he usually did, in doing exactly what he set out to do. His aim was that of Molière: to please. Yet I was breathless before the talent of the young Canadian, Lynn Seymour, of whom (in my second notice) I wrote:

We can (or rather, I can) now accept *The Two Pigeons* as a frame for the performance of Lynn Seymour: and we can pray that Ashton and MacMillan will continue to be inspired by her special qualities to create, as both have done, very special roles for her. Besides being a highly skilled artist, she is also undoubtedly a born one – that is to say, a genius.

In this part of the little love-bird, a kind of Mimi, who is deserted, then rejoined by her painter lover, she is in turn funny, touching, sophisticated and vulnerable. Dancing Ashton's pretty numbers, she never puts a foot wrong – and she has exquisite feet: but she never puts a look wrong either, does everything with the subtlest art and creates what is for ballet an unusually four-dimensional character . . .

Quick as a flash, on the day after Lydia Sokolova read my notice, she put pen to paper.

46 Chipstead Lane, Riverhead,   22 October 1962
Sevenoaks, Kent

Dearest Dicky

     What of the Divine Seymour! Quite lovely. With unspoilt charm & wit. I feel there is a real English Ballerina in the bud at long last. Feet like Pavlova (but they work better).

That is dancing as it should be, for the joy alone.

I am very much better, thank godness, after more than a year of brutal pain.

With my love as always,
from
Lydia

Sokolova had never mentioned that she was feeling unwell when she danced for Massine (and Diaghilev), once more and for the last time, at Covent Garden three months before.

193

CHAPTER 8

❖

China Tea in Hampstead, Indian in Leningrad

In 1967 I had been living for ten years at the corner of Henrietta Street and Covent Garden and, with the help of a mortgage from George Harewood, I had just bought a cottage in Wiltshire. I was working on a pavilion for the Canadians at Expo '67 when I heard to my surprise, in March, that Vera Bowen had asked Sotheby's if they would be interested in selling her collection of Diaghilev ballet costumes. I never knew she had one. Then I remembered the costumes Grigoriev had lent me for the Diaghilev Exhibition, and realized that it must be *his* collection, which for one reason or another he considered it advisable to sell under Vera's name. Grigoriev was obviously hard up, and Vera was helping him to raise money on the old costumes just as she had helped him with his book. Why or how the costumes came to be his in the first place was a question which it was too late in the day to go into. To sell theatrical costumes would be a startling innovation for a famous auction house. '10 March 1967. To Sotheby's. Am invited to run Diaghilev sale in June.' The sale was to be a gala party, tickets for which would be sold in aid of the Royal Ballet School, whose students, I had arranged with Michael Wood, its Director, and Ursula Moreton, its Principal, would pose in the costumes for the catalogue's illustrations and parade in them during the sale.

On 21 March Sotheby's hung the costumes on the hessian-covered walls of a ground-floor room they then occupied across the road from their main Bond Street premises, and invited a few people to drink champagne and look at them. It was a curiously select gathering – Mme Karsavina, Lydia and Ronnie Mahon, Mim Rambert, Michael Duff (son of Juliet, who had died two years before, followed within fourteen months by Simon Fleet), Jake Carter (Sotheby's book expert) and Ernestine, his American wife, who was fashion editor of the *Sunday Times*. Vera Bowen, from whose collection the costumes were said to come, was naturally present; as were Michel Strauss, head of Sotheby's Impressionist Department (under which department the costumes had to be classified), and his assistants David Ellis-Jones and Tassilo von Watzdorf. The last named – always known as Thilo – was new to the firm, of which he later became a director: he also became one of my close friends. I suppose Grigoriev was too infirm to leave his Kensington flat, or he and Tchernicheva would have been there. Looking back on this gathering in later years, I could not remember why Sotheby's had gone to all the trouble, for no press were invited: then David Ellis-Jones (who became in 1981 a director of Christie's) told me that it was planned solely to induce Ernestine Carter to publish in the *Sunday Times* photographs of a few old costumes, shown off by stars of the Royal Ballet: which in fact she did. So the great Sokolova was lured up from Kent and the great Karsavina brought down from her high mountain fastness in NW3 simply to further this strategy. I was to fetch Mme Karsavina in a hired car, take her to dinner afterwards and return her home.

Shortly before Benjie Bruce's death in 1951, he and Tamara had bought an attractive old house, 108 Frognal, on the heights of Hampstead. Nik, with his wife and two children, had at first lived in a top-floor flat above his widowed mother: but finding this arrangement unsatisfactory, moved to Buckinghamshire. In 1967 Mme Karsavina lived alone. I believe there were lodgers lurking above, but I never saw them. The long early-Georgian brick house looked bigger than it was, for part of it was only one room thick. The back

Tamara Karsavina as the Queen of Shemakhan in *Coq d'or*, photographed in her dressing-room at the Paris Opéra, May 1914.

garden, with its trees, sloped uphill, and the front garden was separated from the steep curve of Frognal by a low wall. The secluded character of this dwelling appealed to me in exactly the same way as it did to Mme Karsavina. It was the sort of house about which a child, returning at dusk from school and seeing its lit-up windows through the trees, as in a painting by Atkinson Grimshaw, might invent for himself mysterious stories, deeming it inhabited by an exiled princess who lived in luxurious melancholy among the trophies of her former state. And so it was: the dower house of Armida, Zobeïda, Thamar and the Queen of Shemakhan.

That fine evening in March, Karsavina came out of her door without a hat or coat, carrying a shawl. 'It's a warm day.' Indeed it felt like summer. She had recently taken to wearing a tightly curled blue-grey wig. 1967 was the period of the mini-skirt; and her short-sleeved black dress was skittishly knee-length, worn with a mauve-pink *fichu*. We drove to Bond Street. At Sotheby's little party she inspected the old clothes dispassionately. A hirsute young photographer came closer and closer as I held out Nijinsky's Blue God costume for her appraisal, until I feared for her modesty and wrinkles. Later she settled down with Rambert at a table; and before long they were reciting Pushkin's *Eugene Onegin* to each other, oblivious of the world around them. Sokolova, who was dressed from head to foot in pale cream, held up, to be photographed, the beige lace dress she had once worn as the Hostess in *Les Biches*.

I had booked a table for two at a favourite Greek restaurant in Fitzrovia, the White Tower. It was on the same premises as Stulik's Eiffel Tower, a haunt of genius and depravity in the twenties: and, being at the western end of Percy Street, it faced straight up Charlotte Street, where I had lived in the thirties. At the beginning of its Greek incarnation, shortly before the war, I had been one of the first customers. In those days it was modest: by 1967 it had become smart. Ianni Stais, the genial proprietor, had a habit of telling anyone who would listen the tale of my behaviour during an air-raid in 1941. All his customers had dived under tables, but I went on eating. Being an arrant coward, I always enjoyed recitals of my bravery. It turned out that Mme Karsavina and her husband had also frequented the White Tower during the war: she was fond of it. 'I gave them a Greek flag,' she said; and reminded me of her Byzantine blood.

Reciting Pushkin at Sotheby's, 21 March 1967. *Above:* Marie Rambert begins. *Opposite:* Tamara Karsavina takes over.

We discussed the party. She so much liked Sotheby's young men, Thilo von Watzdorf and David Ellis-Jones, who had been attentive to her. She said that the blue costume for the first act of *Giselle* they had produced was not hers. 'But don't tell them.' (I told Michel Strauss.) Hers had been copied exactly by Benois from that of Carlotta Grisi, thyrsis and all. (When I checked this up in Gautier's *Les Beautés de l'Opéra* I thought Karsavina must have been mistaken: the costume which Sotheby's sold and which she had been photographed wearing in 1910 was a very free adaptation indeed of that in which the divine Carlotta had been portrayed.) I remarked that the big jewelled buckle was missing from Nijinsky's Blue God costume. 'And how it used to scratch me!' she exclaimed.

Looking round the restaurant, she said, 'You know Freda Dudley-Ward?' 'Casa-Maury, yes. I met her staying with Juliet at Bulbridge.' 'She paid me the greatest compliment of my life in this restaurant. She had a party on the other side

of the room, and she came over to tell me, "When you come into a room no man can look at another woman".' I said, 'It's still true.' As dinner progressed, a little tipsy, we chatted more easily and more intimately than ever before, as if we were the same age. I had often thought that, in a way, I was the last of Karsavina's many *beaux*.

A supper at Mdved, in St Petersburg, came into her head – herself, another woman and two merry Guards officers. There was a gallery on the upper floor, off which opened the *salles privées*. Suddenly the Grand Duke Vladimir appeared, huge, deaf and drunk. He sent an ADC to fetch her to sit beside him, made her write on the menu with her 'bad writing' and called upon everyone to admire the calligraphy. 'Look at that! Isn't it wonderful!' (I found her writing almost impossible to decipher.)

When I told her about my tetralogy (the first idea I had for what became the present book), she asked, 'Will you be my biographer?' I said 'But, Madame, you've written your own incomparable autobiography.' 'Not all of it. There were things which my *pudeur* prevented me from having published during my life time. I will put together the documents for you.' 'I cannot refuse.' She gave me a faintly conniving look as she said, 'You live by your wits.' I saw myself as a kind of literary Casanova. 'But it doesn't do to be too cushioned,' she added. I never received the documents, but I am writing about her just the same. I formed the habit of making notes of our conversations.

We talked of the changing shape of women's bodies. I asked, 'Weren't all dancers fat in 1909?' 'Yes. Then a French critic wrote something about me – that I was a *flocon de neige* – and I decided to be thinner. I did not diet: I simply exerted my will-power. I saw myself thinner and became so. One day, on stage, Diaghilev passed me and noticed this. "You have become like an adolescent boy," he said. After that *all* dancers became thinner. But I always ate *everything*.' The most slender and streamlined of all modern ballerinas was the American Suzanne Farrell, loved by Balanchine; and I spoke of her amazing technical prowess. 'I wonder if she will continue to develop after George rejects her when she is about twenty-eight, and go on improving as Margot has done up to forty-eight.' Karsavina said, 'It depends on what you have inside you.'

Yes, she admitted, she was sometimes lonely, and felt 'unsteady' in the evenings. In the morning she had to do her shopping, and in the afternoons, when least disposed for it, she had to write and work. She had no time for *leisure*. She could not say no to requests for her time and company, so wasted her life in boring civilities. In the next day or two, she had to finish an article and judge Royal Academy of Dancing exams. 'But doing everything you do as well as you can is a great source of satisfaction.'

I drove her back to Hampstead. Mme Karsavina said that Marcel Proust had sometimes driven her home after parties. 'He was so green, so over-polite. He wanted to be loved. It's a Jewish weakness.' I spoke of George Painter's amazing book. She thought such analysis diminished Proust and his inspiration. She loved the songs of Reynaldo Hahn, composer of

Le Dieu bleu. 'He was a former *bel ami* of Proust, you know.' I knew. We talked of Romantic music. Karsavina said she adored Berlioz. I exclaimed, 'I so love the "Symphonie fantastique".' 'Oh I cannot hear it enough!' I hummed the *valse*. She added, 'And I adore "Roméo et Juliette" and "Les Nuits d'été".'

As we walked down the path to her door Mme Karsavina asked if I would like tea. I refused. 'You know I have a weakness for you, Dicky.' I kissed her goodnight.

This dinner took place five weeks after I slept in my Wiltshire cottage for the first time.

When I came to write the Introduction to Sotheby's catalogue I realized what a 'Diaghilev revival' had taken place since – and partly because of – my exhibition thirteen years before. I wrote:

> The glory of Diaghilev and interest in his period and his achievement is on the increase. During the last year I have been invited to arrange more than one exhibition about him, to assist with publications about him, to write articles and introductions to catalogues of his work, to advise on and take part in television and radio programmes about him, to authenticate documents and designs relating to his ballets, to help devise new versions of his ballets – and even to attend an exhibition of carpets inspired by his ballets.

I had suggested that Lydia Sokolova should show the young dancers of the Royal Ballet School how to wear their costumes and pose for the catalogue's illustrations. This she did with heartening professionalism.

Sotheby's gave a dinner for Princess Margaret and Lord Snowdon before the sale on 7 June: this was held in the room across the road where Pushkin had been recited. Among the 152 items relating to Diaghilev which were auctioned, there were designs, portraits, posters and contracts. Only eighteen costumes were on sale, but two Nijinsky costumes fetched £920 ($2567) and £420 ($1172). In spite of the parade-ground elocution on which I prided myself, my explanations were inaudible beyond the first few rows because a crowd of customers for whom there were no seats in the hall were making such a noise in the bar. The sale proved something, however. I had not exaggerated the increase of interest in Diaghilev and his Ballet. A scrap of paper bearing his signature could be worth £100; and designs by Gontcharova, Benois and Bakst – particularly the last – had trebled in value since my Diaghilev Exhibition. There was even a market for costumes.

My friend Erich Alport had become increasingly infirm. In the old days he had pursued his researches in Europe and Africa alone, armed only with introductions to remote scholars or officials: by 1967, in case he suffered a blackout in the street, as he had in the previous year, he felt the need of a companion on his travels. He was determined to see the architecture of Leningrad, and he asked me to go with him in September: I was delighted. Of course we had been on jaunts together before. In 1952 he had taken me to Morocco and Spain. We had watched the Chleuh dancers of Marra-kesh, feasted with a *caïd* in the middle of nowhere and frater-nized with the boozy exiles of Tangier. We had sat on the summit of Gibraltar, journeyed from Cadiz to Jerèz de la Frontera and on to Seville for the Féria, then basked in the glory of the Prado and made excursions from Madrid to Toledo and El Escorial. Not only had I seen in Erich's company the 'Meninas' of Velasquez, Goya's frescoes in Sant' Antonio de la Florida and El Greco's 'St Maurice and the Theban Legion'; in 1966, we had visited the house of Rubens in Antwerp together and I had stood breathless with him before van Eyck's 'Adoration of the Lamb' in Ghent. Although Erich was a Jew and a refugee from Hitler, he and his mother had fled Germany in good time; and although after the war they shared a small house in North Oxford (whereas in the 1930s they had occupied two separate houses in Bloomsbury), Erich, motherless since 1960, had never lacked for anything. Yet this obstinate spoilt child, sybaritic in a puritanical way, was prepared to endure hardship in the cause of research. (He filled volumes with sociological and anthropological notes, but published only a few learned papers.) When we had to share a bedroom in a primitive hotel he adapted himself without fuss. On our first night in Rabat he told me, 'I don't mind your peeing in the wash-basin if you wash it out properly afterwards.' I was lazier and more frivolous than he would have wished. After a long morning's sight-seeing, followed by a good lunch, I required a siesta. Then, although Erich liked to drink wine and make love in moderation, he felt himself obliged to curb my tendency to excess. Because I had the habit of wooing sleep with a book, the lamp between us had to be draped with silk handkerchiefs; when I switched it off at last, Erich's snoring would wake me up and I would shout, 'Lie on your side!' We had rows, but it was convenient to pretend next day that these had not happened. Marriage, I supposed, must be something like that.

Erich busied himself with planning every detail of our trip to Leningrad; and I sought what hints I could from friends such as Nigel and Maude Gosling, who gave me advice, as well as an enlarged photograph of a pre-war map of St Petersburg, which proved invaluable. I knew the directors of the Kirov Ballet and of the School, so I wrote to warn them of our arrival.

On 23 August I went to dine with Tamara Karsavina. 'It doesn't look like a kitchen, does it?' she used to ask, with a touch of pride. Well, it wasn't one, because the cooking and washing-up took place in a squalid little room at the back, which held the stove and sink. (Lydia Sokolova could never get over how dirty Karsavina was, and apparently always had been.) The 'kitchen' was more like a cottage dining-room with bright-coloured peasant pottery on the dresser and *images d'Epinal*, watercolours by Konstantin Somov and designs by Claud Lovat Fraser on the walls. That Wednesday my hostess must have been working all day – shopping, cooking and making the table bright with red candles and decorations. She had prepared a *buffet* fit for Grand Dukes. What with the profusion of cold tomato soup with cream, little dishes of olives, radishes and gherkins, chicken with mushroom sauce, spicy Hungarian meat balls and pots of raspberry mousse, Mme Karsavina forgot to serve the salad, and the Brie was left uneaten.

She often made use of charming, slightly archaic expressions, both in speech and in her careful English prose. The verb 'tarry' held an appeal for her. In her book, which I almost knew by heart, she described how, at the Theatre School, maids used to comb the girl pupils' hair after their cold baths. 'It was a sociable corner, and we would have tarried over the combing had it not been for all we had to do before breakfast.' At the Mariinsky Theatre, the *Journal of Orders*, an official weekly gazette, was displayed in a frame, and 'every morning, artists, before entering the rehearsal room, tarried on the landing to scan the page.' 'Fond' and 'fondly' Karsavina used in the sense of 'doting'. Her maternal great-uncle Khomiakov had been a poet and religious philosopher, and her mother 'fondly believed Lev [Tamara's brother] was to perpetuate his fame'. Round the tea-table of the ballet school's secretary and his wife, a former dancer, 'the fond conclave mapped out a victorious career for me'. Describing to me her walks with Fokine, which she had been too discreet to mention in her book, she said, 'And what fond names we called each other!'

That evening I was on the point of remarking how much Diaghilev and Stravinsky came to dislike Fokine, but I thought better of it. I said that Fokine had grown very difficult in later years. 'Prickly,' she conceded. 'But earlier on he was charming. We loved each other very much.'

She reverted to the subject of Pavlova's bitchiness – *that* word is mine. Twice in the 1920s, she reminded me, Pavlova had stolen her partners – first Novikov, then Vladimirov –

which had nearly wrecked her tours. Their place had been taken in turn by Gavrilov and Keith Lester. Once, when she had been dancing at the Arts Theatre in London, Pavlova with two 'escorts' had seats in the front row. In the middle of Karsavina's solo, while she pirouetted at the front of the stage, Pavlova rose with her friends and swept out of the theatre. This caused a stir and threw Tamara off her balance. 'All eyes followed Pavlova.'

I brought up the subject of *épaulement*, that subtle angling of the head and shoulders in relation to the torso and legs – the equivalent of *contrapposto* in Florentine Renaissance sculpture – which gives to classical ballet, with its alternating *croisé* and *effacé*, an added richness and range. '*Epaulement* is lost!' she cried. Then she added, 'Mime too is lost and despised in England.' 'Why, do you think?' 'Because dramatic ballets such as *Le Corsaire* are never given.'

I helped her bolt the shutters. In spite of this nightly fortification she left a window open at the back for the cat, King Florestan XV, who ruled the house, who was known familiarly as 'Diddle' and who, Karsavina thought, when he sat upright, looked just like an Ancient Egyptian cat in the British Museum.

At two in the morning Mme Karsavina remarked, 'I'm not tired, are you?' 'No.' 'Then I shall make tea.' She drank China tea, as I did. It is perhaps necessary to explain that China tea – no longer available in England on railway trains or even in quite expensive hotels – has nothing to do with the green tea served in Chinese restaurants. It is a scented mixture, made over the last century in a number of varieties, specially for the British market. Lapsang Souchong, for instance, has a smoky taste. Both Mme Karsavina and I preferred Earl Grey, which was sold by three different firms. She made it very strong. I said, 'I never know which I like best – Twining's, Fortnum's or Jackson's. One has much more honeysuckle in it than the others.' Karsavina raised her eyebrows, and pronounced, 'Jyackson's is the acknouwledged byest.'

Nobody, as I have said, wrote more tenderly about St Petersburg than Alexandre Benois and Tamara Karsavina. I intended to take Benois' three books of reminiscences and Karsavina's *Theatre Street* with me, to read again in Peter's city. But I was only allowed one suitcase – and I thought I might have to carry Erich's too; the uncertainties of autumn weather dictated a varied wardrobe; everyone wanted me to take presents to Nathalie Dudinskaya; and I was warned to buy quantities of chocolate, chewing-gum and ballpoint pens, which were said to be acceptable in lieu of tips. My suitcase overflowed; and I was obliged to leave behind the Benois, which had never appeared in paperback. Mme Karsavina's book existed in an American paperback edition, and I bought two copies of this, as well as a new life of Pushkin, which I thought I could first read, then give away.

As travellers to the Soviet Union will know, reservations are not always to be relied on, and although we had requested rooms at the old Astoria Hotel it was touch-and-go whether Erich and I might not be put up at one of the big modern hotels far from the centre of the city. Yet we were lucky. We even managed to insist on two single rooms, although urged to share. Erich had paid for our whole trip in London: we had only to produce books of coupons, from which one or two were torn off for every meal. The Astoria, built in the *belle époque* and far from bleak, stands on the huge open space (it is not a square) dominated by the gilded dome and four belfries of St Isaac's Cathedral. On Benois' act-drop for *Petrushka*, which is lowered while scenes are changed to the music of *tambours militaires*, he painted this church looming in the moonlight above the *montagnes russes* (snow switchbacks) and *balagani* (temporary booths) of the pre-Lenten fair. This 'Butter Week' carnival had been held in Admiralty Square, just round the corner from our hotel, on the way to the Winter Palace; and the golden spire – or rather, needle – of the Admiralty, rising so strangely from a dome set on a square tower surrounded by a colonnade, was also familiar

The Admiralty, St Petersburg, with a *montagne russe* and booths imagined in the foreground: a project for *Petrushka*. Watercolour by
Alexandre Benois.

from the décor of the ballet's opening and closing scenes. After dinner on our first evening ('Caviar, sturgeon') we set about ordering breakfast in our bedrooms for the morrow. I doubted whether we should succeed in this, but all went well. The Intourist representative was an amiable, handsome middle-aged woman with dyed hair, who sat behind a desk in the entrance hall; and she spoke English. Suddenly I heard Erich demanding China tea. 'We do not serve Chinese tea. Indian tea is best,' said the lady. 'Not at all, Indian tea is an inferior brand,' Erich insisted. 'China tea is far preferable.' Now, Russia was not on the best of terms with China. I walked away nervously.

When Erich went to bed, I set out alone through the Admiralty Gardens to where Falconet's equestrian statue of Peter the Great, on a rough-hewn granite base, confronts the Neva. This was Pushkin's 'Bronze Horseman'. On my right stretched the long bridge to Vassilievsky Island, where stood the Academy of Arts and Sciences and the University, and where rostral columns framed the former Bourse.

I woke at three-fifteen to hear a swishing sound on the cobbled plain outside my window. It was being washed. Soon after dawn there came a subdued roll of kettledrums, and I rushed to the window. A company of soldiers were diagonalling past the equestrian statue of Nicolas I. In their long grey greatcoats they marched in an easy, slouching, democratic way which I found charming.

Erich and I walked enraptured to the Winter Palace. The trees were turning. When we entered the stupendous building I learned for the first time how insistent Russians are on the shedding of coats the instant one has crossed the threshold. Erich was reluctant to part with his, fought for a while and lost. I will not describe the splendour of the staircases and halls. I had been looking forward to seeing Rembrandt's 'Danaë', which I had known in reproduction since I was a child at Overstrand: but I found the epic compassion of the father in his 'Prodigal Son' more moving than Danaë's golden sensuality. That night we saw a ballet at the Kirov – formerly Mariinsky – Theatre, a heaven of blue and gold, as in Karsavina's day.

'Come on,' I said to Erich next morning. 'We've got to go to the Ballet School.' I knew this was situated in the famous Theatre Street (*Teatralnaya Ulitsa*) which had given Karsavina the title of her book. It was now renamed after its architect, the Italian, Rossi. '*Rossi Ulitsa*,' I told the taxi-driver, showing off one of my three Russian words. Karsavina had described how her mother first took her there for the children's audition on 26 August 1894. 'I was beside myself with fear that I might be refused. I could not drink my tea. On the way to school Mother took me to a hairdresser . . . I kept asking whether it was not time to go.' Theatre Street was indeed magnificent, with its two long identical pinkish-ochre façades, punctuated by white columns, terminating in the back of the Pushkin – formerly Alexandrinsky – Theatre. The Ballet School was in the eastern block. A porter stood at the door. Mme Karsavina, in her Dickensian way, called him 'beadle'. 'The sight of the beadle's livery with the Imperial eagles on it made me feel very small.' But in 1967 the porter had no eagles. 'Natalia Dudinskaya?' I said, naming the former ballerina and present teacher with whom I had made friends in London. This was my 'Open, Sesame'. We were conducted through an arch and directed half-left across a courtyard to a corner door. 'We left our coats and wrappings in the cast hall,' wrote Karsavina, 'and went upstairs.' Erich and I were waved on by a crone-like *concierge*, and mounted the marble stairs, passing commemorative wall-plaques and green plants, to arrive in a babbling office, where there was a lady pianist who spoke French. It was here we left our coats. We were escorted to the rehearsal room. 'In the big room on the first floor,' Karsavina had written, 'we waited for some time, and I took the opportunity of going round looking at the portraits of the Imperial family on the walls before a stern-looking lady in black sailed in with six other ladies in cashmere dresses of light blue.' Erich and I had not long to wait, but I too took the opportunity of looking round me. This sacred hall had seen not only the moulding of Karsavina, but before her of Kchessinskaya, Preobrajenskaya and Pavlova, and after her of Lopoukhova, Spessivtseva, Doubrovska, Danilova, Ulanova – and of Dudinskaya, for whom we were waiting. The ramp of the floor corresponded to that of the Kirov stage. There were windows on both sides, giving a comforting glimpse of trees. The wall at the deep end was covered in mirrors. A gallery ran all round above our heads; from this a bust of the revered teacher Vaganova (shallow end) faced Petipa (deep end). On this walkway there suddenly appeared Mme Dudinskaya. 'Deeky! Deeky!' She vanished briefly, then came through the lower door and welcomed me with kisses.

Mme Karsavina described how in her later years at school she chose to take special classes with Nicolas Legat in the boys' room above, while the girls' regular teacher Mme Sokolova (after whom Diaghilev had named my friend Hilda Munnings) was giving instruction in this room below. 'I always felt uneasy when our small group filed along the narrow gallery overhanging the rehearsal room. Legat, as if flaunting a comic defiance to the official class below, walked first, picking out absurd tunes on his fiddle . . .' Now it was our turn to follow Dudinskaya upstairs and along the gallery to the 'boys' classroom', where she was in the middle of a lesson for girls in their first year. I realized just in time that, following some explanation of my presence, these girls were curtseying to me; and I rose to return their greeting.

Erich soon went off to look at Scythian gold. Dudinskaya had to take her class of perfection in the hall below, but before she left she introduced me to Nureyev's teacher, Mr Pushkin. As his young men began to assemble for their morning lesson I greeted among others the incomparable Soloviev, who soared nearer heaven than any dancer I had seen and landed as silently as an angel. Patrick Procktor had made drawings of him for me in London. Dudinskaya's husband, Konstantin Sergeyev, appeared, embraced me, and went away. Mr Pushkin spoke neither English nor French and I wondered if I dared give him some of the postcards of Nureyev I had in my pocket. I wished I could have watched his class all day long. The male pianist broke into 'If You Were The Only Girl In The World' and I bowled him a smile under a tunnel of *attitudes*, unsure whether this was a tune he always played or whether he was making a funny attempt to breach the language barrier. I remembered Karsavina's description of a famous encounter in this room.

One morning I came up earlier than usual [to join Legat's class]; the boys were finishing their practice. I glanced casually, and could not believe my eyes; one boy in a leap rose far above the heads of the others and seemed to tarry in the air. 'Who is this?' I asked Michael Oboukhov, his master. 'It is Nijinsky; the little devil never comes down with the music.' . . . Like peas falling out of a bag, the boys rushed off, their patter a hollow repercussion in the vaulted passage. In utter amazement I asked Michael why nobody spoke of this remarkable boy, and he about to finish [his schooling]. 'They will soon,' chuckled Michael. 'Don't you worry.'

Downstairs I watched Dudinskaya teaching a class which included Sizova, Maximova and Makarova. Kolpakova, that other favourite with London audiences, was away having a baby. On 30 September 1966 I had given a dinner party at the Opéra Restaurant in Great Queen Street for Sergeyev and Dudinskaya, Semenov, Makarova, Kolpakova and her husband, Soloviev and his wife, Marie Rambert, Nina and Gordon Latta and Patrick Procktor, who spoke Russian. I took my guests back to my flat afterwards and gave them all presents. It happened that I had just bought a postcard by a London photographer of Soloviev and Makarova rehearsing *Giselle*, and I asked them both to sign it. (After Makarova 'defected' in 1970 I counted this as a great rarity, for it was unlikely that they would ever be able to sign the same photograph together again. Then Soloviev committed suicide in 1977.)

It seemed to me so unbelievable that I had spent a morning in the nursery of the classic dance, the school where Fokine, Pavlova, Karsavina, Nijinsky, Lopoukhova and Balanchine had been trained, the temple of tradition whose ministrants were still sending out artist after superb artist to amaze the world! If only, like Diaghilev, I could take these Makarovas and Solovievs and devise a series of perfect ballets for them! But I had almost outgrown my theatrical ambitions. (Almost, but alas! – as time would prove – not quite.) It had needed a century and a half – more – to produce this stable of thoroughbreds. Should we ever, as a result of the long labours of Ninette de Valois, see their like emerging from English schools? I had been too excited that morning, too self-conscious, to take in the fine points of the lessons I had watched: but, like Marius after his visit to the shrine of Aesculapius among the hills of Etruria, I should be strengthened and purified by my pilgrimage.

I walked southwards down Theatre Street to where it emerged into an open space opposite a bridge over the Fontanka. I was still thinking of Tamara Karsavina and remembering her visits as a girl to the market in search of smart second-hand clothes. These she had written about, but I also recalled her amorous walks with Fokine, which she hadn't. 'We spoke of Art – mostly.' I sensed that the markets lay on my right. Going under an arch in the crescent, I found them. After a while I arrived at the little Bankovsky foot suspension bridge over the Griboyedev – formerly Catherine – Canal, guarded by bronze gryphons with gilded wings. Thence it was only a few paces to the neo-classical Kazan Cathedral, with its semi-circle of columns, stretched out like arms to gather in passing Christians from the Nevsky Prospekt. Karsavina's mother had advised her to count these columns as a cure for insomnia. The Cathedral was now a Museum of Religion and Atheism.

That evening we heard *The Queen of Spades* at the Kirov. Both Benois and Diaghilev had been present on the first night of this opera in December 1890. The house where Tchaikovsky had died, and to which Diaghilev had rushed, risking cholera, was round the corner from our hotel, on Gogol Street, formerly Malaya Morskaya, almost opposite the palace traditionally associated with the 'house of the Old Countess'.

Just as Tchaikovsky's operas *Eugene Onegin* and *The Queen of Spades* had been based respectively on a narrative poem and short story of Pushkin's, so was the ballet of *The Bronze Horseman*, which I went to see on the following morning (Sunday matinées being given at 11.30 a.m.), based on another of his stories in verse. Not yet having studied Diaghilev's magazine *Mir Iskusstva* (The World of Art), I did not know that Benois' illustrations to this poem were his finest work, the most loving of many tributes to the capital city whose praises he never ceased to sing. I was amazed by the way in which the stage technicians of the Kirov conveyed the effect of the Neva in flood, with the water rising to the base of Peter's statue, and not only jetsam but whole sentry-boxes drifting by; and I thought the way the hero climbed into a fishing boat and rowed through the storm to find the wrecked home of his beloved was quite wonderful. Erich, meanwhile, had gone to church at the Nicolas Cathedral, whose architecture and ritual made a deep impression on him.

My bedroom at the Astoria was comfortable in a stuffy bourgeois way. The chairs were upholstered in gravy-coloured plush. Breakfast with Indian tea and lemon came up every morning. I made friends with the lady in charge of our second floor. When I had to pay her for the washing of shirts she would cry 'Money!'; and I would execute a mad war-dance in my Carnaby Street dressing-gown, shaking my fists and shouting in mock desperation 'Money! Money! All you want is money!' She quite liked that. Meals in the big restaurant were served rather slowly to palm-court music.

We soon learned to order fish in preference to meat, and discovered a good white wine from the Ukraine. One night when Erich had left me eating and gone to bed early I was drawn into conversation by a party at the next table. A flashy middle-aged man, who said he was a film producer, was entertaining somewhat too lavishly a couple of young sailors with unfinished faces. Oho, I thought. I firmly refused to join them in a second dinner with caviar, but felt I ought to prove that I could drink them under the table. After the third or fourth bottle my host confided, 'I am Georgian duke'.

I pursued my explorations with Karsavina's *Theatre Street* in my hand. For our day's excursion to the country palaces we were provided with an Intourist guide, a woman who studied English at night in the hopes of becoming a teacher of that language. She had heard of Karsavina, but did not know her book, so to reward her for showing us the curving galleries of Pavlovsk, the parade of giants along the façade of Rastrelli's Tsarskoe Selo, and Cameron's staircase at its far end – surely the proudest *perron* in the world – then the water staircase of Peterhof, framed by trees of saffron, copper and blood, I gave her one of my two little paperback volumes. She said she would take it as the subject of her monthly thesis. From Nigel Gosling I had an introduction to Professor Kraminsky, who had initiated and supervised the restoration of Leningrad after the devastations of the German siege. He could not have been more instructive or more anxiously avuncular had he been Benois himself – and indeed he reminded me very much of the old painter. He was really distressed that we had spent several days sightseeing without his supervision, and swept us straight off to the little Hermitage Theatre, which was in process of restoration, and which we should not have seen without his authority. Here in 1908 Benois had watched over the painting of his décor for the Polish Scene in *Boris Godounov*, which Diaghilev was to take to Paris. 'During that period,' he wrote, 'I had grown to look upon the Hermitage Theatre, which formed part of the great

Winter Palace, as something of my own, and it gave me enormous pleasure to frequent it. It was entered from the famous Picture Gallery, by crossing the Venetian Bridge over the Winter Canal. As I was almost an *habitué* of the gallery, and was at that time compiling a guide-book of the pictures, I visited it daily. Crossing over from the gallery, where I worked as an historian of art, to the delightful rooms where I became a theatrical painter, had a peculiar charm for me ...' Erich and I were led by Kraminsky through this *rococo* gallery inside the bridge called 'Venetian', presumably, because it resembles the Bridge of Sighs. It was into the narrow Winter Canal below that that Lise flung herself in Tchaikovsky's *The Queen of Spades*. (In Pushkin's poem she married 'a very well-bred young man'.) I stood on the stage of Quarenghi's little semi-circular court theatre, surveyed its pink marble columns standing out against the white walls, and guessed that it might seat four hundred. At the back of the stage I peered astonished at a road winding down into the darkness, up which I supposed companies of guardsmen must have marched to 'swell a scene or two', or ships and chariots been dragged from a secret entrance on the quay below. Mme Karsavina described a performance here on the night of a fancy-dress ball, when the court wore historical Russian dresses. 'That of the Empress Alexandra Feodorovna was the genuine *sarafan* of the Tsaritsa Miloslavskaya ... the young Empress, in a heavy tiara, put on over a gauze kerchief entirely concealing her hair, looked like an ikon of rigid beauty ... her dress of heavy brocade was sewn over with jewels.' Kraminsky was thrilled to learn that I knew Tamara Karsavina, and sent her 'the homage of one who formerly adored her from afar'. He took us to Pushkin's pretty little house on the Moika Canal, from which the poet had set out to fight his fatal duel.

That night Erich and I heard *Khovanshchina*, which Diaghilev had first shown in Paris and London before the 1914 war: but I still had to telephone my article to the *Sunday*

Times, which I had made an appointment by telegram to do.
Even in Britain it was an exhausting business to dictate one's
piece – from Edinburgh, for example, during the Festival –
instead of sending it round in a taxi to Gray's Inn Road. Every
foreign name, every unusual adjective, even simple words
used in an unexpected way had laboriously to be spelt out,
and every semi-colon given. One's subtler allusions or
obscurer jokes could be ruined by a misprint or misunder-
standing. This time I wrote my five hundred words in the

Opposite: Natalia Makarova and Yuri Soloviev rehearsing *Giselle* at
Covent Garden. Photograph by Jennie Walton, 1966, signed by the
dancers after dinner with the author, 30 September 1966. *Below:*
Soloviev rehearsing *Giselle* during the same London season. Drawing
by Patrick Procktor.

form of a letter to Mme Karsavina, describing how I had wandered through the city with her book in my hand. I sat dictating in my bedroom at the Astoria Hotel; and the telephone call took me from eleven-thirty until one in the morning.

The Ballet Museum was on the top floor of the School in Theatre Street. Its walls were hung with framed photographs and hideous paintings; and bright-eyed boys from the school were seated at one of the long tables. 'They are studying the history of the dance,' I was told by the Curatress, Mme Frangopoulo, who spoke French. Their study was apparently confined to looking at albums of old photographs. I declined the offer to go through several hundreds of these. 'I should like to send you a present for your library,' I told the lady. 'Have you got copies of all my books on ballet?' She said 'I'm afraid I don't know who you are.' Reeling under this blow, I faltered, 'No doubt you have several editions of Tamara Karsavina's *Theatre Street*, but if a new American paperback would be of any interest –'. 'Indeed, we have no copies of the book. You see, it has never been translated into Russian. But we should much appreciate – would you write in it?' *No* copies of that most evocative book ever written by a dancer, that masterpiece, that pearl? I found it hard to believe that the cheap little volume I carried was the first copy of *Theatre Street* to reach Theatre Street, but I inscribed it anyway: 'To the Ballet School Library from РИУАРД ВОКЛЬ.' The Curatress thanked me, and it was clear that the name rang no bell: but my second copy of Karsavina's book had found a home – an 'ideal home', a 'home from home', you might say.

108 Frognal,   21 October 1967
Hampstead, NW3

My dear Dicky
       Your letter from Leningrad makes me proud . . . it was like hearing the echo of my own footsteps . . .
                 Thanks & love
                 Tamara K.

CHAPTER 9

A Film? A Book? A Museum?

The morning after my return from Russia, 13 October 1967, the telephone rang early. I was drinking Earl Grey tea in bed. The conversation went something like this. 'Richard Buckle?' 'Yes.' 'This is Ken Russell. You probably don't know who I am. I make films for television.' 'Didn't you make one on Elgar?' 'Yes.' 'I liked it very much.' 'Good. I want to talk to you about a film on Nijinsky.' 'Oh, everyone wants to make a film about Nijinsky. People write to me about it every month. A lot of time is wasted talking, and the films never come off.' 'This one will. Everything is fixed.' 'That's what they all say.' 'No, seriously. This film is genuine, and Nureyev is to play Nijinsky. Have you heard of Harry Salzman?' 'No.' 'He makes those James Bond films. He's got the Nijinsky film all tied up. You probably know Romola Nijinsky sold the rights of her book to several film companies.' 'Yes, sometimes to two at a time.' 'Well, that took some sorting out. The last man to own the rights was Vidor and he's dead; and Harry has acquired them from his widow. I want you to advise us. Will you have lunch with me?' 'Really, you know, you're wasting your time. And mine. Life is too short. Every week I have to answer letters from girls in Yorkshire or in the Middle West who want advice about their theses on Diaghilev or Bakst or Nijinsky. I can't keep up with it and if I had to lunch with everyone who wanted to make a film about Nijinsky I might as well give up trying to earn a living.' 'But you'll make some money out of this. You can't fail. Harry has got Nureyev under contract.

Please have lunch with me today.' 'Do you realize I only got back from Leningrad yesterday afternoon?' 'All the more reason.' 'Well, come here for a drink and I'll take you to lunch at La Scala in Southampton Street.'

Ken was not yet famous: he had never made a feature film. He was stocky, amiable, full of enthusiasm. He said, 'Do you know you once saved my life?' This was a good beginning, but I had to point out he must be mistaken: I had never set eyes on him before. 'When you were editing *Ballet* I sent you a short story about dancers. I was broke. I didn't know where to turn. You wrote to say you didn't print fiction, but you liked the story and you enclosed five pounds anyway.' 'No wonder the magazine went bust.' We discussed his ideas for the film.

On 17 October I was taken to see Harry Salzman in his office in Audley Square. True to type, he had his feet on the desk and was speaking to Hollywood on two telephones. Christopher Gable was present. He had been a leading dancer of the Royal Ballet, and as the partner of Lynn Seymour in MacMillan's *Invitation* and Ashton's *Two Pigeons* had injected a new and irresistible naturalness into the comportment of the male dancer, but he had given up dancing to act in films by Ken Russell. I thought him very attractive. Perhaps Ken did too, for I suspected he was scheming that Chris should play Nijinsky in Rudolf's place. Melvyn Bragg had written a script for the Nijinsky film; and I was asked to comment on it.

Six years before I had written the synopsis – and one sequence in detail – of a film on Diaghilev for John Sutro (one of Korda's original backers). My idea was that it should be spoken in several languages – Russian, French, German, whatever the situation demanded; then I so much liked some of the dialogue I had invented that I thought it a pity not to have it all in English. Although John paid me £150 for this sketch, nothing more was ever heard of it. I was secretly hoping to write Ken Russell's script myself. I got myself an agent. At that time the big firm of London International dealt as agents not only for actors, directors, playwrights and script writers, but for the authors of printed books: that is to say, they had a literary as well as a drama and film department. Their offices were in a tall block in Park Lane overlooking Marble Arch and Hyde Park. Salzman wanted me not only to advise on the film, but to write a book about Nijinsky which would come out simultaneously – 'the book of the film'. 'Could you do it in a year?' 'No, it would take two years at least.' Through Michael Anderson, the representative of London International who was dealing with my contract as adviser on the film, I met David Machin from the literary department, who persuaded me that a serious biography of Nijinsky should be written, whether Salzman's film was made or not. On 8 November my report on Melvyn Bragg's script was typed; on 1 December Machin told me he had interested Tony Godwin of Weidenfeld and Nicolson in my biography; on the tenth I started writing it. By this time, the confident Ken Russell, initiator of the whole business, had been fired by Harry Salzman.

In the previous May, a month before the sale of Grigoriev's costumes at Sotheby's, reviewing a book on 'Ballet Designs and Illustrations' in the collection of the Victoria and Albert Museum, which was published to coincide with an exhibition, I had written that the museum could be excused for spending no money on display provided that they were saving up to fill in gaps in their collection of ballet designs, which ranged from Buontalenti's sketches for the court masques of the Medici in the 1580s up to the present day. Drawing attention to gaps in their haphazard accumulation of designs for the Diaghilev Ballet – one Benois costume design, four by Bakst for *The Sleeping Princess*, fifteen by Braque for *Les Fâcheux* and a representative group of Gontcharovas and Larionovs, I wrote, 'If the museum boys could visit the last-mentioned artists in their lifetime to buy designs for *Coq d'or, Contes russes, Chout* etc., why couldn't they visit Benois? He had stacks of stuff. No Picasso, no Derain, no Gris, no Matisse, no Sert, no Laurencin, no Pruna, no Tchelitchev, no Rouault, no Chirico, no Utrillo, no Bauchant, no Mirò. It's still not too late. Couldn't we have a Diaghilev Museum within the V and A? Boris Kochno has a fabulous collection of Diaghileviana, whose destiny is undecided. Lifar has fantastic things. In this country, Mr Carr-Doughty of Leicester has a mass of treasures, including Baksts of the exotic early period not represented at the V and A.' I wrote this piece (a week before it was published) on the day before I left for Florence with George Harewood and Patricia Tuckwell, to whom I showed Michelangelo's Medici tombs for the first time, and who didn't much like them. John Pope-Hennessy, who had just succeeded Trenchard Cox as Director of the V and A, rang me up soon after my return (it must have been one of his first acts as Director), and I went to see him on 24 May 1967, to discuss the possibility of forming a Diaghilev collection, a museum within a museum, in South Kensington. I wrote to Boris Kochno about it the same afternoon. Naturally my friends at Sotheby's took an interest in this project.

I had not heard from Anthony Diamantidi since the spring of 1954, when I met him with Olga de Basil in Paris and they had lent me the Utrillo curtain for *Barabau* to hang on the staircase at the Edinburgh College of Art. In May 1967 he must have read about the sale at Sotheby's of the so-called 'Vera Bowen collection'. This had given him a big idea, and he wrote to me about it. (What he did not tell me until much later was that he had rushed over to London, accused Grigoriev of selling what did not belong to him and threatened him with dire penalties. 'I let him keep half the money,' he said.) Tony Diamantidi suggested that I should propose to Sotheby's to sell all the Diaghilev and de Basil wardrobe, curtains and musical scores. He wrote that he was eighty-two, and wanted to find a home for the historic material before he died. He had been paying the warehouse rent for many years.

It was a huge and dubious undertaking. What exactly remained? What condition was it in? Would the large quantity of surviving costumes diminish their market value? Could even a museum give space to display the big drop curtains? Would anyone buy? Peter Wilson, chairman of Sotheby's, decided that David Ellis-Jones and Thilo von Watzdorf should go over to Paris, meet Diamantidi, examine the contents of the warehouse and make a report. As I knew many of the ballets concerned, either from books or from having seen them on the stage, which David and Thilo did not, I was to help sum up the situation. When I flew to Paris on 20 September 1967 and drove to the southern suburb of Bagneux, near Montrouge, Diamantidi and the young men were already there. (On my last brief visit to look at the Diaghilev hoard in 1954 everything had been stored at Pantin, to the north-east of Paris.) We began to unpack, to shift, to pile up and to sort out the hundreds of baskets, trunks and bundles. The dirt was incredible. We were covered in dust and choked with it. Yet it was a real treasure-hunt. I was as thrilled as Aladdin in the cave. From hamper after hamper I pulled famous costumes which I recognized. 'Here are Gontcharova's boyars from *Coq d'or*! These must be something by Juan Gris for *Les Tentations de la bergère*. Look! Here are the Chinese costumes Matisse designed for *Le Chant du rossignol*! Who would ever have thought he might set eyes on the fantastic Indian garments Bakst created for *Le Dieu bleu*, which was never given after 1912?' Holding up an eighteenth-century coat, trimmed with gold lace, obviously designed by Bakst for *The Sleeping Princess* in 1921, I thought from its splendour that it must have been for the King or Prince Charming at least, but no, there were half-a-dozen more exactly like it: it was just a courtier's. We found the costumes for the Hunting Scene, which composed (as Cyril Beaumont had often told me) so autumnal a tapestry of varied greens, turquoise and royal blue, chestnut and orange, against which stood out Tchernicheva's famous yellow velvet riding-habit and Vladimirov's military-looking coat in scarlet and gold. Of Bakst's three hundred costumes for this ballet at least half were there and in good condition. This was the more surprising as it had always been thought that when Sir Oswald Stoll had seized the production until Diaghilev could repay his enormous debt, the entire wardrobe, stored beneath the Coliseum stage, had been ruined by a leaking swimming-pool installed for a music-hall act.

For two days we battled with the ancient dust, and each day Tony Diamantidi took us down the road for lunch in a *bistro*. Bagneux, with its narrow streets of low buildings, might have struck some as a desolate characterless place, but no suburb lacks mystery for me. Through chinks in implacable grey metal gates I caught glimpses of hideous villas with Mansard roofs, flanked by pollarded planes, in which might lurk mayoresses of sickening respectability or the addicts of some nameless vice.

It was tantalizing not to have time to get to the bottom of every basket. We had to guess from the two or three costumes at the top what its other contents might be. We unfolded a few back-cloths by Sert, Gontcharova and Bakst, as well as that of Bérard's *Cotillon*. Diamantidi said there were more, as well as Picasso's famous front curtain for *Le Train bleu*, in store in America.

In the plane on the way back to London, David and Thilo asked me if I thought the sale – or, more likely, several sales – would justify the expense involved. How could I guess? I was confident in our ability to 'put on a show' which would attract and amaze the public, so I felt optimistic and said yes. Although my opinion was asked, the decision rested with Peter Wilson and his fellow directors. Would they shoulder the labours of Hercules? If Sotheby's could come to an agreement with Diamantidi they would have to consider the shipping, the customs, the finding of a London warehouse, the sorting, the taking of photographs for the catalogue, a location in which to display the exhibits before the sale, somewhere to hold the sale, and a method of selling. Not only must living models – presumably young dancers, as in the June sale – be procured to pose in their spare time and form appropriate groups to show off the costumes so that a catalogue could be prepared months in advance, but the same dancers – or others of similar shape and size – would have to be reassembled and rehearsed to parade at the sale itself. Pictures, furniture, silver or jewels are always shown to the public for three days before an auction, but Sotheby's sale-rooms could not accommodate costumes, much less drop-curtains. It seemed inevitable that a theatre must be found: and if the sale were to take place in a theatre some sort of performance would have to be given. This entailed staff, lighting, choreography, music, make-up. Could expenses be covered, let alone a profit made? To sell a few costumes worn by Nijinsky, Lopoukhova, Tchernicheva or Sokolova, as had been done as a freak experiment a few months before, was one thing: to sell whole productions was another. Was there a market? At the most the whole undertaking, which would keep so many people busy for so long, could hardly, when expenses were deducted, bring in the price of one painting by Cézanne! On the other hand, the publicity might be valuable to Sotheby's, who were always trying to keep one step ahead of their rivals. Then there were less mercenary considerations, such as the possibility of a Theatre Museum.

The day after our return from Paris I wrote in my diary: 'David Ellis-Jones rings to say Sotheby's will buy Diaghilev material.' It was six days later that I flew with Erich Alport to Leningrad.

On 8 February 1968 John Pope-Hennessy came to lunch and I showed him the view down on to Covent Garden. I had bought some daffodils to put in the Blue Office over-looking the Market. The fruit, vegetable and flower market had been on the point of moving south of the river for years, for the traffic problem had become acute. (In fact it did not move till 1974.) I told John that I thought the new theatre museum ought to be in Covent Garden, for it was the heart of 'theatre land'. The first two theatres to be given charters by Charles II after the Commonwealth, when play-acting was forbidden, were Covent Garden and Drury Lane. My street, Henrietta Street, and the parallel King Street, which both ran into the market, were named after Charles's parents. The square itself, laid out by another of my ancestors, Bedford, was the first in England, built in imitation of the Place Royale in Paris, which Henri IV (father of Queen Henrietta Maria) and Marie de Medici had derived from the Piazza d'Arme in Livorno and the Piazza Santissima Annunziata in Florence. What is more, the original 'piazza', with its arcades and its church in the Tuscan style, had been designed for Bedford by Inigo Jones, the first great English stage designer.

John Pope-Hennessy was entirely in favour of a new museum, which would, like Apsley House and Osterley, be a dependency of the V and A, but he said there was no question, in these lean years, of seeking public money to finance it. I talked over the museum project with Peter Wilson, David Ellis-Jones and Thilo von Watzdorf, who all hoped that the Sotheby sales might help to bring a museum into existence. It was decided that there should be at least two auctions of the Diaghilev material, the first on 17 July. As I was to catalogue these, I was anxious for a kind of unity, and urged that all the surviving costumes of any one ballet should be sold together: but it was explained to me that sales must have variety and that to sell fifty costumes for *Thamar* or a hundred costumes for *The Sleeping Princess* all at once would not only depreciate their value, but depress and discourage potential customers. The Picasso curtain for *Le Train bleu*, which we knew from photographs, but had not yet seen, was considered to be an object of prime importance. Peter Wilson was in favour of keeping it for the second sale: I begged him to include it in the first, for I thought that if we did not do all we could to ensure the success of the first sale there could be no second. We had once more arranged with Michael Wood and Ursula Moreton to borrow young dancers not only to pose in the costumes for the catalogue illustrations, but to parade in them for the sale. Lydia Sokolova would again arrange the choreography of these poses and parades.

Throughout the winter Thilo had been sorting the costumes in a bleak warehouse in Fulham. This was cold, dirty and tedious work, though interesting. I taught him all I knew about Diaghilev's designers, but as he began to classify the old wardrobe, comparing costumes with photographs, he came to know more about them than I did. It was easy at first glance to confuse Gontcharova's Russian peasant costumes for *Coq d'or* with Larionov's for *Chout*, until one discerned the element of Cubist asymmetry in the latter; to mix up the Bakst costumes for two Greek ballets such as *Narcisse* and *Daphnis et Chloë*; or to think one of Roerich's for *The Rite of Spring* belonged to *Prince Igor*.

It was during April, when I was dictating long descriptions of the Diaghilev costumes to a secretary in the warehouse, and when the curtains were being photographed at the Scala Theatre in dear old Charlotte Street where the sale was to take place, that George Harewood introduced me over lunch to Lord Goodman, the Chairman of the Arts Council. I gave an account of my talks with Pope-Hennessy and mentioned the opportunity offered by the forthcoming sales to start a Diaghilev collection. There were already at least two collections of theatre material in England, apart from the gallery attached to the Memorial Theatre at Stratford. That of Raymond Mander and Joe Mitchenson, two Cockney dandies out of Dickens who were to be seen at first nights finishing each other's sentences, was housed at their home in a South London suburb, and had been in existence since the war. This was run as a business: by writing books, by

227

providing information and by arranging small exhibitions of prints, playbills and programmes in the foyers of theatres, Raymond and Joe made money for new purchases. The British Theatre Museum (founded 1955), over which Lord Norwich presided, had also built up a considerable archive, and held temporary exhibitions in a corner of Leighton House, Kensington; but it had no money, and John Julius Norwich was always writing to *The Times* about this. These two collections were not on speaking terms. If there were to be one Theatre Museum, possibly including one or both of the existing collections, possibly attached to the V and A – whose own Department of Prints and Drawing, plus the Enthoven Collection, constituted a precious nucleus – it should obviously not confine itself to the work of Diaghilev, even if the chance of making a big haul of Diaghilev material – a chance which might never recur – was our starting point. George's main interest was opera: and we were all conscious that Shakespeare had been the greatest contribution to the world's civilization made by our sceptred isle. What could be done, in view of the money shortage? Goodman was the great fixer, an ambassador between the worlds of big business and the arts. He asked me to sum up the situation in a report, which I did.

For several days before the sale of 17 July the costumes were on view at South Lodge, 253 Knightsbridge, a curious Edwardian mansion, partly derelict, overlooking Hyde Park, which had recently been bought by the Royal Academy of Dancing, and from which they moved to less central and less expensive premises shortly afterwards. 'The curtains,' announced the catalogue, 'may be viewed on the 15th, 16th and 17th July between the hours of 10.30 a.m. and 12 noon only at the Scala Theatre, London (Scala Street entrance).' It was at the Scala that Lydia Sokolova put her young dancer-models through their paces. My work on the catalogue had naturally been finished months before, and the handsome book had been disseminated throughout the world. In spite of my talks to Pope-Hennessy and Goodman, no one had come forward with offers of money for a new museum, and I had no idea up to the day of the sale of buying costumes for myself or for anybody else. Lincoln Kirstein, it is true, had written to ask if the *Thamar* décor and costumes were original or if they had been recreated for de Basil; and I telephoned Tchernicheva to ask her to ask Grigoriev, who said they were original. I supposed Balanchine was contemplating a new production of the old ballet. The *Thamar* material was any-way not included in this first sale (and Balanchine never revived the ballet). Apart from this I had no idea who might be interested in bidding. I was busy preparing the exhibition of Cecil Beaton Portraits for the National Portrait Gallery, and there was nothing I could do to help Sotheby's and Diamantidi any more.

On the morning of the sale I walked round to the Scala Theatre to see how Sokolova and her kids were getting on. They were not there. There was, however, a small audience waiting in the dimly lit auditorium to 'view' the curtains – not more than a dozen people, of whom Charlotte Bonham-Carter was one; and the stage staff, hired for the occasion, told me that no one from Sotheby's had turned up to make the necessary explanations from the stage. I stepped into the breach and told the story of the exhibits: Gontcharova's three sets for *Coq d'or*, Bakst's one surviving décor for *The Sleeping Princess*, Picasso's *Train bleu* curtain, and another in the style of Persian miniatures which I had found out – simply by re-reading the *Reminiscences* of Benois – had been designed as a belated frontispiece for *Scheherazade* by the great Valentin Serov, not in 1910 but in 1911, the year of his death. (This was bought that evening by the Russian state for £1200 ($3348).) My 'spiel' took a quarter-of-an-hour. Since more potential customers arrived I repeated it twice. As I finished my final speech Tony Diamantidi, who had just arrived from Switzerland, leant across the empty orchestra pit to say hello. He asked me to lunch, and I

accepted. 'Where can you recommend in the neighbour-
hood?' I suggested the White Tower, where I had taken
Karsavina fifteen months before. (After all, he too was of
Greek descent.) 'Is there anyone else you would like to ask?'
I thought a pretty girl might gladden his octogenarian heart,
so I grabbed Bonnie Prandato, whose hopeless passion for
Nureyev had caused her to seek transfer from Sotheby's
Parke-Bernet Galleries in New York to their London branch.

Before we had even spread our toast with *taramasalata*
Tony asked how my plans for a 'Covent Garden Museum'
were going. I told him that while everyone liked the idea,
we still had no committee and no funds. He seemed to think
that we were very slow about things in England, and proposed that as he was in London only till the following day
we should try to advance matters that afternoon. While
Diamantidi, as President of the Diaghilev and de Basil
Ballets Foundation, was determined to get the best price
possible for the material on sale, as a private individual he
wanted to see the works of art – for so the costumes and
scenery appeared in the hands of Sotheby's to have become –
preserved with suitable reverence for the benefit of posterity.
He therefore announced that he would give out of his own
pocket £25,000 ($69,750) if English backers would make
up the sum of £100,000 ($279,000), so that we could take
advantage of the sale to buy unique objects for the future
museum. It was still not one o'clock, so I thought I might
catch John Pope-Hennessy before he went out to lunch. I did:
but he had all along disliked the idea of being landed with a
lot of costumes, and he said he thought it was an impossible
task to raise the sum Diamantidi named that very afternoon.
I returned to eat my lunch.

Back at my flat in Covent Garden I began to telephone,
but in between calls I went through the catalogue making a
list of lots which I thought most essential to buy if any money
were forthcoming. I had trouble tracing the busy Lord Goodman, and left messages. I thought he might well have

forgotten who I was, but he was civil enough to ring me back. He considered Diamantidi's offer too good to refuse, and asked me to get Tony to telephone him. I spoke to Tony at the Devonshire Club. He rang Goodman, then rang me back. Goodman had undertaken to raise £75,000 ($209,250) not that afternoon, but in three months, and Tony and I were to meet him at his flat at 6 p.m.

It occurred to me that although the British Theatre Museum and the Royal Opera House had expressed goodwill towards our museum project, I had not yet spoken to the London Museum, so I rang up John Hayes, its director, and had a talk. I then spoke to Pope-Hennessy again and to Lord Goodman. The latter said that John was now afraid of having to display the Picasso curtain, and suggested buying some costumes. I said he had formerly been terrified of costumes. Goodman said that his long experience of artistic people had taught him they sometimes changed their minds. I rang Peter Wilson about John's fear of the Picasso curtain, and he said, 'He's afraid of having to move the Raphael cartoons.' I had a bath and changed before taxi-ing to Lord Goodman's in Portland Place.

I was early, and walked round the corner into Park Crescent. It was a fine evening. When I had been at Heatherley's art school I had planned – and even, I think, begun – a painting of a huge naked giant looming against the curve of Park Crescent, but I was held up by the technical difficulty of rendering the extraordinary hemicycle of columns, a conception worthy of Rossi and St Petersburg. My picture would have owed something to Surrealism, to the early Chirico, to Picasso's classical or gigantic period and even to Michelangelo: but I now think that statues of giants, like towers, had always appealed to me. Had I not asked Rosoman to design a couple for the sculpture court in Edinburgh, and renamed the room 'The Hall of Giants'?

In Park Crescent I ran into Gabriel White, Director of Art at the Arts Council, who had also been summoned to the conference. I told him what was going on. At six we entered Goodman's block of flats, took the lift to the third floor and found he had not yet arrived. Tony Diamantidi came next; then our host appeared. Goodman said he had to ring up Henry Moore. It was, apparently, the sculptor's birthday. Moore was on his way to show the Picasso curtain to some American museum directors. 'We don't want competition,' exclaimed Goodman. 'Tell them it's terrible.' He said that Moore told him the curtain had been a landmark in his youth, and even changed his life. How interesting to think of the young sculptor executing in 1929 his first public commission, the relief of the floating 'West Wind', high up on the London Transport Building in Westminster, with the thought of Picasso's running giantesses, first seen at the Coliseum music-hall in 1924, at the back of his mind! George Harewood rang, returning a call of Goodman's, but he could not come round. Max Rayne arrived, calm, dapper and amused.

Time was short, for the sale began at eight. Goodman pressed matters forward. He and Rayne thought that between them they could undertake to raise not £75,000 but £50,000 within three months to match Diamantidi's £25,000. Tony accepted this, and when Goodman asked shamelessly, 'Will you not only give us the £25,000 but lend us the £50,000 for three months?' he agreed. I was told to bid for the Picasso curtain only. We knew that Diamantidi had placed a reserve of £50,000 on this, but no one had any idea if there would be competition. Tony began to leave, and while he was in the hall Goodman said to me, 'Don't stop at £75,000. Go to £76,000. No, £76,500.' As a new discussion seemed to be developing between him, Gabriel White and Max Rayne, I left too. I found Tony had gone ahead.

The Scala Theatre was only ten minutes walk away. I crossed Great Portland Street, where I had watched Idzikovsky's classes in 1937, walked along Maple Street, where I had had my first 'studio', and down Fitzroy Street, where I had been living when I founded *Ballet* in 1939. As I approached the Scala Theatre I saw on the pavement a pride of peacocking young people, bright with flowers and beads. (This was, after all, the 'Swinging Sixties'.) I realized that the sale had been turned into a festive occasion, and felt gay. My party was waiting for me, scattered in pairs about the front of the dress circle – Alicia Markova, June Churchill, Viva King, Astrid Zydower the sculptor, Barry Kay the designer and Philip Dossé. I sat next to Alicia in the front row, on the corner of the right-hand gangway. I looked round what Pevsner called 'the exceedingly baroque interior' of the theatre (Verity, 1904), which was soon to be pulled down. I had watched Jamaican dancers there on the night Juliet died; and in the forties had attended there a Mr Universe Competition, after which I was introduced to the beautiful giant, Steve Reeves.

Peter Wilson mounted his rostrum to the left (stage right) of the stage. He was surrounded by David, Thilo and various clerks and secretaries. After some good-natured laughter and shouting caused by the initial failure of the microphone, the sale began. The first fourteen lots were costumes by Bakst for *Le Dieu bleu*, an unimportant though spectacular ballet for which Cocteau had devised a libretto, Reynaldo Hahn had written a score and Fokine had invented some would-be oriental choreography in 1912. Lot 1. 'Costume for one of the Temple Servants. Short-sleeved gown of plum-coloured face-cloth, the sleeves bordered with a band of slate-blue, with *appliqué* zig-zags of white, trimmed with gold embroidery . . .' and so on. (My descriptions were much too long.) £80 (about $220). Lot 2 – £20. Lot 3 – made up of three costumes – £180. Lot 4 – £40. Lot 5 – £50 . . . I had not realized that Lord Goodman was sitting a few rows behind me with Annie Fleming (with whose brother Hugo Charteris I had shared a room at the IRTD at Rotondi in Italy during the war). Suddenly I became aware that Mrs Fleming, widow of the creator of James Bond, was crouching on the step beside me to whisper, 'Arnold says that if the costumes continue to go for so little you can spend £2000 ($5580) on them, as well as bidding for the curtain.' As I knew I was incapable of doing sums in my head, I turned round and asked Philip Dossé, who was in the seat behind me, to keep count of how much I spent on costumes, so that I could know at any moment how much money I had left. This proved invaluable.

I bought Lot 14, 'Frohman's costume as the Young Man', in *Le Dieu bleu*, for £200 ($558). It was one of Bakst's most elaborate creations, brilliant in colour, sewn with innumerable jewels. In the ballet Max Frohman had been an initiate for the priesthood whose girl-friend, Karsavina, was condemned to death for trying to dissuade him from taking his vows. She had been saved at the last moment by the apparition of Nijinsky as Krishna, the Blue God. I had remarked to Mme Karsavina how handsome Frohman appeared in his photographs. 'Yes,' she said, 'and Diaghilev soon had his eye on him!' His costume was paraded by a young man called David Ashmole, who later became a principal dancer in the Royal Ballet. It was the first acquisition of the yet unestablished Theatre Museum.

During and after the sale I learned that apart from private individuals – and a number of flower children were buying costumes to wear at parties – we had active opposition from George Howard's costume collection at Castle Howard in Yorkshire, from the Swedish Dance Museum, the Theatre Museum in Amsterdam, the Los Angeles County Museum and Robert Tobin, a big collector in Texas. I bought eight Matisse costumes for *Le Chant du rossignol* for £380 ($1060), one by Juan Gris for *Les Tentations de la bergère* for £100 ($279), and nine Chirico costumes for *Le Bal* for £315 ($879). Then came the interval.

The Picasso curtain, looking magnificent but a little faded, like a Pompeian fresco, now filled the stage. Diaghilev had first ordered it to be painted as a 'frontispiece' for his 1924 spring season at the Théâtre des Champs-Elysées, and while it was lowered a specially commissioned fanfare by Georges Auric was played. It was the enlargement of a gouache and, though Diaghilev was doubtless struck by the epic splendour of Picasso's little painting, it may also have occurred to him that nothing could be more appropriate to mark that year of the 8th Olympiad than these two running giantesses on the shore of a timeless Mediterranean. The curtain was painted by Prince Schervashidze (whose ancestors, according to Iain Moncreiffe, had been sovereign princes in Georgia so very long ago), and the imitation of the hatched strokes of dry paint with which Picasso had rendered the girls' ruddy flesh was a marvel of scene-painting. To ensure that no part of the bold design should be lost when shown on tour in smaller theatres than the Champs-Elysées, Diaghilev had sensibly decided that the picture should not cover a whole curtain, but be surrounded by a wide white border. The overall size of the curtain was 10 metres by 11: the painted area 6.78 metres by 8. Because of the low opening of the Scala's proscenium the white border at the foot had to be tucked under and the foremost girl appeared to be treading on the stage. The curtain, it was said, had been painted in a hurry in twenty-four hours, and Picasso was so thrilled by the skill of its execution that he took a brush and wrote in the bottom left-hand corner 'Dédié à Diaghilew. Picasso'. He thus put his stamp of authenticity on the fake. It was intoxicating – as I knew myself, in my insignificant way – to see one's small idea enlarged to cover a high wall or fill a huge proscenium arch. In 1924 Diaghilev had been in love with my old acquaintance Pat (Anton) Dolin, and Cocteau had devised *Le Train bleu* – a ballet with Bronislava Nijinska as a tennis-player *à la* Suzanne Lenglen, Woizikovsky as a golfer in plus-fours like those of the Prince of Wales, and Sokolova and Dolin in Chanel bathing costumes – mainly to show off Pat's acrobatic feats and boyish English charm. In *Le Train bleu* Dolin enjoyed his first great triumph: and when the company danced the ballet at the London Coliseum

The curtain for *Le Train bleu*. Painting by Prince Alexander Scher-vashidze after a gouache by Picasso, May 1924. Bought for the future Theatre Museum, London on 17 July 1968.

later in the year, the doting Diaghilev had allotted to it the enlarged Picasso as a front curtain.

Bidding for the curtain began at £5,000 ($13,950). Goodman again sent Annie Fleming down to tell me, 'Don't start bidding until all but one bidder has dropped out.' I waited till the known reserve had been passed and there seemed to be only one bidder left. I bought the curtain for £69,000 ($192,510); and I admit that when Peter Wilson said in his quiet throw-away manner, 'Bought by Mr Richard Buckle for the nation' – and there was a burst of applause – I felt rather proud, though I tried not to look it. Of course I knew that nobody could have thought for a moment that I was bidding with my own money.

I bought over thirty Bakst costumes for *The Sleeping Princess*. Next day, when it was found that a number of lots had not reached their reserves I was able to buy these too for slightly lower prices. The total of the first sale was £88,245 ($246,204), which was more than had been expected. The extra £50,000 ($139,500) on top of Tony's £25,000 was eventually put up not by a number of people but by one. Sir Lew (later Lord) Grade made this princely gesture.*

Over the next six years took place a series of meetings of a group of well-wishers who called themselves first 'Friends of the Museum of Performing Arts', then, at my suggestion, 'Friends of the Theatre Museum': these meetings were attended not only by Lord Goodman, George Harewood and Max Rayne, but by John Pope-Hennessy of the Victoria and Albert Museum, John Hayes of the London Museum, Roy Strong of the National Portrait Gallery, Ken Davison of the Friends of Covent Garden, Keith Jeffery of the Arts Council, Lord Norwich of the British Theatre Museum, Raymond Mander and Joe Mitchenson. I felt it was an achievement to have got representatives of the two last-named 'rival' collections round a table together, and both expressing goodwill for our project to form one national Theatre Museum. Although I was ambitious that the new museum, when it came into being, should incorporate every existing collection in the country – which was why I had thought of it in the first place as a department of the V and A – I realized that since everyone's treasures could never be on display at one time it was unnecessary to house them under one roof. Provided an agreement existed that we should work together over future exhibitions and publications and in the furthering of research, the bond of common goodwill would be better than nothing.

Because I felt England must make some effort on its own behalf, rather than rely entirely on Diamantidi, I exerted

---

* Born Lev Winogradsky in Russia, from being a poor refugee Lord Grade had become head of Associated Television.

myself to raise money privately for the second sale, which was to be held on 19 December 1969 at the Theatre Royal, Drury Lane. I set about writing innumerable letters. Would Michael Duff give a group of costumes in memory of his grandmother, Lady Ripon, who had been such a friend to Diaghilev? Would Lord Rothermere buy a costume as a souvenir of his father who had backed the Russian Ballet in its later years? Would a group of stage designers subscribe a pound or two each towards a certain lot? Would six friends of the late Simon Fleet buy another lot as a memorial to him? In the few weeks before the sale I managed to raise £5,000 ($13,950): but I must admit that although I had expended hours of time in extracting £10 each from several friends, only £1,000 was subscribed by forty supporters, while the remaining £4,000 was the gift of one member of our committee. Tony Diamantidi viewed my efforts with scorn, but I liked to think of the museum depending to some extent on widow's mites, given with love.

Through the continued generosity of Tony Diamantidi, the further efforts of Arnold Goodman and the kindness of some of my friends I was able to spend £15,000 ($41,850) on curtains by Robert Delaunay,* Utrillo,† and Gontcharova.‡ I also spent £8,000 ($23,320) on costumes by Roerich for *Prince Igor* and *The Rite of Spring*, by Benois for *Giselle*, by Bakst for *Narcisse* and *Daphnis et Chloë*, by Larionov for *Chout*, by Marie Laurencin for *Les Biches*, by Chanel for *Le Train bleu*, by Utrillo for *Barabau*, by Mirò for *Jeux d'enfants* and by Tchelitchev for *Balustrade*.

I deemed particularly historic the costumes of *Prince Igor*, which had been worn on the very first night of the Russian ballet in Paris on 9 May 1909. The mottled, spotted and irregular zig-zag patterns of the Polovtsian girls' and boys'

---

* For the 1918 revival of *Cléopâtre*.

† For *Barabau*. This was the curtain I had shown in Edinburgh.

‡ The backdrop of a hundred onion-domed Moscow churches for the wedding in *Firebird*.

tunics which appeared to have been produced by dipping the material haphazardly into pots of purple, magenta, green or lemon-yellow dye, were in fact woven into the material. They were made of a special silk from Turkestan, which Nicolas Roerich had doubtless bought in rolls in the old covered markets of St Petersburg between Theatre Street and the Catherine Canal; and the fact that they were woven, not printed, accounted for their survival, for ordinary silk or taffeta is more perishable than cotton or linen. As for the stencilled woollen smocks designed by Roerich for *The Rite of Spring*, they seemed to me like sacred relics of that heroic occasion in 1913, when the masterpiece of Stravinsky and Nijinsky had caused such an uproar in Astruc's new theatre – almost like regimental Colours borne off the field of a bloody battle, to be gazed at in awe by generations yet unborn. From that conflict on the barricades of art Marie Rambert, Lubov Tchernicheva and Lydia Sokolova survived, like King Harry's companions, to strip their sleeves and show their scars. Lydia, one of the *corps* in Nijinsky's original version of the ballet, and the Chosen Maiden in Massine's version (which was given in the same costumes intermittently between 1920 and 1929), arranged a short episode of dance in the style of Nijinsky for the young dancers of the Royal Ballet School to show off these Roerich costumes which I bought for the Theatre Museum. After this, she was led on to the stage of Drury Lane, where she had danced for Diaghilev in 1914, to receive a round of applause. It was her last curtain call.

CHAPTER 10

Well, a Book and a Museum Anyway

When I began to write my life of Nijinsky in 1967 it was just on thirty-five years since Romola's had appeared. This had been through many editions and was still in print: not a comma had been changed, not a lie corrected. It was time to review Nijinsky's career and his part in the Diaghilev epic in the light of what other witnesses than his wife had written about him. His reputation had not diminished: if anything, it was greater than ever before. Some of Romola's libels against Diaghilev had been contradicted in Haskell's biography: but it was important that the truth – or as much of it as could be established – should be stated in a life of Nijinsky himself. There was a new interest, too, in Nijinsky as a forerunner of the so-called 'modern dance'. When Martha Graham, the great American pioneer, had first brought her troupe to London in 1954 I had been conquered at one glance by her new poetry of movement which seemed able to express states of mind ignored by classical ballet choreographers. For a week or two she played to almost empty houses, but I had written, 'I conjure every idle habit-formed fellow in need of a third eye to see new beauty that he should visit the Saville Theatre and watch Martha Graham . . . she has enlarged the language of the soul.' After that, business looked up; and Martha's season at the Prince of Wales's in 1963 had been a triumph. It was partly to her that I attributed the 'new wave' in British drama, which began in 1956. Encouraged by Marie Rambert, who had worked with Nijinsky, and by Lincoln Kirstein, who had long been interested in the analysis of Nijinsky's *The Rite of Spring* by Jacques Rivière in *La Nouvelle Revue Française* (November 1913), a number of students had begun to believe that Nijinsky's experimental ballets – only one of which (*L'Après-midi d'un faune*) had survived his dismissal by Diaghilev, the others being subsequently forgotten and lost – might have been wonderfully ahead of their time. I ought to find out what I could about these while there was still someone alive who could even faintly recall them.

I was all too aware how many people who might have helped me with my book on Nijinsky had died before I could ask them the essential questions – not only the essential questions, either, for invaluable little details of dates and journeys might have been confirmed. Of the most important survivors Karsavina, Rambert and Grigoriev were in London: others were further afield. I began to compile lists of questions for my friends, as well as for Stravinsky who lived in California and whom I had never met.

Luckily old people enjoy answering intelligent questions about their past. (Of course the banal queries of ill-informed journalists can be merely irritating.) They like to be reminded of happier days; and to fill in a verbal or written questionnaire becomes a kind of game to pass the time, like a crossword puzzle.

Marie Rambert, who suffered from claustrophobia, was a fresh-air fiend. Our first long discussion took us from her home on Campden Hill on a bus to Kew Gardens and back; during our second we paced and picnicked beneath the trees of Holland Park. I sent her transcripts of what I thought she had said, and she would telephone corrections at great length, insisting that I take down certain of her own words. Among the notes of her conversation I sent her was one about the rather plain Nelidova, whom Nijinsky had chosen, because of her height and distinctive nose, to be the chief Nymph in his *L'Après-midi d'un faune*. 'Nelidova loathed this ballet,' I wrote, summarizing Rambert's words, 'and longed to be back in Moscow. "Have I come all this way for this?" But Nijinsky moulded her into Pallas Athene.' Next time I saw Rambert she dictated to me an amplification. 'By eliminating from Nelidova's technique all her personal idiosyncrasies, Nijinsky moulded her into a goddess.' Most of this found its way not only into my book, but into Rambert's autobiography which she was induced to write soon after: but her general comment on the refining process of artistic creation, which was added for my benefit to her description of Nijinsky teaching Nelidova, has remained with me for life. 'In dancing or writing you must strip away all the "you", and be left with what can't be stripped away, and that is what God created you for.' I wrote this down in her presence during the afternoon of 2 August 1968.

As I suggested earlier, Mim Rambert had something of the effusive – even explosive – character of my Grandmother Buckle, so I was able to tune in to a familiar wave-length. When, over a year after our first talks, she read a few of my typed chapters she told me on the telephone: 'I have never read before a line about Nijinsky that had a drop of his blood. You will make him live.' To my notes on this telephone conversation I added: 'She thought it would be a great "classical" book, so I must work at perfecting certain passages – which I will.'

I did not go to see Grigoriev and Tchernicheva, partly because I was not sure how ill he was and feared that he might feel obliged to dress up for my visit. I posted him long lists of questions, which Tchernicheva returned, with his answers translated into English. I sometimes wondered if they thought me mad.

Whether or not Stravinsky would be helpful depended entirely on the co-operation of his indispensable companion, Robert Craft. Now, Craft's greed for detailed information about the past was as great as mine, so I found him more than ready to play the game; and I have no doubt that a triangular game provided some amusement in far-off Hollywood, as

Craft brought up question after question for discussion by the composer and his second wife. While Craft was equipped to ask every conceivable musical question of his beloved master, there were certain matters of ballet history which I had studied in greater detail than he, so my questions and Stravinsky's answers were of value to us both. Already, in his fifth letter (of 16 July 1968), Robert Craft was asking, 'Please send more questions.'

With regard to *The Rite of Spring* of 1913, which I believed to be a revolutionary masterpiece not only of music, but also of choreography, it was vital to know what its composer thought of Nijinsky's work: but it was possible that Rambert, who had merely been chosen from among the pupils of Dalcroze to help Nijinsky analyse the unprecedented, broken and constantly changing rhythms of the score, might well remember more – since she was a dancer – of what the choreography had been like. I knew it was pointless to ask Grigoriev about the ballet, the quality of which he was unable to comprehend; and I could not imagine that Karsavina (who had never danced in it) would have liked it either. However, Stravinsky, who had allowed Walter Nouvel to 'ghost' his first essay in autobiography, *Chronique de ma vie*, in 1931, and to express in it the opinion that Nijinsky was a musical ignoramus with no talent for choreography, began in the 1960s to tell Craft and anyone else who was interested that Nijinsky's version of *The Rite* was far superior to Massine's version of 1920, or to any other. Stravinsky had a brilliant, far-ranging mind: he was an intellectual and a wit who could seldom resist giving friends and journalists his unconsidered opinion, embellished with a wisecrack. These opinions and wisecracks had often to be lived down in later years.

Perhaps Diaghilev and Stravinsky owed more to each other than any two men in the artistic history of our century. Diaghilev had given Stravinsky his first great opportunity in *Firebird* in 1910: and as the composer continued to deliver more master-works – *Petrushka*, *The Rite of Spring*, *Renard*,

243

Les Noces, Pulcinella, Apollo, Oedipus Rex – Diaghilev presented them in succession to the world. Yet in 1913 Nijinsky was more famous than either of them (just as Burbage had been more famous than Shakespeare) and he risked his reputation as God of the Dance to devise for *The Rite* the kind of choreography demanded by its amazing newness. He even abstained from creating in it a role for himself.

While Stravinsky still indulged in snide observations on Diaghilev's and Nijinsky's musical shortcomings, exaggerating the former's appetite for vengeance and what he considered the outrageous homosexuality of his entourage, Rambert sought to glorify Diaghilev's relationship with Nijinsky, which had been so productive of miracles, and Grigoriev did his best to pretend it had not taken place.

And what of Massine, Nijinsky's successor – not only as Diaghilev's favourite, but as his principal dancer and choreographer? Having been 'discovered' by Diaghilev only five months after Nijinsky's surprising marriage, his genius seemed almost to have been called into being by Diaghilev's will-power, to fill the gap. Yet Diaghilev had 'forgiven' Nijinsky and secured his release from internment in Austro-Hungary in 1916 – admittedly Nijinsky's name and fame were needed to fill houses on the enforced wartime American tours; so that Massine and Nijinsky, in New York and in Spain, had worked for some weeks side by side in the Diaghilev Company. Would Massine be disparaging of his great rival?

As early as the thirties my friend André Eglevsky had described to me how precisely Massine ordered his life – so many hours every day for work, a rest after luncheon, love-making from five to six, etc. – and the gossips of the ballet world had labelled Massine (as they had Stravinsky) a miser over money. It has often been suggested that he was even grudging of praise, for fear someone might turn it to profit. Agnes de Mille related in her *Dance to the Piper* how, after the twenty-two curtain calls following the première of her *Rodeo*

in New York, Massine merely said, 'You have done a charac-
teristic ballet, and in Europe I think it will have success.' I
remembered how, when I was planning the Diaghilev
Exhibition, Massine would lend us his portraits only on
condition that certain warehouse charges were paid, and that
his representative was remunerated for visiting the Manhattan
warehouse to identify them. (Perhaps, after all, this was
perfectly reasonable.) My own theory was that once Massine
had bought – no doubt with Diaghilev's help – his Siren
Islands (those alluring rocks off the coast of Positano) he
could not allow himself to be out of work for a single week
or to incur any avoidable expense for fear of holding up a
costly, unending programme of cultivation and embellish-
ment. There was also the burden of Massine's multiple
alimony to be considered. To how many of those attractive
ladies had he actually been married? After reading about the
success of my Diaghilev Exhibition, which he never saw,
Massine had written to offer me what amounted to a secre-
tarial job. I was to tour with him and deal with his correspondence. In return (and in payment) for this I was to be
allowed to write his memoirs, and to keep the advance paid
for these by the publishers. I replied truthfully that I should not
be much use because I could not type, adding, untruthfully,
that I never got up before two in the afternoon. (I regretted
this later, as Massine's memoirs, when they were finally
published in 1968, could have been ten times more informa-
tive.) However, Leonide – we were by the sixties on Christian
name terms – had come to regard me as a friend of Diaghilev's
fame, and he eyed me affectionately.

Our conversations about Nijinsky took place, oddly
enough, at Stratford-upon-Avon. In the off-season the Royal
Shakespeare Theatre was visited by touring companies, the
Royal Ballet among them, and we critics were invited there in
January 1968 to see revivals Massine had staged of his
La Boutique fantasque and *Mam'zelle Angot*. I was staying as
usual at the Shakespeare Hotel, but Massine was at the Falcon

opposite; so it was at the latter hotel that I entertained him to dinner after his rehearsals on the nights of 29 and 30 January. We spoke in French and English. Leonide had mellowed with age. He poured out praise of Nijinsky, whom he first saw (except for once when Nijinsky made a guest appearance in Moscow) dancing *La Princesse enchantée* (the Blue Bird *pas de deux*) in New York in 1916; and although Nijinsky had been isolated from the company for two years Leonide found him 'unbelievable'. In *Le Spectre de la rose*, when he jumped, raising both legs behind him in *temps levé*, it was like '*une arabesque sans l'appui* [without the support of one leg standing on the ground]: he seemed to lie flat in the air.' The point of Nijinsky's too-famous exit jump through the window was that you saw him going up and up on an ascending arc, but never saw him beginning to come down. 'Vassili caught him.' It was moving to hear from Leonide's lips the story, later printed in his book, of how, in the Uffizi in 1915, and in the room with the Cimabue and Giotto madonnas, Diaghilev had asked him if he thought he could make a ballet, and he had said No: then, a few minutes later, in front of Simone Martini's 'Annunciation', he had said to Diaghilev, 'Yes, I think I can make a ballet. I'll make you a hundred, I promise you.' As we left the Falcon Hotel to walk to the theatre I pointed out to him the Guild Chapel opposite, next to the school which Shakespeare had attended. Leonide, to whom Diaghilev had shown all the wonders of Italy, thus learned for the first time what the long half-timbered building was. We crossed the road. 'I must touch it,' he said.

I had been present during the opening season in 1965 of the New York State Theater, part of the Lincoln Center complex, Manhattan's Parnassus, where the State Theater, the new Metropolitan Opera House and the Philharmonic Hall were to form three sides of a plaza. My friend Kirstein had helped to establish this; and now, in a building on a second secluded square, the New York Public Library had a branch to hold its theatrical and musical collections, the

Library and Museum of Performing Arts. Kirstein had also been a benefactor of the Dance Collection, which housed papers hardly put in order until then, invaluable for my research. On 1 May 1968 I flew to New York. Through the kindness of Genevieve Oswald, Curator of the Dance Collection, boxes of rare photographs of Nijinsky and many folders of the Astruc papers were laid out on one of her big tables. Gabriel Astruc (whose daughter Lucienne, the close friend of Jean Hugo's sister, Maggie, had lent me posters for the Diaghilev Exhibition) was the musical impresario who had made possible Diaghilev's seasons in Paris between 1908 and 1914. He had also built the Théâtre des Champs-Elysées, presented Nijinsky's *The Rite of Spring* during its opening season in 1913, and gone bankrupt as a result. The spate of telegrams with which Diaghilev had showered him, from 1908 onwards, had all been kept, along with other relevant papers recording bitter quarrels and arduous reconciliations, hopes, struggles and despair; and the whole of this documentation was waiting to be explored by me. Lincoln Kirstein had long hoped (though he kept quiet about it) to write the life of Nijinsky himself, but he stepped aside without a murmur, and did all he could to expedite my research. He urged me to fly to San Francisco to interview Schollar and Vilzak and to Hollywood to visit Bronislava Nijinska: he also paid for my trip.

Ludmila Schollar, plump and amusing, was eighty: with Karsavina and Nijinsky she had made up the trio of flirting tennis-players in Nijinsky's *Jeux*. She remembered little about this strange ballet, of which Debussy's wonderful score, written so reluctantly to the order of Diaghilev and specifications of Nijinsky, had enriched us all: but she tried to explain to me the steps in Nijinsky's *variation* in *Le Pavillon d'Armide*, with which he had captivated Paris in 1909. Her twelve-year-younger husband, Anatole Vilzak, had joined Diaghilev only in 1921. Had I but known in 1968 that I should one day write Diaghilev's life as well as Nijinsky's, how many questions

I should have had to ask him! I remembered him as the swaggering hero of Fokine's *Don Juan* at the Alhambra in London before the war.

It was with some hesitation that I went to Hollywood to confront Bronislava Nijinska, whom I had never met, for her second husband Singayevsky had died only a few weeks before. Lincoln Kirstein had brushed aside my scruples. Nijinska was to be approached through her daughter Irina, who was a friend of Tamara Toumanova, whom John Taras had rung up from New York to warn of my impending visit. As David Hockney and Peter Schlesinger dropped me opposite the house where Tamara lived with her mother, I watched a middle-aged woman park her small car and walk up the unfenced lawn to the one-storeyed villa. From Irina's high cheek-bones and slanting eyes, as well as from her muscular legs, I recognized the royal blood of the Nijinsky family. Toumanova, my beautiful heroine of Balanchine's *Cotillon* in the 1930s, and her battling mother, as inseparable from her as a Siamese twin, had been preserved unchanged by some Shangri-la of singlemindedness, which the atmosphere of California's dreamland had rendered possible. In a perfectly appointed studio Tamara did her daily exercises, as if awaiting some unknown prince's call to resume her rightful place, stage centre, at a moment's notice. Regaled by Tamara's and Mama's Russian plenty and by the warmth of their welcome, I made friends with Irina Nijinska-Raetz. It was because Bronislava had been pregnant with her in 1917 that Nijinsky had travelled without his sister to South America.

Next day I paid my first visit to Mme Bronislava in her little house at Pacific Palisades, overhanging the ocean. I knew what she would look like – stout, with Tartar features and flattened hair parted in the middle (in fact she had a hair-net over her pale hair, and wore a brown silk shirt and baggy black trousers) – but I was doubtful as to how she would receive me, a pestering journalist, callous of her bereavement, intent on writing a book about her brother which might turn out as mendacious and superficial as that of Nijinsky's old classmate, Anatole Bourman. However, she had cuttings of what I had written about her revival of *Les Noces* at Covent Garden, and she was predisposed in my favour. The flowers I handed her were not conventional roses, but a huge bunch of mixed white, pink and mauve stocks, bought on the sidewalk. (I knew she was unworldly and unsnobbish.) Mme Bronislava, Irina and I sat on three sides of a table covered in oilcloth for our conference. I had been warned that Mme Bronislava was deaf and spoke little English, and I was ready to shout in French: but she preferred that I should use Irina as an interpreter, so it was English into Russian. I had expected a high seriousness about the history of her brother and his art. The warmth and sweetness hidden behind her rugged features were a bonus. We saw eye to eye.

I had to check with her about the accuracy of certain statements in Romola's biography of her husband; I had to ask her whether she believed in the authenticity of Vaslav's *Diary*, said to have been written when he was on the verge of madness, which Romola published; and I had to find out if any of Bourman's sensational biography was true. I also had to ask certain intimate questions. For instance, was Vaslav Nijinsky basically homosexual? (I did not think he was.) His sister turned out to have no false prudery. I will quote from the notes I made immediately after each of my sessions with Mme Bronislava. I had no doubt that on this cliff at the western edge of the world I had come to the ultimate repository of truth about the great dancer who had given my life its direction, although I had never seen him dance.

> At the back of Romola's mind the thought of making a film was always present. She liked money. She despised Bronislava Nijinska for not staying in chic hotels, not understanding that B.N. might prefer simple ones . . . Nevertheless B.N. has tried not to quarrel openly with Romola. They speak . . . Eleonora's father [maternal grand-

father of Vaslav and Bronislava] did not kill himself [as stated by Romola]. Thomas [the father] did *not* have fits of insanity. But he had a terrible temper and could seem mad . . . as Vaslav could. But V's rages soon blew over. Eleonora's father, Bereda, was a carpenter – made furniture. E. was a genius of a mother. Thomas's father had nothing to do with dancing either . . . Thomas jumped higher than Vaslav and showed V. certain steps which V. could not do. She, Bronia, had inherited this jump, and so had her daughter Irina. V's looks came from his father. Bronia, Irina, Leon [Bronia's son who was killed in a motor accident, aged sixteen] and George [Irina's son] all have the Tartar face. George is Leon's double, brilliant at physics and mathematics and a fine pianist. He always regarded his mother as a sister and Bronia as his mother, as if he were a reincarnation of Leon.

Romola's lies about Stanislav [elder brother of Vaslav and Bronislava, who was simple-minded and confined in a hospital]. He died in bed of a liver complaint [not in a fire]. B. thinks Romola took V. to the sanatorium [in Zürich] when he was in one of his fits of rage, and if she had not he would never have gone mad. If Bronislava had not been in St Petersburg having her first baby [Irina], Romola would never have had the opportunity to seduce and marry Vaslav. And he would probably never have gone mad. Asked [by Bronislava] if it would not have been decent to defer the marriage till Eleonora could give her consent, Romola said she was not such a fool, as she knew it would be refused. So she was not an honourable woman. People [on the ship to South America in 1913] thought Romola was after Bolm, and Bolm's girl-friend was jealous and tried to flirt with Gunzbourg.

Nijinsky's Diary. [Soon after Bronislava came out of Russia in 1921, Romola showed her] two notebooks, with only about 20pp written by V.N. Romola later told her she had found some more. But B.N. can hear 2 voices in the diary and can distinguish her brother's words. Does not want to accuse R. of faking, but thinks she may have written some of it based on things V.N. said. The philosophical

The revival of *Les Biches* at Covent Garden. *On the sofa*: Robert Mead, Svetlana Beriosova, Bronislava Nijinska, David Blair. *Standing behind*: Keith Rosson, Georgina Parkinson. Photograph by G. B. L. Wilson, 2 December 1964.

part quite unlike her brother. He would only have written very short sentences. She remembers reading in the note-book the words: 'I should never have married Romola because I loved Diaghilev.'

Nijinsky sometimes [in his youth] fell in love with girls, but lost interest when he found they did not take ballet seriously. The story in the *Diary* of running after prostitutes in Paris is completely untrue.

Stravinsky wrote that N. was musically ignorant, and she had not hitherto contradicted him in print, admiring him as she does and because of the friendship V. and she had for him: but she will now do so. In choreography N. did not represent the notes but the sense of the music. V.N. much preferred music to literature. He studied music for six years and passed out top of his class in it. He was not good at reading, but played by ear. If someone played a chord he could say what notes it was made up of. She

251

remembered him playing [a transcription for piano of] the Overture to *Tannhaüser* without a mistake. He played the piano, mandoline, balalaika, flute and accordeon. Eleonora didn't like him playing the accordeon [because it was 'common']. N. was the first choreographer to set dances in detail – '*avec justesse*'. Petipa and Fokine sketched the pattern and left dancers to fill in the interpretation. It was Vaslav who gave her the detail of her own role of Papillon [in Fokine's *Carnaval*]. He showed her the fluttering hands and danced it for her, and she was up all night practising in front of a mirror. When she saw a rehearsal of Fokine's *Spectre de la rose* she was depressed by the banality of the movements. It was Vaslav who gave it a special strange quality – for instance, by drooping his arms over his face. She agreed that N. had probably invented Petrushka's jerky movements, as he heard the music long before Fokine. B.N. thought Fokine's *Polovtsian Dances* [from *Prince Igor*] were not genuinely barbaric: they were arranged in lines and conventional formations like a Petipa ballet. Fokine was not an inventor like Vaslav, being obsessed by the *folklorique*.

N. had worked out *Faune* in detail before rehearsals began. It was to have been given in 1911, but was put off for a year. The reason it took so many rehearsals was not that N. was slow at inventing, but that the dancers were slow in learning . . . *Jeux* was worked out on her and Vassilievska in Monte Carlo during holidays in 1912, while Diaghilev was in Russia. It was not so much a result of association with Rodin, as I suggested, but of studying Gauguin. He had a Gauguin book open while he worked on it. *Le Sacre du printemps* was worked out at rehearsals. Marie Rambert may have been a help with the counting: she could not [by Mme Bronislava's standards] dance at all. B.N. thought *Le Sacre* was certainly a good ballet. Was her own choreography a continuation of V.N.'s experiments? They were two individuals. She had her own ideas.

When Mme Bronislava showed me her garden, I realized that she had a precipice on two sides, for hers was the last house but one on a promontory. She said she 'loved to feel like a bird'.

Christopher Isherwood fetched me after my second visit to Nijinska. Although she had first editions of *Nicholas Nickleby* and *Bleak House* in her glass-fronted bookshelf (as well as a first edition of Byron's *Cain*, bought in Edinburgh) I thought it too complicated to explain who Christopher was. His own house, not far away, in Santa Monica, as he told me with a chortle, was one of the oldest in Hollywood – built 1926. For that matter, David Hockney was fascinated by my modest hotel, the Montecito (recommended by Taras), and photographed me against the gilt bronze 1930 swing doors. I loved my lush suburb, with its avenues of blue paulonia in flower. When I explored the winding lanes higher up the hill, peering through bushes at the variegated villas – homes, I supposed, of artificially animated art directors of the twenties, who were served by mindless boys with perfect bodies – I was the only pedestrian for miles, a suspicious character. Below my window the brick bell-tower of a heretical church, soaring from bougainvillea, played the Overture of *Tannhaüser* every midday to remind me how musical Nijinsky was. On the night before I left, Tamara and Mama Toumanova, suffused with sympathy for what they imagined to be my lonely life, expounded over their laden dinner-table a plan they had just hatched between them: namely that I should give up my work in England and move in to share their home. They showed me my room. The astounding prospect of reincarnation in the hot-house of Hollywood rose before me: but duty called, and I resisted the lure of platonic bigamy in Shangri-la.

I had been unable to make up my mind whether or not to discuss my projected book with Romola Nijinsky. When Lincoln Kirstein told me that spring in New York that he had received a cable from her, challenging (fifteen years late) Jerome Robbins's right to stage a new version of *L'Après-midi d'un faune*, I realized that her megalomania, of which one symptom was a passion to make money out of litigation, was gaining on her. Then Kenneth MacMillan told me that Romola was exacting *droits d'auteur* from *his* version of *The Rite of Spring*. This was going too far. Stravinsky's musical rights, of course, were due, but if authors' rights were to be paid for the scenario, which perhaps they were in certain countries, there was no question but that the authors were Stravinsky and Roerich. The painter had died, a hermit in the Himalayas, in 1947. Although I could foresee Romola creating every sort of difficulty I decided that as I should have to quote some of what she had written, true or false, I had better re-establish relations with her, and try to be nice. The warm-hearted Margaret Power, who not only acted as Romola's honorary Secretary of State for England, but paid quite handsomely for the privilege in energy, time, and petty cash, kept me informed of the gadabout lady's global peregrinations. In March 1969 she arrived in London at the newly magnified Cavendish Hotel, and on the fifth I picked her up and took her to dine at Boulestin in Covent Garden.

Romola Nijinsky had been hard-up (in a luxurious way) for so long: but now, according to Margaret, she was better off. A cousin, Paul von Bohus, who had shared her gipsy wanderings and privations with Vaslav during the last war, had recovered a property in Italy sequestered by the Fascists and been paid compensation: he helped to keep Romola going. Meanwhile, she sensibly tried to extract every ounce of possible profit from the name and posthumous fame of Nijinsky. Romola's hair was now red. The contrast with her Sèvres-blue eyes, which were usually half hidden by seductively lowered lids, was striking. There could be no doubt that she was a charming, *chic* and attractive woman, if a little stout. Her manner was flattering, but I was always conscious of the underlying menace.

There were still amusing decorations by Marie Laurencin in the ante-room of Boulestin; and the walls of the restaurant had acquired a mellow lacquered patina, as if constantly revarnished over the years. The *banquette* on which we sat, however, had been re-covered in sticky red plastic, and I felt apologetic about this.

There was one particular question I wanted to ask Romola. 'When you travelled with the Diaghilev Ballet to South America, were you in love with Nijinsky?' 'No,' she replied without hesitation – and I knew she was telling the truth. She added, 'I came to love him later because he was so good.' I realized that Romola had not re-read her life of Nijinsky perhaps for thirty years. (In fact no corrections to it were ever made, and it continued to be reprinted from photographic plates, every page identical with the first edition, up to her death.) She had forgotten that the whole point of her story, written with one eye on Hollywood, was that the love of a pure young girl for the great genius of dancing saved· him from the clutches of a perverted and ruthless villain, Diaghilev. If the truth were not simplified (and twisted) in this way, the tale became far more complicated and much harder to put across to the masses through the medium of film. If it was not for *love* of Nijinsky that she had got herself attached to the Russian Ballet and followed him across the Atlantic, she had merely been a 'fan' who hoped to link herself in some way to the great man and bask in his reflected glory. When I thought this over I realized that there was nothing wrong with 'fans' unless they ruined the lives and careers of their idols. Romola had written in her book that Nijinsky's proposal of marriage, conveyed by Baron de Gunzbourg (who had reasons for wishing to separate Nijinsky from Diaghilev), had taken her by surprise. How could the 'fan' resist being married to the star she adulated? Visions of wealth and social prominence glittered before her: she would outshine her dominating mother, Hungary's greatest actress. That her marriage to Nijinsky might separate him from Diaghilev and upset the whole apple-cart of the Russian Ballet, even if the thought occurred to her, would not have perturbed her unduly. I knew from experience that young people did not look ahead. I also knew that Romola was a lesbian.

The biography of Nijinsky, the book which had changed my life, was based on a lie. All the same, I could not altogether blame Romola for marrying Nijinsky out of ambition without loving him, even if I blamed her for writing an untruthful and sensational book. Yet most books were written to make money (mine certainly were); and she needed money to take care of her sick husband as well as to live in comfort. Instead of reigning over society as the wife of a god, she had been lumbered with a lunatic. This had been her punishment. Even if she continued throughout the thirty years of Nijinsky's eclipse to try to make money out of his legend, it was one way of paying the bills for his medical care. She never abandoned him, and when he was released from an asylum, she cared for him in war and peace up to the end.

During the next year Romola read the chapters of my book as I wrote them. I accepted most of her comments and made the changes she required. Over a few matters I judged her more exact than Grigoriev – who had died in September, 1968. Alert to the potential danger of my probing questions, she called me 'Tricky Dicky' (which was how people referred to President Richard Nixon). Later, because of an imagined relationship through Charles II, she came to address me as 'Dear Coz' – but she spelt it 'Couze'. When my book appeared many readers thought she came out of it a more sympathetic character than she did from her own. Of course there were a few facts I had to suppress during her lifetime, for fear of her going to law. I could not call her a liar, and she would not have liked me to write that she was a lesbian, whatever revelations she had dared about Diaghilev – and they were very outspoken for 1933. Some old members of Diaghilev's troupe thought I had been seduced by her into painting too flattering a picture. In a way, I had. Through her agent she exacted five per cent of all my royalties.

From Zürich (October 1969) she wrote: 'I have been very

impressed of what you had to say about Vaslav's ballets and
creations . . . a tremendous research work . . .' Then (13
November 1969): 'I am leaving on Nove 22 for Rome . . .
for about ten days . . . after which I am flying to California
and Japan. I won't be back in Europe until late in April as I
have to go for Easter to Leningrad. If you think your book
won't go to press until then we could wait to see each other.
Otherwise we should meet before my departure for Rome
. . . I will be staying at the Grand Hotel . . .' From Rome
(9 December 1969): 'I agree with your suggestion that we
should meet in Leningrad in March . . . I got your wire
giving me Sotheby's [estimated] price for the Nijinsky
costume. I am afraid I cannot bid at so high a price, as my
grand-daughter is getting married in January and I have
promised to buy them a house . . .' (Neither of us went to
Leningrad.) From Rome, where Bronislava Nijinska was
producing *Les Biches*, helped by Irina (13 April 1970): 'I
have asked you several times, dear Dicky, to show me the
entier manuscript *before it goes to the publishers* . . . I just heard
from New York, that your manuscript arrived, at the Simon
& Schuster . . . Irina is just now translating the part of your
manuscript, to Bronia . . . Bronia states that many of your
statements in reference to Vaslav's youth are erroneous. You
must know, that nobody knows Vaslav's youth better than
Bronia . . . The rest of Vaslav's life *I know the best* as we were
married for thirty-eight year.' Well, of course I knew; and
I accepted all Bronislava's and Romola's corrections and
gratefully incorporated their suggestions. Romola continued:
'Mme Sokolova was not a member of original Russian Ballet
[she joined in 1913]. What she told you, in her memories,
are *not correct* always . . . Don't forget she is a British girl of
middle-class family, who knew little of the Russian nature
and very little about Vaslav himself . . . The rest I will tell
you personally. I will be at the Cavendish Hotel Jermyn
Street. Arriving 19th the evening.'

On 22 April I took Romola, her erstwhile rival for

Romola Nijinsky, Marie Rambert, the author and the Polish ambassador, with the back of Astrid Zydower's head in the foreground, at a party at the Polish embassy. Photograph by Munson, 22 April 1969.

Nijinsky's affections, Mim Rambert, Astrid Zydower, the sculptor and David Dougill, who had recently become my secretary, to see the Polish Pantomime Theatre at Sadler's Wells, and we had supper at my flat afterwards. Two days later I went with the same three ladies to a party at the Polish Embassy, and drove them back afterwards, stopping first at the Cavendish Hotel, next at Campden Hill Gardens and finally at Willes Road, Kentish Town. During the middle lap of this long taxi-drive it occurred to me that Astrid ought to make a portrait of Mim, and that as it was possible Mim had lonely moments in her old age she might be willing to pose. It probably would not work out, but it was worth trying. I told Mim that Astrid was a Polish Jew like herself and a refugee from Hitler, and took on myself to commission a bust for the future Theatre Museum. (In fact the first cast in bronze of the finished work was ordered by Roy Strong for the National Portrait Gallery.) That the bust turned out a kind of masterpiece, the finest portrait in sculpture since the death of Epstein, did not surprise me at all: what I had not bargained for was that Mim and Astrid would become such inseparable friends that if I ever wanted to ask Astrid to dinner in future years I had to plan it weeks in advance. I could never again get her to keep me company at the ballet, because she always went with Mim.

On 29 April I arranged for Romola to watch the horse Nijinsky running in the Two Thousand Guineas, and she arrived at my flat with Margaret Power after the race in tearing spirits, for the horse had won. She then gave me detailed notes on my chapters, and I showed due docility. Margaret later told David and me that she had snatched from Romola some pages of my text which were on the point of being torn up. 'What lies!' Romola exclaimed. Margaret pointed out to her that they were in fact an almost verbatim description of Nijinsky's last days written by Romola herself.

David Dougill, mentioned above, had come into my life in the following way. Various reminiscences of Ronald Firbank which I collected during the war from Evan Tredegar, Nina Hamnett, Duncan Grant and other people who knew him, had been quoted in a book on the epicene and neglected novelist. Reading this, David, who was an enthusiast for Firbank, came across my name and wrote to me. A native of Blackpool but educated at King's College, London, he was then a part-time teacher; but he began in his spare afternoons to file my untidy accumulations of paper. Then, despairing of the task of imparting knowledge to unmanageable classes, David took up my offer to employ him as a full-time secretary. I could only afford this because I had earned more than usual that year. David was then twenty-five with a mop of black curls which prompted my mother, when she met him, to enquire in a perfectly audible stage whisper, 'Is it a wig?'

In May 1970 I took David (by Channel steamer, as he feared the air) on his first visit to Paris; and we had a *séance* on the twelfth in the double bedroom of Mme Bronislava and Irina at the Hôtel Chambiges. During this both David and I made copious notes. When we were talking about Nijinsky's *Giselle* costume designed by Benois, which had been the cause of his dismissal by the Imperial Theatre on the absurd charge of indecency, Mme Nijinska said, smoothing her behind, 'Both Vaslav and I were very flat at the back.' Then the two women spoke Russian, giggling; and Irina translated, pointing between her legs, 'My mother says Vaslav was very small here!' We all laughed at this revelation, which, all the same, seemed to me to hold a curious psychological and historical importance. David made a note: 'B.N. says Dicky's theory about Vaslav & sex is right.' This referred to my idea that when Nijinsky was on the *Avon* in summer weather, he found himself longing to make love to a woman; and this was how Romola was unlucky enough to catch him. David's next note recorded: 'Diaghilev wrote to Bronia "You mustn't marry Kotchetovsky" [her first husband and the father of Irina].' Yet she married him in the Russian Orthodox Church in London on 15 July 1912. My own note on the same subject is in French, so our conversation must have been tri-lingual. '*D. écrivait pas marier K. Mélangez le bleu et le jaune vous avez le vert.*' Diaghilev's curiously expressed eugenic fears had clearly been groundless: for the loquacious, energetic Irina, who was so devoted to her mother, struck me as true-blue throughout. David noted: 'B. believes that Vaslav without art or the theatre [i.e. when isolated from the Ballets Russes by marriage, by Romola's suspicions of Diaghilev and by the war] was like a fish out of water – hence he became ill.' But 'In last war Romola was in rags – gave all her money to keep Vaslav. She should be forgiven all.'

To me Bronislava Njinska's word is law. As far as I am concerned, Romola has been forgiven all.

Four months later I had Mmes Bronislava and Romola together, with Irina, at the Cavendish Hotel in London. The

Kirov Ballet were at Covent Garden, and Konstantin Sergeyev wanted to reproduce Nijinsky's *L'Après-midi d'un faune*. Romola had undertaken to help, had called in Bronislava and Irina (and was paying their expenses) and would enlist Marie Rambert, in the repertory of whose company a version of the ballet survived, handed on by Woizikovsky in 1931.

In a corner of the empty first-floor dining-room I sat, putting my questions to the three ladies. I was answered sometimes by them each in turn, sometimes by all three together; and I took notes. It was a sort of Verdian quartet. Mme Bronislava was so totally devoid of artifice, Irina was her *alter ego*, and Romola was as subtle as Mme de Merteuil in *Les Liaisons dangereuses*. I warmed to Romola when she described her youth in a flat of the Academy of Arts in Budapest, brought up among works of art. Instead of fairy-stories her father read her Vasari's *Lives of the Painters*: she dreamed of playing a part in a second Renaissance, and had the sense to see in the Diaghilev Ballet the new art movement she had been waiting for. (Later it struck me that she might have found her true *métier* as publicity agent for the company.) I was interested in Nijinsky's preferences among works of art. She said he liked studying paintings with big groups (looking for possible choreographic compositions). She mentioned the boy breaking a stick on his knee in the foreground of Raphael's 'Sposalizio' in the Brera. Vaslav had wanted to 'show his back first in *Les Sylphides*' – like a big figure looming in shadow in the foreground corner of a tapestry, I imagined, who led the spectator's eye inwards to the heart of the painting.

Bronislava corrected something I had written about her brother's movements at the beginning of *L'Après-midi d'un faune*. Up on his rock 'He doesn't lick the grapes. He *squeezes* them, one hand above the other.' It was 'his breakfast'. When she mentioned his one jump in the ballet, she said it was across an imaginary stream (the one in which the Nymph had come to bathe); and I pointed out that in the backcloth of Bakst, to right of the centre, there was a waterfall.

She said that Nijinsky's gesture in *Les Sylphides* of brushing his cheek with the back of his hand was in order 'to be taller'. I think she meant that the elbow in the air would help to give the illusion of his being on the point of taking off from the ground. When Vladimirov did this it was merely 'silly'. All other men who danced *Le Spectre de la rose* performed 'as if they were offering a sandwich'. Serge Golovine had come closest to Nijinsky. Vaslav 'created an atmosphere with his gestures'. At one moment it was as if he were 'fanning Karsavina, creating the aroma of a rose'.

I noticed that, when I said goodbye, Mme Bronislava and I kissed each other, whereas with Mme Romola, whom I had known longer, I was still on more formal terms. After these gossips at the Cavendish Hotel (on 28 August 1970 from four till seven, and on the twenty-ninth from two to four), although we continued to correspond, it happened that I never saw either of the sisters-in-law again.

Although, from 1969 onwards, gifts to our nascent museum had begun to come in – from Jean Hugo, from Nadia Nerina and others – I felt powerless to beg on a large scale until we had some proper writing-paper. Yet we could not print paper with an official heading until we had a chairman: and nobody wanted to take on the responsibility. Goodman, Harewood and Rayne all said they were too busy. Lord Drogheda declined. From the time of my first conversation with John Pope-Hennessy in 1967 I had kept Boris Kochno informed of my plans, because I hoped that his collection might come to us. I also had my eye on Lifar's. Many opportunities were missed, I felt, because of this lack of a chairman and writing-paper.

At one moment, oddly enough, Goodman offered the St Pancras Hotel to the future museum. Although this pinnacled dream palace, which my grandmother Lily had sketched from her bedroom window in the 1880s when she was engaged to Chris Buckle, and where my parents had spent the first night of their married life, had long been one of my favourite buildings, I refused it point blank, because I felt so sure that our museum, if it were to attract foreign visitors as well as scholars, must be in the district hallowed by three centuries of theatre-going. Lord Goodman told me that I should never see the Theatre Museum sited in Covent Garden in my life-time. Since he knew all about property deals and I knew nothing, I was not in a position to argue.

In 1974 John Pope-Hennessy became Director of the British Museum and Roy Strong succeeded him at the V and A, while John Hayes moved from the London Museum to the National Portrait Gallery. Donald Sinden had taken over from Lord Norwich the Chairmanship of the British Theatre Museum, while Mander and Mitchenson showed signs of wishing to disociate themselves from our enterprise. I was going through a personal crisis (which is irrelevant to this volume) at the time when Pope-Hennessy and Sinden arranged through Lord Eccles, Minister of Works, that the newly refurbished state rooms of Somerset House should be assigned to the Theatre Museum. I could not but be grateful for the princely mansion, built on the site of a palace where my ancestor the Protector Somerset had held court.

Because the V and A, of which our Theatre Museum was to be a part, was not a Trustee museum (like the British Museum, the National Gallery and the National Portrait Gallery), all its members were Civil Servants, and as the law laid down that high offices in the Civil Service had to be advertised for, Roy Strong invited applications in *The Times* for a Curator to the Theatre Museum. (I was considered too old to run the museum which I had helped to found, and it was obvious to myself, as well as to Pope-Hennessy, that I was not cut out to be a civil servant.) A lot of people appeared before a board, and all were rejected. Another advertisement was placed, explaining that practical experience in the theatre would count for more than service in a museum. Guided for once by archangels, the Board appointed Alexander Schouvaloff. Although he had worked for H. M. Tennent, had been assistant to George Harewood at the Edinburgh Festival, and had administered the North Western Arts Association, I had never met him. He was descended from Count Ivan Ivanovitch Schouvaloff, a favourite of Catherine the Great: together these two had founded the St Petersburg Academy of Arts and Sciences – not that anyone but myself would have considered this a qualification for Alexander's appointment. He was even a cousin of Diaghilev's first cousin (and first love), Dmitri Filosofov.

The Theatre Museum came officially into existence on 16 September 1974. I guessed that future historians might regard it as a continuation and enlargement of the *British* Theatre Museum, which had battled obscurely for recognition since 1955. Yet until I told Goodman and Harewood about the latter, shortly before the first sale of the Diaghilev wardrobe, I think, they had hardly been aware of its existence; and its members had never imagined linking their body to the V and A. If I had not walked round to the Scala Theatre on the morning of 17 July 1968 on the chance of watching a rehearsal of Sokolova and her students (who were not there) and if a stage-hand (hired for the week) had not appealed to me in the absence of Sotheby's young men to explain the curtains to a waiting audience – so that I was still in the theatre when Tony Diamantidi arrived to ask me to lunch – I think the V and A would never have acquired a new department, the British Theatre Museum would still be where it was and John Julius Norwich would still be writing his valiant letters to *The Times*. Luck had been on our side.

On 19 December 1974 George Harewood, who had been since 1972 managing director of English National Opera (formerly Sadler's Wells Opera), which occupied the Coliseum, presided in Lord Goodman's absence over a last meeting of our little committee in the boardroom of that theatre. George used the funny expression 'Sheer cheek' in describing the part I had played in bringing about the existing state of affairs; and the collections of the Friends of the Theatre Museum were handed over to Roy Strong and Alexander Schouvaloff.

Early in 1975 it became clear to Schouvaloff that storage space at Somerset House was quite inadequate. Furthermore, although the allotment to the Theatre Museum of the rooms designed by Sir William Chambers in the 1770s had been the act of the Department of Science and Education, the maintenance of their fabric came under the Ministry of Works, who had recently restored them to their pristine splendour. The marble chimney-pieces and the plasterwork of cornices and ceilings were not to be hidden. No heavy weights might be placed in the middle of rooms: no nail was to be inserted in a wall. The palace was quite unsuited to our purpose. Roy Strong and Alexander Schouvaloff rejected it. In connivance with the architect of the Greater London Council, Schouvaloff turned his attention to the old Flower Market in Covent Garden, which had been vacant since the market's move to Nine Elms, south of the river. The long saga of accepted estimates, rising costs, changing governments and cancelled grants need not be sung here. Meanwhile the Theatre Museum was housed in a suite of rooms on the top floor of the V and A. It mounted a series of small exhibitions, and its archives were accessible to students for research.

When I was in New York on my way to Hollywood in May 1968 Jerome Robbins had said to me, 'I think we are rivals.' 'Why?' 'Both working on Nijinsky: you on your book, I on the film.' 'Have *you* been asked to direct a film?' 'Yes, by Harry Salzman.' 'My God! Well, you know I was supposed to be advising Ken Russell on *his* film for Harry? And then Harry fired him.' 'Yes. What happened exactly?' 'I don't know. I have a feeling Ken tried to persuade Harry that Christopher Gable would play Nijinsky better than

Rudolf. Anyway, watch out. And do try to get me the job as *your* adviser. I could use the dough.' Jerry got me the job. By the end of June he was in London, at the Savoy, and on the thirtieth, a Sunday, he and I drove together to lunch at Harry Salzman's country house in Buckinghamshire. On 18 July I was sent to interest Harold Pinter in writing the script, and failed. On 28 November I had a telephone conversation with David Storey, who also refused to collaborate. During December I incorporated some of Jerry's and my ideas in a 'treatment', which I posted to New York. On 3 January 1969 Jerry rang me to say he thought 'they' were trying to get him out. On the eighth he told me by transatlantic telephone that he was pleased with some of the treatment. Salzman wasn't. I do not know if it was what Dolly Sandford would have called my *'frightfully* good ideas' that cooked Jerry's goose, but no sooner had Harry Salzman read our few pages of typescript than he fired Jerry. I was sent for by Harry on 19 February. When he said, 'If I'd wanted an Ingmar Bergman picture I'd have hired Ingmar,' I kept quiet about the part I had played in composing the treatment. Harry announced that my old wartime friend, Franco Zeffirelli, would be taking over as director of the film. Shortly after this Franco had a serious motor accident and was out of the running. On 19 June Edward Bond, the author of *Saved*, came to lunch with me, and we had a long talk about Nijinsky. I was told by those who read it, which I was never allowed to, that Bond's script was very good. However, he was fired without delay. By the end of that month I had signed a contract with Salzman: my fee of £15,000 ($36,000) was to be divisible into three parts – for my pre-production advice to the script-writer and director, for my comments in the course of production and for my post-production suggestions on editing. As things turned out, only the first third was ever paid. However, by 2 January 1970 I was lunching with Salzman's latest potential director, Tony Richardson, who tended to see Nijinsky as the type of

Common Man, victim of Capitalist Oppressors. Obsequiously I tried to adjust my ideas. Edward Albee just had time to write a script before Harry fired Tony. Later, Ken Russell, who had by this time made his name with a series of sensational movies, and whose horrific film about Tchaikovsky had proved his ability to squeeze the last ounce of drama out of the lives of Russian homosexuals, was re-engaged by Salzman for the Nijinsky picture. I never heard what provoked his second dismissal, which was not long delayed. But I was told that when Nureyev was given another film test (after six years had passed) it was decided that he was too old to play Nijinsky. He had a contract, however, which specified that he was due for compensation to the tune of thousands if the film were *not* made with him in the leading role: and this fine had to be paid.

My book *Nijinsky* was published at the end of 1971. On a Christmas card Mme Bronislava called it 'wonderful'. She died in the following February; and on 14 March 1972 Romola wrote, in reference to the obituary I had done for the *Sunday Times*, 'I want to thank you, that you so beautifully wrote about Bronia.'

Richard Attenborough rang me up after reading my book in January 1972 to say that nothing on earth would stop him making a film of it. I told him I thought my contract with Salzman had lapsed, and wrote: 'It would save time if you could take advantage of the Ballet Rambert's being in or near London to give a film test *at once* to Christopher Bruce, who might be a godsent Nijinsky. Please arrange this . . . the biggest difficulty will be having a ballet company when you want one. Incidentally, Festival Ballet have a respectable production of *Scheherazade*, a *Sylphides* and an improvable *Petrushka* . . . I recall that when Salzman told Jerry Robbins he had secured the Royal Ballet for three whole months, Jerry said, "But I may not need a ballet company."' Neither by letter nor by telephone did I ever again hear from Dickie Attenborough about the project of this film.

On 2 March 1973 I had lunch in Soho with Cedric Messina and Nicholas Lom of BBC Television, who wanted Terence Rattigan to write a play about Nijinsky. On 8 June we lunched with Terry Rattigan in Albany and talked about it. Terry had read my book twice, and he set off for a remote hotel in Scotland, where he remained *incommunicado* until he had finished the play. I never read it, but was told that Romola had made difficulties, as might have been expected, and that the project had been shelved for the time being. Terry died in 1977 without the play ever being produced.

Early in 1973 I had begun to get letters from a solicitor in Piccadilly, whose client, 'an internationally known film director and producer', was intending to make a film of the life of Nijinsky and was anxious for my help. Now, an address in Piccadilly, though desirable in certain businesses, hardly 'inspires confidence', as Lady Bracknell would have put it, in a solicitor. Moreover, the lawyer in question declined to reveal the identity of his internationally famous client. On 9 April I wrote to him: 'I think my secretary will have explained to you that conversations about films on *Nijinsky's* life have been a regular feature of *mine* for twenty years. None of these films came to anything, and only in the case of one planned by Harry Salzman did I receive any money. [It is true I had received £150 ($360) from John Sutro.] You will therefore understand that in order not to waste any more of my life having futile lunches and discussions I have made a rule to be paid a fee *before* the discussions take place, apart from any fees or salaries if the film is actually made. I think you will sympathize when I tell you that letters asking for information about Nijinsky and the Diaghilev Ballet arrive by every post, and that strangers telephone daily . . . I go to Canada on May 17th.' The Piccadilly lawyer was undaunted. 'My client . . . will be in London from the United States within the next four weeks.' Telephone calls followed: 'My client is on the way . . .' 'My client is in London . . .' 'My client is in the room with me . . .' I refused to talk to him. His patience exhausted, 'my client' seized the telephone and announced, 'This is George Cukor. If you will have lunch with me at the Savoy I will tell you anything you want to know about any star in Hollywood, alive or dead.' 'Oh,' I said, 'I always heard such nice things about you from my darling friends Juliet Duff and Simon Fleet. They were so fond of you. I should love to meet you.'

It was a sunny day on 27 April 1973 when I arrived at the Savoy, and was admitted to Mr Cukor's suite by a handsome young man dressed in beige velvet. The great director who had made me cry in Norwich in the 1930s with Garbo's *Camille*, and in Leicester Square in the 1960s with Judy Garland's *A Star is Born*, had not yet arrived; and I admired with rapture the curve of the river from the window of his sitting-room, counting nine bridges, from London Bridge on the left, to Vauxhall Bridge on the right. I was full of enthusiasm for the Arts Council's exhibition of 'The French Impressionists in London', which had recently been held at the new Hayward Gallery opposite, and I began to expatiate on Monet's miraculous series of views painted between 1899 and 1904 from the windows of the Savoy Hotel. (Twenty of these had been gathered for the exhibition from collections as far apart as Copenhagen, Hamburg, Dublin, Ottawa, Chicago, Santa Barbara, St Louis, Baltimore, Philadelphia and Massachusetts.) Before long it dawned on me that the young man had never heard of Monet and did not know what I was talking about.

George Cukor burst in, short, square, energetic, with piercing dark brown eyes which I thought had soon started summing me up from my greying head down to my ready-made shoes. He ordered lunch and began to tell me his plans for the Nijinsky film. 'Now that Nijinsky's difficult widow is dead we can go ahead without the danger of her causing trouble over money and litigation.' 'Romola?' said I. 'But she's not dead. I heard from her last month.' '*Not dead?*'

cried Cukor, aghast. 'But I read it in the papers!' I told him that it was Nijinsky's sister, Bronislava, who had died in February, not Romola, his wife. Cukor's eyes flashed cold fury at Romola's audacity in remaining alive. For once the intriguing woman had caused trouble without having deliberately instigated it: she had made Hollywood's most celebrated director cross the Atlantic for nothing. (I never told Romola of her involuntary achievement.) Mr Cukor barely managed to remain civil until the end of lunch.

CHAPTER 11

Giving up Ballet for Ever

I had already given up writing about ballet 'for ever' once in the 1950s, for shortly after *Ballet* magazine closed down I resigned from the *Observer* and set about trying to write plays. Two of these actually reached the stage, though not the West End of London. I wrote ten comedies in all, but when in 1956 John Osborne's *Look Back in Anger* burst upon the world (partly through the exertions of George Harewood, who was a founder of the English Stage Company at the Royal Court) my kind of artificial comedy, influenced by Coward and Sacha Guitry, in the writing of which I had been encouraged by Peter Daubeny, became out-of-date overnight. From that moment, for quite twenty years, working-class types (such as my Cockney spivs and charwomen) became the principal characters of plays, changing places with the gentry, who were relegated to clownish minor roles.

When I was jobless from 1955 for a year or two I was also homeless, because Barclay's Bank, with the foresight for which banks are famous, had declared that my twenty-five year lease of Bloomfield Terrace was insufficient security against an overdraft of £5000 ($13,950); and they made me sell it. After an excursion to the Middle East I camped out with various friends, and of course my mother was always glad to have me at Overstrand between visits. I remember the face of Violet Kinnaird when I arrived to stay with a taxi full of luggage. She had a mania for tidiness and she exclaimed, 'I don't mind having you, but I can't have that

271

luggage.' I left her on the door-step and drove away. It was then that the Goslings took pity on me and put me up for several weeks. After settling in the flat at Henrietta Street, Covent Garden, in 1957 I worked for two years on Sokolova's memoirs, which was a kind of return to writing about ballet – the Diaghilev Ballet, at least. In 1959, partly at the instigation of Juliet Duff and Simon Fleet, the *Sunday Times* had asked me to replace Cyril Beaumont as their critic of ballet. The value of money changes so rapidly in this century that figures lose their meaning within half a generation: but I may as well record that when I left the *Observer* I was earning £8 ($22) a week, which was not in 1955 enough to live on, whereas the £1500 ($4215) a year the *Sunday Times* offered me in 1959 was. (The rent of my large flat in Covent Garden was £10 ($28) a week.) I could not refuse the *Sunday Times*'s offer, for I had no regular income at all. My first assignment for the paper was to cover events at the Edinburgh Festival, and I had to sell two Buckle silver candlesticks in order to travel north. Lydia Sokolova recommended a silversmith opposite Ronnie's bank, in Burlington Gardens, who paid fair prices. When Simon Fleet asked, 'What does it feel like, coming back to writing about ballet again?' I replied, 'Oh, I just feel I know everything'; and he laughed his high fluting laugh. I little realized how much I had to learn. For a start, the finest inventions of Jerome Robbins, who brought his Ballets USA to Edinburgh that year, were about to burst upon me; and my unbounded admiration for the versatility he showed in his one perfect programme, composed of the silent, timeless *Moves*, the newly thought-out *Afternoon of a Faun*, the raw vision of the lives of young city-dwellers offered by *Opus Jazz* and the Thurber-esque wit of *The Concert*, made us close friends overnight. I was shortly to witness the mature flowering of two other very different choreographers, Martha Graham and George Balanchine. London was no longer the capital of the world of ballet: because of these three geniuses – besides a number of other

Above: Jerome Robbins with the author at the Ristorante Cocchetto, Trevi, during the Spoleto Festival. Photograph by Jerome Robbins, 13 July 1961. *Below:* Martha Graham cutting her Come-back-soon cake at a last-night party, 34 Henrietta Street, 14 September 1963. Photograph by Hans Wild.

experimental choreographers – New York had taken London's place. I began to travel there regularly.

The Bolshoi Ballet had come for the first time to London in 1956, during the interregnum, when I was attached to no newspaper: I had written about them for *Dance and Dancers*. The schooling of these Russian dancers was as good as – probably better than – that of their predecessors in the early years of the century, when under Diaghilev's banner Fokine, Karsavina and Nijinsky had broken away: but from the point of view of music, design and choreographic invention the Russians were back in 1900 – Diaghilev might never have lived. Stalin had suppressed the revolutionary artists of the 1920s, and it was said that Krushchev ordained that ballets such as *Swan Lake* must have a happy ending: both insisted that art should be, if not propaganda, at least opium for the masses. So Russia bred a stable of superb dancers, but entered them for no important races. When Leningrad's Kirov company came to London in 1961, we realized that they excelled in style, just as in the early years of the century, whereas the Moscow artists we had seen still put more emphasis on virtuosity.

Two sentences I improvised on an impulse to fill a gap in an article for the *Sunday Times*★ contain a hint of the essential difference between British and Russian dancers in the 1960s and 1970s. 'Leonardo wrote in his notebook that it is the extremities which lend grace to the body; and invented the early English school of dancing. Michelangelo, who had seen the newly unearthed Belvedere Torso, went one further, twisted the body into a shape more expressive of the soul; and invented the Russian school.' I added that it was hard for a layman to divine the secret skill of turning bodies into works of art and moving sculpture: but I was sure it had something to do with movement starting from the small of the back, with following through, with the crossing of limbs and with the varying relationships of the head to the arms

★ On 28 May 1972.

and legs which is called 'épaulement' (and which I had discussed with Karsavina, as mentioned earlier.) The Russians danced with their whole bodies: the British did not. The process by which Balanchine, whether consciously or not, devised a streamlined neo-classical style suited to athletic Americans and to his new ballets in which expression was subordinated to the invention of a visual parallel with music, and in which épaulement became of minor importance, is a question worthy of study in depth. In the course of forging this new style he created some of the master-works of the twentieth century.

You can't make good ballets without a good company or without a good choreographer who is, or has been, a good dancer; and both these elements must emerge from a good school. Once you have established a school and a company you just have to hope that a choreographer or dancer of genius will emerge every ten, twenty or fifty years to produce or inspire works of art. In the meanwhile all you can do is to maintain standards and entertain the bourgeoisie. (After all, ballet is perfect after-dinner entertainment for the half-artistic half-educated, and there will always be bird-watching businessmen with soulful wives who can afford to remain half-awake to the music of Tchaikovsky.) Rambert could animate young dancers: she was hardly equipped to teach them the tremendous vocabulary of the classical technique. Her troupe, and in fact all classical ballet companies, had their range extended by the innovations of Martha Graham; and Robin Howard, inflamed by Graham, had founded with her former dancer, Robert Cohan, the London Contemporary Dance Theatre. De Valois realized her own deficiences, and while she systematically built up the edifice of her school and companies, hankered after help from Russia. When Vera Volkova, a pupil of the celebrated Agrippina Vaganova, came to England in the 1940s Ninette de Valois did not enlist her to serve on her board of instructors, thus missing, as I think, her first big chance to improve the English school;

and perhaps she regretted this later, when Vera was established in 1950 in Copenhagen. Fonteyn went to Volkova for classes. (I too took private lessons with her until she told me I could join a class. Being over thirty I was too shy to expose myself.)

Margot Fonteyn, the most wonderful – yet a typical – product of the British school, was an example of the victory of mind over matter. Her torso was inflexible, and her by no means perfect legs were limited in their range of movement: but she *thought herself* into becoming a great dancer. (Taglioni had some serious physical defects, but she too had captivated a whole generation and gone down in history.) One could say that Fonteyn's body was a stiffish stem with expressive flower (head) and foliage (arms) attached. She acquired real theatrical know-how, and seldom failed to score her points. The sad eyes and the inclinations of her head lent such expression to the gestures of her lovely arms, that her torso and legs were overlooked. She was an actress of exceptional power. When I discussed the neglect of *épaulement* in England with Karsavina she had said, 'Even Margot only approximates.' (Karsavina did not go often to the theatre, but I think she would have missed emotional content in Balanchine's latest ballets. Lopoukhova found them 'cold'.)

The South African Nadia Nerina had three times Fonteyn's strength and technique, but although she created delightfully the leading role in *La Fille mal gardée*, Ashton's most popular ballet, she never imposed herself to the same degree as Fonteyn as a personality. Other much-loved ballerinas – Beryl Grey, who combined sweetness with authority, the radiant Moira Shearer and the languorous Beriosova with melting eyes – left their mark on history.

With what patient labour and propaganda de Valois built up from scratch a fine body of male dancers, and what prejudices had to be overcome by her and by Arnold Haskell and Michael Wood, who in turn directed her school, before

British parents could be persuaded that ballet was a suitable career for young men! Then in 1961 Rudolf Nureyev arrived, defecting from Russia, and such worthy home-grown artists as David Blair, Somes's heirs as *danseurs nobles,* were indignant to find themselves put in the shade. Nureyev was in a sense Ninette de Valois' second chance from Russia. She took to him in a big way. Though only a guest artist, he was at once assimilated as leading dancer of the Royal Ballet, and his partnership with Margot Fonteyn began on 21 February 1962.

Ashton succeeded de Valois as Director of the Royal Ballet in 1963 and ruled it until 1970. He did not like administration and found that it interfered with his invention of new works, the most recent of which was a 'vehicle' for Fonteyn and Nureyev, immediately world-famous. *Marguerite and Armand* (clumsy title) did not amount to much choreographically, but it was splendid theatre, Romanticism to the nth degree, a Puccini opera in miniature – with music by Liszt, arranged by my old acquaintance Humphrey Searle. It was never danced except by the artists for whom it was created. (Alas that the same could not be said of *Le Spectre de la rose* and Pavlova's *Dying Swan*!) Although I was vaguely aware that there were kindly old widows, backwoods peers and despairing young aesthetes scattered about Britain who looked forward to my brief candles of comment in the *Sunday Times,* it was extremely rare that anyone told me in so many words that they had liked what I had written. It is because Fred Ashton remarked to me in the bar at Covent Garden that a piece I had done on *Marguerite and Armand* was 'just what ballet criticism ought to be' that it occurs to me to quote it here.

> Watch Fonteyn's face when the love-at-first-sight takes place. She is such a cool pussy-cat at first, almost sucking in her cheeks and primly pursing her pretty mouth, perhaps to stop herself smiling with too broad a joy. Then his uninhibited monkey yearning. She looks slowly and

277

bashfully down, recognizing the *coup de foudre*. And, after all, they are at a party and she is the cynosure of neighbouring eyes. But in the ensuing *pas de deux* he becomes catlike in his different way and possesses her utterly, a cheetah gorging.

In the country scene Fonteyn's white dress [by Beaton] with its fluttering satin ribbons reminded me of Herrick's 'When as in silks my Julia goes,/Then, then (me-thinks) how sweetly flowes/That liquifaction of her clothes.' Michael Somes as Armand's father, the god of Duty, comes and strikes his tragic gong and goes. Marguerite loving Armand before renouncing him – a white battle.

Next the party: Fonteyn coughing in black with camellias in her hair and a new diamond necklace. Nureyev comes in and yearns. He twirls her round, then madlier; flings her to the ground; lifts her with one finger under her chin; stares; suddenly pulls off and rejects her necklace; does low pirouettes in arabesque on a bent knee. With a change of mood he seems to try to sweep her off. But no, he flings banknotes at her and wipes his hands down his sides with a grimace of repellence. But when his back is turned his right arm is drawn back miserably towards her and his face is piteous. 'Oh now, for ever/Farewell the tranquil mind; farewell content.' Turning again to the sobbing Fonteyn, he seems to relent, then points at her with dagger derision and backs out, fiendish, laughing.

To her death-bed, cloak swooping, a desperate night-rider, he soars. Whisks her up, whirls her round, cuddles her on the floor, smothers her with smiling, mocking sympathy. Mad embraces. She is lifted, diving to the sky; then falls. She raises a hand, touches his brow, gazes wildly. Her hand drops. Death. Sour chords.

Ashton's *Enigma Variations* set out to be the evocation of an exact day at the end of the last century, probably 17 October 1898, with realistic falling oak leaves, 'a staircase for children to wave goodnight from', 'a hammock for the cream of British womanhood to be swung in by the best type of Englishman', and Elgar, 'in tweeds and a genuine watch-chain . . . expressing feeling by a *rond de jambe*'. I found it clever but ridiculous. Ashton's sentiment and humour, whether in *La Fille mal gardée*, *The Two Pigeons* or *The Dream* (with which he celebrated Shakespeare's Quatercentenary in 1964), together with his nostalgia for the nineteenth century and his choice of easy-to-like music, ensured the popularity of his ballets with the conservative British public, and earned him a knighthood, the CH and the OM. What honours! I could not help feeling that Fred's inventions were seldom in the spirit of the age (at the time of *The Two Pigeons* someone told me that Fred's sister Edith had said she knew exactly what Buckle would write about the new ballet: he would complain that no one wore blue jeans in it): yet when I find my hero Kenneth Clark deriding scholars who deplore that the Hellenistic Venus of Milo should be an imitation of the 'heroic age of Phidias', and denouncing them for their 'contemporary critical cant that a work of art must express its own epoch', I feel scolded. Still, I admired Ashton most when he most approximated to the *dépouillé* style of Balanchine. I loved his two trios of white statuary in Satie's *Monotones*, and wrote:

> These *pas de trois* are not storyless to me, though they plunge me into uncritical dreams of '*luxe, calme et volupté*'. In *Trois Gnossiennes* watchers on a roof-top await the arrival of their prince from another island. In *Trois Gymnopédies* a doll-girl is rehearsed in love-knots for her lord. The bustle of the fish market is miles below.

The partnership of Fonteyn and Nureyev became world-famous. She learned a lot from him, though old enough to be his mother (she was two years younger than I). By the time Kenneth MacMillan succeeded Ashton as Director of the Royal Ballet in 1970, Nureyev had already for some time been complaining that he was booked by Covent Garden with decreasing frequency. MacMillan used him, certainly, but perhaps he was more interested in budding youth than in so ripe and resplendent a blossom as Rudolf. MacMillan's muse was the young Canadian Lynn Seymour, for whom he created *The Invitation, Romeo and Juliet* and *Anastasia*. MacMillan cannot take more than a fraction of the blame, however, for the incessant travels of Fonteyn and Nureyev. They commanded higher fees than Covent Garden could regularly afford; and while Fonteyn had a crippled husband to support, Nureyev had an agent who kept him flying from continent to continent as busily as President Nixon sent Dr Kissinger, and doubtless with the same philanthropic motives. Anyway, Nureyev was insatiable for work. He would cross the Atlantic twice in a week so as to squeeze in an extra performance. The chart of his bookings over five months reproduced in one of Nigel Gosling's biographies of him has to be seen to be believed. It cannot therefore be said that Nureyev devoted his energies to improving the quality of teaching in the Royal Ballet School. Even so, he inspired a new generation of brilliant male dancers, notably Anthony Dowell and David Wall. He also staged one or two fine productions at Covent Garden.

In Lynn Seymour we had at last a ballerina whose whole body was as expressive as a Russian's. God knows where she learned to use it the way she did. She was an even more wonderful actress than Fonteyn, less romantic and far more a child of the period, with an appeal which went straight to the hearts of young people in the sixties and seventies. Whereas Fonteyn's effects were long calculated, Seymour seemed to need to live her roles – and this is taxing to the nerves. Ashton, seeing into her soul, invented some little dances for her in the style of Isadora, whom he had admired and pitied in his youth. Alas! It was Seymour's very resemblance in private life to the generous, emotionally self-indulgent Isadora which was her downfall.

Led by Seymour, Antoinette Sibley, the Rhodesian Merle Park, David Wall and Anthony Dowell (all of whom had passed through the Royal Ballet School) the company was never so strong as under Kenneth MacMillan. Yet MacMillan, who dared more than Ashton, could not sustain so steady a level of public acclaim, and his diffident character led to failures of communication. John Field, appointed his co-ajutor, decided within a few weeks to part company with him and the Royal Ballet. (He later succeeded Beryl Grey as Director of Festival Ballet.) Critics began to scheme openly for MacMillan's replacement by Nureyev.

I loathed plots and anything approximating to mutiny, but I did think that when the time came Nureyev, with his drive to work, his intelligence, imagination, humour and choreographic talent, could be the ideal leader of a company. The time came and passed. Nureyev was offered the Royal Ballet on condition that he gave up dancing. This he was unwilling to do. The New York City Ballet had Balanchine; and perhaps Nureyev considered the French, Milanese, Austrian, Canadian and Australian companies – for all of whom he staged ballets – unworthy of him. Having no firm base, he was obliged to keep on the move, and this continued after Fonteyn had begun a slow withdrawal from the stage. It happened that Nureyev's finest choreographic achievement in Britain was his staging of *The Sleeping Beauty* for Festival Ballet in 1975.

Despite the incredible achievements of Ninette de Valois, British ballet could not compete during the 1970s with the invention, diversity or performance of Balanchine's company. The apogee of New York City Ballet's golden age was the Stravinsky Festival of 1972. For one week only there were performed thirty-two ballets by seven choreographers to Stravinsky's music; and no single work was repeated. This amazing repertoire was conducted by my old friend Robert Irving, who had been at Oxford with me, and at the end Robert Craft conducted the 'Symphony of Psalms'. There were a few old favourites, such as Balanchine's *Apollo*, *Orpheus*, *Firebird*, *Agon*, *Monumentum pro Gesualdo* and *Movements*, Robbins's *The Cage* and Taras's *Ebony Concerto*: but most works were new. Taras arranged *Scènes de ballet* and *The Song of the Nightingale*; Robbins *Scherzo fantastique*, *Dumbarton Oaks* and *Requiem Canticles*. The sixty-eight-year-old Balanchine created at least three new masterpieces: *Violin Concerto*, *Duo Concertant* and *Symphony in Three Movements* became jewels of the repertory. There was no doubt in my mind that George Balanchine was the most imaginative choreographer who ever lived: his classicism was an extension of Petipa's, while his vision of new forms kept pace with those of twentieth-century composers. For years his best ballets had been in demand throughout the world; and it was usually John Taras who remembered their details and staged them for other troupes. For instance, Balanchine's *Apollo*, made for Diaghilev in 1928, was reproduced by Taras for twelve companies – rather more, he thought, but he had lost count.

As the years went by I found it harder to sustain the zest with which I had flung myself into working for the *Sunday Times* in 1959. 'Do you think writing about ballet is a ridiculous way of passing one's life?' I demanded of Erich Alport. 'Not as you write about it,' was the reply. Still I was ashamed of my limited occupation. When Berenson had asked me at Settignano in 1944, 'What do you do in peacetime?' I had answered almost boastfully, 'I am a ballet critic' – and he had gone into an aria of amazement about the multiplicity of human callings. At fifty, when I was asked by strangers what I did, I felt a fool. In spite of my trips to New York and although every kind of company – classical, modern and exotic – came to London, I began to develop a mental crick in the neck from looking half-left at the stage of the Royal Opera House from my seats, A29 and 30, in the front row of the stalls circle. A large part of the repertory was annually repeated, and as the Royal Ballet drew from its school more and more skilled dancers, and these were given the chance to tread the tightrope of leading roles, critics were invited to compare ever more varied cast-changes in familiar ballets. One day I found myself writing, 'We are thinking of taking on a special *Swan Lake* critic': and at Christmas 1972 I wrote, 'Well, we are one more *Nutcracker* nearer death.' These were the jokes of a desperate man. My few close friends began to fear invitations to keep me company at the ballet. Had they not seen it all before? But could I be sure of earning a living by writing books? However, I worked hard to make my short articles constructive and readable. I should have been a better critic had I not been drunk most of the time. I don't mean that I was drunk when I wrote my articles in the early hours of the morning but when I was watching ballets at night. How was I to get through those long intervals, surrounded by the same silly faces, without whisky? Yet I went to operas, plays, concerts and art exhibitions and tried to relate ballet to the other arts. It was a grave danger that ballet should exist in a little hothouse of its own, unruffled by the breeze of new ideas. One reason that I admired Nureyev was that he longed to see and experience everything. When he had a free night he was always at a movie or a play.

Conditions of work became more difficult with the passing of time. When in London, I always put my article in a taxi on Thursday or Friday mornings, and the fare was paid by the porter in Gray's Inn Road. During my first years with the *Sunday Times* a boy would then bring me a proof and wait while I cut or corrected it. This practice died out, and I began to go round to the newspaper on Thursday or Friday afternoons. I enjoyed my visits because I liked the feeling of being one of a team. When the Royal Ballet invited critics on Friday nights, which they did increasingly, I used to get up at six on the Saturday morning, write my piece, taxi to the *Sunday Times* before nine and wait while it was set up, to cut and correct it. By lunch-time it was hardly worthwhile going away for a weekend. I could not have complained of being obliged to go to the ballet nearly every night of my life, or of having to spend a great part of my days in receiving critics, writers or students from all over the world, or in answering letters from strangers – for the *Sunday Times* had turned me into a sort of oracle – if my salary had risen with the tide of work and the cost of living: but it did not. One fantastic example of how I spent a morning will suffice. The Royal Ballet was to perform in Korea on the way to China; and a Korean newspaper went to the trouble of flying a lady journalist to London for two days' research, so that she should be able to greet the company in Seoul with an informed article. She arrived at Henrietta Street with the cultural attaché from her Embassy to act as interpreter. Her first question went straight to the point. 'Could you tell me, please, the history of the Royal Ballet?' I looked at the clock: two hours to lunch. 'In 1931,' I began, 'Ninette de Valois –' 'Could you spell, please?' It turned out that this charming lady, who, by the way, rewarded me with a fan and a topaz ring, had made no plan to spend her one night in London actually *watching* the Royal Ballet at Covent Garden. I exerted myself on her behalf, and although the house was full, obtained for her a standing pass.

I felt my life was slipping away. The editor of the *Sunday Times* had no idea how much my little five-hundred-word articles cost me in work, expense and the loss of leisure to write books. Nobody thanked me for extra work or lost weekends because nobody gave the matter a thought. The paper had no pension scheme for contributors. I wrote several times about this to the editor, Harold Evans, who made vague promises: I also told him that I reckoned I was sub-sidizing the paper at the rate of £2000 ($4780) or so a year, and that I had no more aunts left to die. He said he did not like my tone. I had not for years taken the month's holiday with pay to which I was entitled. Foreseeing a rare lull on the ballet scene, I wrote in September 1974 that I was going away and should not return until he implemented his promises. Nevertheless, because the Frankfurt Ballet were visiting England for the first time to appear in Birmingham, I decided (out of fairness to them) to go over from Oxford for a night to see a performance. It was at Oxford station, as

I carried luggage down the metal-edged steps of the staircase which led to the passage under the railway, that I slipped and broke my thigh. Shortly afterwards, the promise was made that contributors who had worked for at least twelve years for the *Sunday Times* could retire on half-pay. This was better than nothing. The age of retirement was left in doubt. In 1975 I should be sixty and should have worked sixteen years with the newspaper. As it turned out, the circumstances in which I parted with the *Sunday Times* in 1975 made it possible for them to exclude me from the promised benefit; and the pension scheme which I had extorted (by using a tone the editor did not like) never came into force. Because at my suggestion David Dougill had stood in for me when my leg was broken, and had done well, the *Sunday Times* would appoint him as my successor when I resigned. This was one of several happy results of my impetuous resignation.

In 1975 Festival Ballet were celebrating their twenty-fifth anniversary with a tour of Australia, and, in the same way that Colonel de Basil had invited Arnold Haskell to travel there in 1936, they asked me to go with them, observe how things went and, presumably, record their triumphs. They could not pay my fare there and back, but offered free transport and accommodation inside Australia. I knew the *Sunday Times* would not pay for my flight, but Philip Dossé stepped into the breach. He had an arrangement with Air India to give advertising space in his magazines in exchange for air travel; this enabled him to reward certain contributors with tickets in lieu of cash. The *Sunday Times* offered expenses in return for two 1200-word articles, which were to be of a general nature. I did not know, when I accepted Festival Ballet's offer, that Nureyev's production of *The Sleeping Beauty*, which I had loved and praised when it was first shown at the Coliseum that April, would be given nightly for successive weeks in Perth, Melbourne, Adelaide and Sydney, or that Rudolf himself was under contract to dance at every performance. My last three weeks as a ballet critic would be spent in his society.

When Nureyev first came to England we had not immediately become friends: it had taken several years. In fact, when Erik Bruhn brought him to dinner (on 30 October 1961) I sensed a wall of animosity. It was eighteen years before he told me the reason for this: but in early days I was merely puzzled, because I felt we were cut out to be friends. I loved wild gipsies. Nigel and Maude Gosling 'adopted' Rudolf. Their own son had married and made a home apart: Rudolf became the son of their middle age. Their devotion was so great that they would rise at four in the morning to cook him steaks *à point*.

When the barrier was broken down I would sometimes be summoned at very short notice to supper at Nureyev's house on the fringe of Richmond Park. The voice on the telephone, heard perhaps for the first time in six months, was gentle and unassuming. 'Dicky, this is Rudolf.' In East Sheen Road, later given up for tax reasons, hospitality was medieval, baronial: a blazing log fire, immense brass candelabra with wax candles, Spanish leather, a life-size portrait of Peter the Great, a refectory table to seat twenty, a dresser fifteen foot long, twelve courses served on silver plate, whisky in pint goblets. Nureyev was always called at nine, so as to drive himself very fast in a tiny car to class at ten: but it was seldom before half-past three in the morning that I left the castle of the unsleeping prince.

I do not know how much value Rudolf placed on friendship: but he seemed to need a court, and I could never be a courtier. I know I was thrilled when he remembered and quoted a phrase which had struck him in one of my old articles. I described him in *Don Quixote* 'clowning like a tipsy monkey'. The words were repeated months later with relish. Once he telephoned his great friend Erik Bruhn across the Atlantic to quote a line of praise I had given to the latter's miraculous performance as Dr Coppelius, 'Shelley turned Frankenstein, the artist gone mad with dreams of power.'

On 18 May 1975, my second morning in Australia, I walked alone to Edgley's Entertainments Centre, which stood next to the Bus Station in a *terrain vague* where the civic splendours of Perth petered out into ring-roads and railways. This theatre was round and seated 8003. Going on stage, I approached for the first time from the rear Nico Georgiadis's handsome curving staircase, which, after a flight of nine thousand miles, had already been erected. In a little clear space behind this a portable *barre* had been placed, and Donald Barclay, who played the King, was conducting a class of three. This included Nureyev, just arrived from New York *via* San Francisco and Sydney. 'Hello, Dicky,' he said, doing a *plié*. I wandered into the vast auditorium, whose blocks of seats were painted red, purple, orange and pink. It was the large capacity of this Entertainments Centre, built in his home town by our impresario Michael Edgley, that made Festival Ballet's tour financially feasible, for the theatres in the other three cities would only be a fraction of its size. Since its opening, five months before, this popular palace had already held Shirley Bassey and Disneyland on Ice. Michael Edgley, an attractive stocky young man about thirty, who came from a theatrical family, fascinated me, not only because he was said to have made his first million before he was twenty-one. He had a beautiful, witty wife, Jeni, a son and heir in a well-tailored patchwork blue jean suit, a sister, secretaries and a closest friend, Jack, who wore the same sort of leather jackets and fantastic shoes as Michael, though not always on the same day. This Napoleon – if not the Diaghilev, at least the Astruc or Hurok of Australia – who was that week to reveal the masterpiece of Tchaikovsky and Petipa to forty thousand of his fellow citizens, was conferring with his Marshals in the front row. Reluctant to intrude, but afraid that if I didn't say anything about his theatre he would think I didn't like it, I went up and told him how wonderful it was. Love was born. Jeni was sent to get me something to eat. 'Rump-steak sandwiches for Dicky and me,' called Michael. 'Hamburgers for the *corps de ballet*.'

Standing on a corner of the specially built forestage, by his comparison of which to iron he had upset Michael Edgley, Rudolf told me about his hellish trip. He had been mounting his production of *Raymonda* for American Ballet Theatre. They were in Washington and he had been obliged to travel backwards and forwards from New York, where Martha Graham was inventing a dance for him. Because of union regulations he never got more than an hour or so rehearsal time in Washington: then back to New York, and to Washington again next day. 'Then I came from San Francisco on small plane. It was awful. I had four hours to wait in Sydney, so I took class with Australian Ballet. I saw press. Then I came here. Press again.' I said, 'I saw you on television in my bedroom. You looked dead. Is Martha all right?' 'She's fine. She had her face lifted, so she feels better.' 'I love her.' 'I do too.'

Poor Rudolf, whose fate it was to fly continually zig-zag around the earth, was terrified of air travel. Once, when we flew to Paris together, I was amazed to see him before take-off duck his head between his legs and pull his coat over it. Ten minutes later he came up for air, pouring with sweat. I have never beheld this animal panic in any other human being. What courage, I thought, to keep going as he does!

Rudolf always professed that to take a class when you were really exhausted was good for you. I thought it was just another way of proving you were Superman. Yet Vladimirov told me that Nijinsky did exercises *after* an evening's performance. I cannot think this happened often.

When Eva Evdokimova came to rehearse her Rose Adage, Rudolf took the role of all her four partners in turn. Picturesque stage-hands with long hair emerged to watch the fabled hero.

Later, in the *cabana* of an Edgley swimming pool in a
terraced garden sloping down to the Swan River, somebody
said something about taking risks. 'All of life is a risk,'
pronounced Rudolf. 'Art is a risk.' (Nobody took more risks
on stage than Rudolf did, which was why he danced better
on some nights than others. I admired him for his nerve,
that most aristocratic of qualities.) He had had his blue steak
cooked twenty seconds longer, and was eating it quickly
because Donald had to take a class at four. He said this gave
him 'heartburn'. I said that was rather a Shakespearean word.
Rudolf was always eager to requisition new words, and
sometimes grew impatient with his shortcomings: but I never
ceased to be amazed at his range and the speed with which he
enlarged his vocabulary. Shortly after this, discussing *The
Sleeping Beauty*, I complained of the series of crashing chords
with which Tchaikovsky postponed the fall of his final
curtain, in the same way that Beethoven hammered home
the closing of a symphony. 'You have to crown it,' said
Rudolf; and I thought his well-chosen verb went far to answer
my criticism of the two composers.

Rudolf always started laughing when I talked earnestly
about the Theatre Museum. That night, the eve of the company's opening in Perth, he listened to my harangues till half-
past-two in the morning. When he showed me politely to
the door, I realized he was going out for a walk. This
pampered pussy, surrounded by courtiers, became in the
early hours a cat that walked by himself. I had never before
spent several consecutive days in his company, and was
obliged to remind myself that gipsies do not like to be hedged
in. After dining alone with Rudolf two days running, I
decided to make myself scarce. I did not want him to think
I was in love with him. Everybody else was. Well, nearly
everyone. There was trouble a day or two later with dressers,
new to the privilege of serfdom. Rudolf's favourite masseur
had to be flown out from Italy at Edgley's expense. We all
expected Adonis, and were disappointed.

Rudolf Nureyev rehearsing Festival Ballet in *The Sleeping Beauty*, Perth, Western Australia. Linda Darrell, who played the Queen, is on the left. Photograph by Graeme Dalton, 18 May 1975.

There was a party in the theatre after the first night in Perth, so that when we came out of the stage door between one and two we found only one small girl of about ten waiting for an autograph. Her mother, who must have been a saint, was seated at the wheel of her car in the almost empty car-park. I had in the past seen Nureyev push angrily through crowds of autograph-hunters and refuse well-dressed ladies in restaurants or in the stalls of theatres, saying, 'If I sign your programme everyone else will follow and my evening will be ruined.' This time he obliged. The girl's reaction was immediate and unexpected: she burst into tears. Nureyev is the least sentimental of men: but as we walked away he began talking rapidly about his youth at Ufa on the western slopes of the Ural Mountains which divide European from Asian Russia. 'I used to hang around outside the theatre, trying to beg the price of a ticket from people in the street.'

Even before I went to look over the Entertainments Centre on the morning after my arrival at Perth I had visited the Art Gallery, where I was greeted by Epstein's bronze of the black girl, Lydia. A temporary show of drawings by West Australian artists prompted me to ask the Exhibitions Officer whether I could not lure one or two of these, whose work I liked, to draw dancers at the theatre. I was thinking I might get some good illustrations for my articles. Two artists who turned up, and for whom I arranged tickets, were annoyed by Rudolf's refusal to pose, but one of them sent along a tall, persuasive young man with long dark hair and a Che Guevara moustache, who said he was working on pictures of 'the drag scene' in Perth and who seemed ready to brave the dressing-rooms. Sam Abercromby not only drew extremely well, he had a knack for getting likenesses.

It had never occurred to me in England that I should go to *The Sleeping Beauty* almost every night in Australia, but I became involved with the company and anxious to see them appreciated; and I found I had turned into a regular Stage-

Door Johnny, or the follower of a football team. Nureyev's production was so richly wrought that I enjoyed studying it, and watching its effect on the Australians.

One of Nureyev's happy ideas had been to restore the music of the Sarabande, which we in England were used to hearing in the Hunting Scene, to the beginning of the last act and to use it for a *ballet de cour*. These formal spectacles, such as Gissey or Berain used to design for the young Louis XIV, and in which *le roi soleil* himself loved to dance, were known to us only from old prints, and had always appeared tedious to me. Yet when the curtain rose in silence on a ruddy tableau of the court, led by the tall King with his tumbling mane of feathers, poised to tread a solemn measure, I caught my breath. The minimal movements of Donald Barclay and his Queen, so carefully rehearsed by Rudolf, who had even prepared himself by reading Saint-Simon, gave me a shuddering recognition of the awe inspired by absolute monarchy. The towering men in their high heels executed no movement more difficult than a *changement de pieds*; and as the Royal couple later passed down a diagonal of courtiers, the ladies sank backwards into the arms of their cavaliers in a ceremonial swoon. After this short stilted ritual, Georgiadis's red, black, brown and gold picture was invaded by the pale blue and silver river of dancers for the *polacca*. (Rudolf explained to me that he had meant these to stand for youth succeeding age, or spring following winter.) By thought, care and willpower Nureyev had turned Festival Ballet, then directed by Beryl Grey, into something grander than it had ever been before.

On the last night in Perth I got to the Entertainments Centre early, watched cars converging, and looked across the railway to a little park where I guessed an old aboriginal in a feathered cap, whom I had dubbed in my mind the (dis-possessed) King of Australia, was sitting beneath a Moreton Bay fig-tree, while his subjects begged drink-money from the passers-by. Michael Edgley had told me that Roe Street, which ran parallel to the other side of the railway, had once been famous for its brothels: but the nymphs had departed. Backstage, Linda Darrell, a miner's daughter from Durham, who played the Queen as to the manner born, had nobly donned her last-act costume and feathers, to pose for Sam Abercromby. His drawing-board was propped against a clothes basket. I slipped out silently; and found myself alone on the stage from which, for a week, there had irradiated an unfamiliar vision of the European past. I climbed Nico's staircase, the mobile backbone of the production. At the top, on a crude, unpainted shelf contrived behind the baroque 'marble', the infant Aurora in her portable cradle was stowed away until needed. Looking over the Versailles balustrade, I saw below me that evening's living, grown-up Aurora, Eva Evdokimova, 'at the still centre of the turning world', clutching the architecture as she practised *ronds de jambe*.

At the end of the evening everyone was delighted with Sam's drawings of Linda, of Donald as the King and of Terry Hayworth as Catalabutte. A little bearded and spectacled sculptor called Robert Hitchcock, who had already made a wax model of Rudolf suspended in the air in a turning *manège*, appeared with a second sculpture showing the preparation for a *pirouette*, which he had worked on all day after 'the happiest night of my life'. Michael Edgley was as struck as I was by the way Robert had brought off the former difficult pose, and he promised him a free air passage to Melbourne in exchange for a cast of the eventual bronze. Thinking of the Theatre Museum, I offered $200 expenses (about £120 or US $290). I also undertook to pay Sam Abercromby's expenses, so that he could make more drawings, if Michael could squeeze him on the plane next morning. I found Rudolf, who was to fly on ahead of us that night, bent over his foot bandage, looking white and pinched. He asked, 'Do you want to see *Godfather 2* in Melbourne at 6.45 tomorrow?' 'Love to.' 'OK.'

Old Melbourne, in contrast to the expansive garden city

of new-rich Perth, had a monumental centre, and looked to me like a cross between Paris and Glasgow; while the Windsor Hotel on a Sunday was my idea of an Anglo-Indian club from which the *sahibs* had been urgently summoned to a punitive expedition in the hills. The Forum Cinema, however, was a more incredible relic of the aspirations of the twenties and thirties than any surviving movie-house in England, not excepting the Granada, Tooting – one of many people's palaces which adventurous Sidney Bernstein had so surprisingly commissioned Komisarjevsky to design – or the subaqueous dream world of the New Victoria, with its effulgent stalactites (E. Walmsley-Lewis, 1930), where Festival Ballet sometimes held their winter season. Outside, the architecture of Melbourne's Forum was Moghul, with a clock that told Mecca Mean Time; inside, there were domed Greek temples with statues flanking the stage, and the intervals were heralded by the dawning over our heads of a Milky Way. Festival Ballet performed in another cinema in the suburb of St Kilda, next to Luna Park and backing on the sea. The front-of-house was amusing, with sweeping staircases (on one of which a dog slept permanently); and on the Chinese-Plantagenet-Commedia dell'Arte landings a few tapestry thrones were drawn up to flickering electric logs. Backstage, on the other hand, was hell. People were almost changing in the sea. To walk down the narrow passage off which the dressing-rooms opened, with dancers bulging out of the doors at you, was like running the gauntlet in the brothel quarter of Marrakesh.

My friend Bill Lieberman from the Museum of Modern Art in New York had staged a spectacular exhibition 'Manet to Matisse' in the Art Gallery of Victoria. He was also busy planning for his museum a big show of Fred Williams, whose epic empty landscapes were a revelation to me, and of whom no one in slow-coach England had at that time heard. I was driven out to lunch in the country with Pam Vestey, the widow of a fellow-Scots Guardsman, who turned out to be

Melba's grand-daughter and produced all the great singer's stage costumes, made by Worth, from a cupboard.

On Saturday night our stage director, David Mogridge, had to repeat the ghastly miracle he had performed once already in Perth, of moving the company's cumbersome sets and costumes from the theatre, flying them on to our next city – in this case Adelaide – and setting them up before the company arrived to rehearse on the Monday morning. I was in Nureyev's small dressing-room, which he shared with Patrice Bart and Paul Clarke, after the show. The whole move was held up because the backstage passage and the space outside the stage door of the Palais Theatre were blocked by autograph hunters. The trunks on wheels could not be got out. David was imploring Rudolf to sign programmes and disperse the crowd: but Rudolf was preoccupied in doing a good deed. At every city a number of children from local drama or ballet schools were engaged and rehearsed to walk in certain simple processions, to spread out the Queen's train or to be taunted by the Witch's monsters. Rudolf had noticed one of the Melbourne boys taking a class with the company, and thought he had talent. I too had observed his interesting egg-like face, topped with an elfin bonnet: he was of Danish descent. There he stood with his mother while Rudolf composed a letter to Stanley Williams, another Dane, who taught at the School of American Ballet in New York. David Mogridge pleaded in vain. Rudolf (who never wrote letters, and from whom I had never received so much as a postcard) was determined to get his spelling and English right. The boy's mother said she thought her son was too young to leave home. I said that the sooner he had the best teachers the better. Rudolf discarded his first draft and began again. 'Scholarship' was spelt correctly at last; the letter was finished – 'Love, Rudolf'; mother and son departed; a hundred autographs were bestowed; trunks were wheeled down the corridor; *The Sleeping Beauty* set off for Adelaide; we went to supper.

Because I had to be in Venice on a certain day to put the final touches to an exhibition of Diaghilev designs and costumes I had rashly undertaken to arrange at very short notice, I planned to leave Sydney after the opening night. In order to spend five nights there and see the sights, I decided to stay only four nights in Adelaide. This delectable city, ringed by leafy boulevards, still retained its original plan of 1836. From its centre straight streets ran out towards the surrounding hills, on which *vignerons* of German origin, such as my friend David Wynn, had their vineyards and made delicious wine. On the banks of the Torrens river stood the fine new theatre, where the ballet was to perform: its airy surrounding galleries were adorned with big paintings by Sidney Nolan and Fred Williams. My impression of this community was that its members passed their Firbankian lives in providing entertainment for their art-loving Premier, Don Dunstan. This charming gentleman, an admirer of Nureyev's, invited him and myself to a dinner *à trois* at Ayers House in a handsome and comparatively ancient (1859) ballroom for official entertaining (which made me feel like La Périchole, a Viceroy's mistress); and he won my heart when I arrived at his home for a supper cooked by himself because he had one of my favourite songs on his record-player, 'La Captive' by Berlioz, to words of Victor Hugo. My big moment of hysterical suspense in Adelaide came when a lady, recording live an interview with Rudolf, asked him, 'When you are not working, what do you like doing best?' The answer could not be 'eating' or 'sleeping'.

Being abroad always gives me a sense of unreality which makes me spend too much money and believe I can get away with anything. The discovery of Australia, whose landscape, cities and people I liked so much, certainly went to my head. When I became over-expansive and raved at dinner, Rudolf used to smile and pronounce the words 'Dickybuckle Star!' (This was the name of a newspaper-pamphlet, two numbers of which I had published at the time of my Great Madness in

1971.) Indeed, my intoxication with the possibilities of Australia, the kindness with which I was entertained and the brief chance to bask in Nureyev's reflected glory had over-excited me. Both in Melbourne and Sydney I found flowers from old friends waiting for me; and the girls behind the desks at the Adelaide and Sydney hotels roared with laughter every time I opened my mouth. When I am feeling on top of the world I have too many good ideas which are not good enough, and think up too many jokes which are not funny.

The first article I sent to the *Sunday Times* from Sydney brought a telegram from my literary editor Jack Lambert: 'Personal touch welcome but most of material so far sent totally unusable . . .' I had already discovered how slow the post was between England and Australia, and had trouble in telephoning; and I was struck by the impossibility of ex-plaining what I was leading up to in my second piece, or of discussing acceptable modifications. I also rebelled against Lambert's intransigence, for I had experienced how, after a good lunch (and probably because he would like to have been sleeping it off, just as I should) he tended to vent his temper on colleagues. He had once, just as I was going in to a crucial meeting of the Friends of the Museum of Performing Arts, rung me up at the Arts Council to abuse me for writing too little copy to fill my space; and as I always dreaded these meetings dominated by the cynical John Pope-Hennessy and by Arnold Goodman, who never read my brief until he was seated at the table, Jack might well have thrown me off balance and prevented the foundation of the Theatre Museum. I cabled that unless my piece was printed uncut and unchanged I should resign from the *Sunday Times*. This was idiotic; and rereading today the manuscript of my article, with its references to Michael Edgley's wardrobe and Sam Aber-cromby's cat, I realize that Jack Lambert had a point: but like many foolish actions my resignation was a blessing in more ways than one. It was high time I gave up writing ballet criticism for ever.

Before flying off to Italy, I saw the Sydney Opera House, which had landed with a beating of wings beside the bay; I fell in love with the city; I was given an Yves Saint-Laurent tie in the middle of lunch by the divine Jeni Edgley's mother; I advanced the sculptor Robert Hitchcock £750 (about $1790) on account for his sculptures, of which by this time there were six; I had a row with Sam Abercromby and sent him back to Perth, but kept a pile of his drawings; I suffered a fit of remorse for having got above myself and took communion in the Cathedral, which had fragments of stone from Iona, Salisbury and the Houses of Parliament let into its walls; and I gave the usual interviews. At the Ballet's opening night at the Capitol, another quaint cinema decked with statues of Venus, Augustus, Antinous and Meleager, the stage was too narrow to hold the set and too shallow to allow for proper lighting. Beryl Grey and I sat with the Governor-General and Lady Kerr, and I spent much of the evening explaining what *should* be happening and extolling the genius of Nureyev. I was all the angrier, afterwards, when Rudolf broke one of Robert Hitchcock's statuettes. My farewell dinner, held in a flamboyant Chinese restaurant, was much the best meal I ate in Australia, but when I rebuked Rudolf for his iconoclasm he flung a plate of delicious food at my head and rushed from the room, followed by Michael Edgley. Shortly after this I bade farewell to Jeni (whom I still love, though I have never seen her since), to Beryl, who had been so hospitable and patient with my excesses and who still had a few of Nureyev's prawns clinging to her immaculate *coiffure*, to Patricia Ruanne, who cried a little, and to Paul Clarke, one of the kindest and funniest – as well as prettiest – boys I have ever known, and who died during an operation without my ever setting eyes on him again. I had to pack, but I also had an exciting date with someone who never turned up.

My break with Rudolf was soon mended (on the stage of Covent Garden on 4 December, to be exact); and a year or so later I told him how my Australian euphoria had met with retribution. In response to an urgent cable from the sculptor Hitchcock, I had sent him, with the permission of the Bank of England, a further thousand pounds. Rudolf had always maintained that I over-rated these rapidly modelled sketches, and that only the first was good. The BBC ran a weekly radio programme at the time called *The Arts Worldwide*. I was writing at my cottage before lunch on 7 October 1975, when I heard Hitchcock in Australia being interviewed about his Nureyev sculptures. He described how I had admired and subsidized them; and how he was about to have an operation on his eyes. If this was not successful he would at least have achieved *something*. That something, I thought, belonged to me: but although I wrote and telegraphed not only to Robert Hitchcock but to everyone in Australia who might be able to trace him, I heard no further word from the sculptor. I never saw him, his works or my money again. When I told Rudolf this in New York he clapped his hand to his mouth with an expression of fiendish glee.

On the morning of my arrival in Rome from Sydney, I ascertained that there were three flights a day to Venice, but after being told that I had missed two because the planes were full up, I realized – for I had been sitting in solitude by the correct gate – that the airport authorities were lying: if they had not gathered enough passengers to make a flight worthwhile they cancelled it. It was Wednesday, and my exhibition was due to open on the Saturday evening, so the situation was serious. I had not a penny of Italian money on me, but I took a taxi for Venice. I stopped when we were nearing our destination to telephone Sir Ashley Clarke and ask him to meet me with the equivalent of £150 (about $360). Slightly surprised, he did as I asked. My action had not been as mad as it appeared, for when I arrived in the evening at the Palazzo Grassi, although David, back in England, had worked assiduously at collecting exhibits and perfecting my catalogue (which was printed on the island of the Armenian monks), although Pip Dyer and others were slaving in an attic studio and although the Picasso curtain was hanging in the covered courtyard, looking superb, I found that the remaining eleven huge and splendid rooms were completely empty. I had three days to rig up some sort of show.

On 15 June, the day my exhibition, 'Omaggio ai Disegnatori di Diaghilev', was open to the public, the *Sunday Times* printed a garbled version of my Australian article, together with a pointless drawing of a kangaroo in ballet shoes. I deliberately refrained from replying to the kind and conciliatory telegrams with which my friend and sub-editor John Whitley tried to stop me from taking an irrevocable step. I stuck to my ultimatum and considered that my engagement with that admirable newspaper was at an end.

My exhibition was part of a dance festival, and once I had done my damnedest, I stayed on to see ballets by some of the companies who performed not only in La Fenice, but in the pretty open-air theatre on the island of San Giorgio Maggiore and on a vast stage erected in the Piazza San Marco. A number of old friends were in Venice: Irina Baronova, Yvette Chauviré, Rosella Hightower, Maina Gielgud, Roland Petit and the Ballet Rambert. I noticed that Maurice Béjart was regarded as the King of European Dance: the rest were nowhere.

On the scorching afternoon of 24 June, St John the Baptist's Day, I walked back from watching Béjart give a class in one of the Biennale pavilions in the Public Gardens, and arrived thirsty at Florian's in the Piazza San Marco at about five. The square was deserted except for some dancers rehearsing on the stage at the western end, surrounded by several thousand empty seats. I climbed under ropes and walked towards them. The young American John Neumeier was rehearsing his Hamburg Ballet for their performance of Mahler's Third Symphony that evening. He had liked my book on Nijinsky and he was pleased that I had come. After leaving him, I walked towards the passage that leads from the western extremity of the Piazza towards San Moisè, my parish church (which Ruskin thought so hideous), and to the Regina Hotel, where I was staying. I looked over my shoulder at John and his dancers. They were all staring after me. I had a sensation of riding my white horse away into the sunset at the end of a heroic movie, 'leaving the spring faint with Mercutio'.

Peggy Guggenheim was expecting me to take her to the Mahler Symphony. As I dressed I looked out of my window down on the Grand Canal. Waiters were laying tables for dinner on the terrace below. Ten minutes afterwards I heard a clatter of plates. The same waiters were stripping the tables and gazing anxiously at the eastern sky. They were just in time. A deluge fell on Venice. It was dramatic. I rang up Miss Guggenheim, for it was obvious that even if the weather improved no performance could take place: stage and seats would be sodden. Poor Neumeier! A *vaporetto* landed passengers at the Salute opposite. They dispersed helter-skelter in the drenching rain. Those who climbed the little hump-backed bridge towards the Abbey of San Gregorio were leaning at a desperate angle, just like Tintoretto's Alexandrians who fled up the steps of the arcaded piazza in his 'Removal of the Body of St Mark', scattered by super-natural thunder.

As it turned out I had not given up ballet for ever, because in November I agreed to undertake the long-dreaded task, which Nigel Gosling had for years been urging on me, of writing the life of Diaghilev.

CHAPTER 12

Dance of Death

As one grows older one is kept busy burying the dead. I usually accepted, if asked, to speak at the memorial services of my friends. I got rather a name for this, and discovered to my embarrassment that just as in Proust's novel Dr Dieulafoy was always sent for to sanctify deathbeds with the assurance that everything possible was being done, so people automatically exclaimed 'Send for Buckle!' when it was a question of enthusing over a corpse.

In the world of ballet, it struck me that directors, choreographers and dancers were over-eager to remind their forgetful public that they were still alive, if no longer kicking, by commemorating the foundation of their companies, or marking the milestones on their own path to the grave.

Marie Rambert was especially afflicted with anniversaries, both personal and professional (she lived to be ninety-four). The Mercury Theatre Trust, Mary Clarke and Peter Williams gave her a party for her eightieth birthday on 20 February 1968. This took place at the Arts Council, 4 St James's Square, the former home of Lord and Lady Astor. (It was very shortly after this that the Council moved to the house in Piccadilly where most of the meetings of our Friends of the Theatre Museum took place.) At the southern end of the gilded drawing-room there had been erected a platform on which Mim would be honoured and perhaps turn cartwheels.

A number of Diaghilev's old stagers were there, some of whom were seeing each other for the last time: Karsavina, Sokolova, Grigoriev, Tchernicheva and de Valois. Then there were Phyllis Bedells, who among 'English' non-Diaghilev dancers had been second only to the Danish-born Adeline Genée; as well as de Basil's ballerina Irina Baronova, whom I had adored since the thirties, and whose husband, Cecil Tennant, had recently been killed in a motor accident.

Mme Karsavina spoke in praise of Mim: and Mim said how pleased she was to have become British. In gratitude for all England had given her – including Ashley Dukes, her late husband – she presented her famous and very valuable collection of Romantic Ballet prints and music titles to the Victoria and Albert Museum. During the applause which followed this announcement, it was observed that Mim's elder daughter and son-in-law, Angela and David Ellis, were not sharing in the nation's gratitude. I was standing beside Ninette de Valois, and as she watched the two old ladies on the platform with a kind of baleful fascination, she murmured, 'It's very curious. About fifty years ago, Karsavina was acknowledged as one of the most beautiful women in the world, and Rambert was quite plain. Now, they seem to have changed places.' It was true. Mim had a fine head (which Astrid Zydower was shortly to sculpt); whereas Mme Karsavina, beneath the tight bluish curls of her wig, was puffy and wrinkled and the famous eyes were almost hidden by dome-like lids.

I gave Lydia Sokolova a lift back to Charing Cross Station. Next morning she wrote to thank me. The civility was typical: so was the humanity of her letter. There was something golden about Sokolova's character. Ancient feuds, rivalries and mis-representations were forgotten. She had looked round at her old colleagues and had seen good in them all. 'How Grigoriev rallied when he found himself amongst his own environment was nothing short of miraculous. As I told you, when I met him downstairs I was horrified . . . Tamara with a knee full of fluid. Ninette I did not know had had an awful accident. Kathleen Gordon [of the Royal Academy of Dancing] with a leg like a lamp-post, with torn

303

ligaments. Irina, trying – poor sweet – to surmount her ghastly tragedy. They were all so courageous and brave, and then, shining superbly over it all, Mim. Sweet and gentle, mellowed, after bullying everybody for years . . .'

The other Lydia and I had drifted apart. One day in the mid-sixties, anticipating a visit to the opera at Glyndebourne, I rang her up three or four days in advance to say that I would stay the night with my cousin Violet in Alfriston if she would like me to lunch with her on the following day. 'Can't say. Too far ahead,' Lopoukhova almost snapped. I don't know if she had crossed me off her list or if she had reached the point of finding all visits a nuisance. I felt a little hurt, but it was soon after this that she went into a nursing home for good.

From the time of Mim's birthday party in 1968 Mme Karsavina was increasingly unwell, and she found it hard to be cheerful. Yet, in her aristocratic way, she disdained to ask for pity. She admitted to taking a benzedrine pill every morning – 'You know, purple hearts' – to help her face the day; but she minimized her predicament: 'There's nothing I lack except time, health and spirits.' Karsavina had an operation on her eyelids, which 'kept closing', and treatment for her bad leg. Then a lorry knocked down part of the low wall of her front garden. The roof gave trouble. There was tubular scaffolding in the Dutch Room and in her bedroom in case the ceiling fell down. 'It is like sleeping in a grotesque four-poster bed.' 1969, she said, had been 'a bad year' for her. It was, however, during this bad year that I saw more of her, and talked to her more often on the telephone, than during any other. On a portable tape-recorder-cum-record player which John Taras had given me, and which she greatly admired, I played her passages of *Carnaval* and *Scheherazade*, while she explained to me what had happened at which point in the music. Seated in the Dutch Room, she demonstrated some of the *ports de bras* of her *variation* in the *pas de trois* from *Le Pavillon d'Armide* with Nijinsky and Baldina which had first conquered Paris in 1909. She held her arms now over her head, now in a pretty loop over her extended front leg, leaning forward and looking down at her hands without inclining her head, but with a delicate eighteenth-century smile and eyebrows raised in an *accent circonflexe*. When she was 'dancing' her beauty returned.

An odd thing happened when I flew out in April 1971 to Stravinsky's funeral in Venice. With two friends I entered the church of SS Giovanni e Paolo by a side door, expecting to take my chance like other strangers and stand with the crowd. A tall man I had never set eyes on before loomed up before me and asked, 'Are you Richard Buckle?' He had not only guessed that 'that' was what I should look like, but felt sure I should come to the funeral (which I had decided to do on an impulse only the day before) and had kept a seat for me in the second row of the choir. He was Brendan Fitzgerald, the Rome correspondent of an American paper. We faced the Stravinsky family across the catafalque, which was surrounded by towering municipal wreaths. Some English daffodils I laid on the floor before it were removed by the police. While Robert Craft conducted 'Requiem Canticles' I made two bad drawings. Afterwards, from my friends' motor launch, I made another drawing of the coffin landing from its gondola at the island of San Michele, to be laid near that of Diaghilev: but we did not go ashore. It is curious that although I visited the graves of Diaghilev's friends Tchaikovsky and Rimsky-Korsakov at the Alexander Nevsky monastery in Leningrad, I have never seen Diaghilev's own. Perhaps the idea of Lifar being photographed beside it annually on 19 August put me off.

Two years later Nik, Karsavina's son, decided that it was no longer safe for her to live in Frognal without supervision, and he arranged for her to move to a nursing home. The Hampstead house and most of its contents were to be sold. Before the great dispersal Mme Karsavina remembered the Theatre Museum. On Tuesday, 8 January 1974 I was summoned to Frognal for a last visit. I was due at noon, but the tube was quicker than usual; I arrived early and walked to the very summit of Hampstead, where so many 'shining ones' had dwelt in plain brick palaces amid blossoming trees – at Admiral's House, Sir George Gilbert Scott, designer of my favourite fantastic St Pancras Hotel, and at Upper Terrace House, Kenneth Clark, whose writings on art had enhanced my life. I never stood on the top of Hampstead without thinking of John Keats who had heard the nightingale a little lower down to the east, in the Vale of Health, or of John Constable who had sketched every view in every light, and who was buried in St John's Churchyard just behind Mme Karsavina's house. I walked down Frognal to the home of my friend, which I thought must also become in time the goal of pilgrims.

Over the last twenty years I had visited 108 Frognal at all hours, in all seasons, in all weathers. In the cold light of day the late Victorian flats, Frognal Mansions, which blocked Karsavina's view on the other side of the road, were not beautiful, and yet the fact that they rose up like an irregular cliff and had to be approached by ramps and flights of steps, gave them an eccentric charm, as if a suburban Neuschwanstein. Karsavina made friends with Kathleen Ferrier when she lived there (until a few months before her death in 1953), and used to hear the strains of Gluck and Mahler floating from the windows. On winter nights, when I went upstairs to close the shutters at No. 108, the lighted windows of Frognal Mansions, seen through a black filigree of trees, had inspired in me romantic musings. On summer afternoons the sun would slant through the yellow curtains of Karsavina's drawing-room on to paler yellow walls: two yellow marbled columns held candelabra (later stolen). There were two tall engraved Venetian mirrors between the western windows. On the chimney-piece reclined a pair of Staffordshire figures, of which the female was based, like the nymph in the grotto at Stourhead, on the Vatican 'Cleopatra' or

'Ariadne'. 'Antony and Cleopatra,' I had said. 'No, Neptune and – who was Neptune's wife?' (Mme Karsavina had her own mythology, so I didn't argue.) 'Amphitrite.' Another much bigger Staffordshire group stood in the little panelled Dutch Room, which was green, with crimson curtains, and took its name from a blackened landscape over the fireplace. This pottery sculpture by Enoch Wood was intended as Cupid and Psyche, but Karsavina insisted that it was Daphnis and Chloë. In her study, her huge desk was *retour d'Egypte*: this had been an exceptional extravagance, bought for Benjie on the Quai Voltaire. Over it hung Karsavina's portrait by Oswald Birley, which had once been full-length, but which the artist had compliantly cut down to an oval at his sitter's request. If I went to telephone in the dressing-room next to Mme Karsavina's bedroom, I found hanging there Benois' design for the autumnal décor of the first act of *Giselle*, which he must have given her when she danced the old ballet with Nijinsky at the Paris Opéra in 1910, as well as the design by Bakst for her chaste white ball gown in *Le Spectre de la rose*, which was first presented at the Théâtre de Monte Carlo in the following year. If I had lingered with Mme Karsavina over tea until the 'rush hour', the sound of expensive cars changing gear in Frognal for their final climb, instead of annoying me, gave me a luxurious feeling of being at least on the higher slopes of Olympus, to whose summit were bound these god-like drivers, impatient for the cock-tails of Ganymede and supper at their golden tables.

The door was opened, on the day of my farewell visit, by a little woman I had never set eyes on before. Indeed, every-thing about the occasion was strange. While this lady whis-pered excitedly to me in the hall about the gift which was about to be bestowed, I gazed at the painted and gilded figure of St Florian (bought in Salzburg for fifty shillings). Its baroque pose, according to Karsavina, was that of Fokine at the moment of his transformation by a theatrical trick from Vicomte René de Beaugency into Rinaldo, beloved of

Armida. The old staircase creaked as a tall smiling Negro came down and said good morning. Who he was or why he was there I have never known. I remembered black Hannibal, Pushkin's ancestor, and the court *Araps* who stood outside the doors of the Emperor's apartments at the Winter Palace and at Tsarskoe Selo, and whom Bakst had included, dressed in amazing turbans, in *The Sleeping Princess*.

My princess was awake but I thought a little drowsy, and awaiting me in the study. She had prepared herself for the interview, but she no longer sat as erect as when Benjie Bruce had drawn her in her flat overlooking the Kriukov Canal in St Petersburg: in fact she looked slightly mummified, and her eyelids were heavy. 'Brightness falls from the air,/ Dust hath closed Helen's eye.' Here sat the former toast of Europe. (Kenneth Clark, who called her 'the idol of my youth', would later include her photograph, along with the Venuses of Botticelli, Titian and Tiepolo, in his book *Feminine Beauty*.) Few women had been so adored but, as she once assured me, 'I was virtuous.' 'Fokine asked me to run away with him . . . He never kissed me.' Even Diaghilev had been smitten – if I was to believe what Karsavina liked to believe. In Paris, in 1909, he had exclaimed, 'I am in love like a boy of eighteen.' In Brussels, in 1910, he told her, 'Tata, I am hopelessly in love.' 'Who with?' 'She doesn't care for me any more than for the Emperor of China.' But in Rome, in 1911, when he took her and Nijinsky driving in the spring sunshine to see the sights, he had admitted, 'I should make a very bad husband – but a very good father.'

My present, wrapped in tissue paper, was on the table beside Mme Karsavina. It was a fan. The sticks were blond tortoise-shell, the material chocolate-brown net decorated with glittering arabesques and lyres cut from foil. Taglioni had carried it on the stage when she appeared in Russia in the late 1830s; and her grandson, Comte Gilbert de Voisins, an ardent admirer of Karsavina's from 1909 onwards, had made her a present of it after the first performance of *Petrushka* at the Châtelet on 13 June 1911.

I walked all the way back to Covent Garden with the historic fan, which now belonged to England, in my pocket.

Lydia Sokolova died in February 1974. In her last letter to me she had written something kind, as so often before, about an article of mine in the *Sunday Times*. It was in that paper that I wrote her obituary. I spoke at Lydia's Memorial Service at St Martin-in-the-Fields. Lydia left me in her will the manuscripts of our book, which contained much unused material, and the original plaster cast of Nijinsky's head. She also left me for the Theatre Museum the pear-shaped pearl ear-rings which Nijinsky had worn as the Golden Slave in *Scheherazade* before he was dismissed by Diaghilev, the castanets of Felix Fernandez who taught Massine his *farruca*, and the silver-framed photograph of Enrico Cecchetti which he had inscribed and given her as a 'prize for good work' in summer 1913.

Flowers meant a lot to Lydia Sokolova, and since she was not a pampered, *blasée* beauty she remembered the bouquets of time past. I should like to hang garlands of flowers on my memorial to her, but since it is a literary monument, my flowers will be ghostly ones, remembered by her and recorded in her own words.

In 1921, when Lydia was dancing *The Rite of Spring* on the cramping stage of the Prince's (now Shaftesbury) Theatre, Mrs Sickert sent her 'a trellis gate covered with white roses, which was so large that two ushers had to carry it on to the stage'. As it would not go into her dressing-room it stood for the rest of the evening on the stairs; when Lydia went to collect it at the end of the performance there were only two roses left. Then, towards the close of the 1926 London season Lydia was rushed for an operation to the Chelsea Hospital for Women. She had letters of sympathy from all over the country, including one addressed 'Lydia Sokolova, London', and Lord Rothermere sent so many immense bouquets and boxes of roses that they overflowed into every ward in the hospital. Usually – I think in memory of the kindness she had received at the time of her abortion in 1920, she took her superfluity of flowers to the Charing Cross Hospital.

This is my favourite bouquet story, as it appeared in our book.

[In 1927] Diaghilev told us that he intended reviving *L'Oiseau de feu*. This was a considerable undertaking as the ballet had not been given since 1921, when Massine had danced the Prince, while of those who had known the production in Fokine's day hardly anyone remained but Grigoriev, Tchernicheva, Kremnev and myself. We worked on the great ballet in Paris and tried to reconstruct it day by day. I felt it was a bit hard, now that I was a principal dancer, still to have to dance my old part as one of the twelve Princesses. Also, having recently recovered from my operation, I felt it would be wise to reserve my energy as much as possible for leading roles. I therefore asked Diaghilev during a rehearsal whether someone else could not be a Princess in my place . . . He was outwardly calm but inwardly furious. In front of everybody he told me I should consider it an honour to dance in his *corps de ballet*, which was only good because principal dancers took their turn to dance in it. He reminded me how Doubrovska danced with twenty-three others in *Le Lac des cygnes*, and how Tchernicheva was one of the Nurses in *Petroushka*. It was his right, he said, to decide which ballets I should dance, not mine; and there was a clause in the new contract I had signed the day before to that effect . . . By this time tears were pouring down my cheeks. There were two of us in the company whom Diaghilev could always make cry whenever he wished, Nijinska and myself . . .

So I was back in my old place as one of the Princesses, and although the production had changed I loved every minute of it. On the first night of the revival, *L'Oiseau de feu* was given as the middle ballet, following *Les Biches*. I noticed that there were several bouquets waiting for me;

and one, especially beautiful, was an enormous mass of pure white flowers. On the envelope pinned to it was written 'After *L'Oiseau de feu*'. I told Grigoriev that I would not have this outstanding bouquet handed to me while I stood in a group of the *corps de ballet*, and that I should like it after *Les Biches*. He said, 'It says on the envelope "After *The Firebird*" and you'll get it then.' Our discipline was severe even in such matters as this . . .

As we took our calls after *L'Oiseau de feu*, myself standing in the big semi-circle behind the principals, the enormous bouquet of white flowers was handed to me. I had a sensation of opera glasses being raised to every eye in the theatre, as the audience wondered what this girl in the background had done to be singled out with such flowers; and I longed for the curtain to stay down. The card inside the envelope was inscribed with the words:

Sokolova's 'old trouper' side made it possible to envisage her as a slightly comic secondary character in the saga of the Diaghilev Ballet: and some years later I began to ponder whether my close alliance with her over her autobiography, and the love I felt for her, might not have blinded me to certain absurdities and caused me to exaggerate the splendour of her artistry, which I could only celebrate at second hand. I decided to consult the two most sophisticated oracles of my acquaintance, both of whom had seen her often on the stage. I wrote to Boris Kochno, 'Was Sokolova sometimes ridiculous?' He replied, '*Sokolova n'était jamais ridicule.*' I asked Cecil Beaton, 'What was Sokolova really like?' He said, 'She was *wonderful*!'

Karsavina took up residence in a small nursing-home on the outskirts of Beaconsfield. The contents of 108 Frognal were sold at auction in May 1974. I bought the Staffordshire group by Enoch Wood, which Karsavina called 'Daphnis and Chloë'. I only once visited my old friend in her 'home', with John Drummond and Bob Lockyer, who drove me down; but Mary Clarke, the editor of the *Dancing Times* and Karsavina's close friend, thoughtfully organized a small fund to enable Dolly Watkins, a former theatrical dressmaker and the ballerina's devoted Maid of Honour in later years, to travel weekly to see her, across country by car, and I think this one regular visit, along with glimpses of her son and grand-children, was preferable to haphazard incursions of other admirers.

Kathleen Gordon of the Royal Academy of Dancing, which Karsavina had served as Vice-President up to 1955, sent out invitations to the latter's ninetieth birthday-party on 10 March 1975. About sixty people were asked. I was driven down by Nigel and Maude Gosling. The party was held near Karsavina's nursing-home in the Church Hall of St Michael and All Angels, so the night air above this unpretentious building was alive with beating wings.

Nothing could have been more commonplace than the interior of the hall. The Queen had lent no Mortlake tapestries after Raphael's cartoons, the Hermitage no urns of jasper or malachite; there were no festoons of orchids. A few paper chains had been left over from Christmas, the lights were harsh, and on the bare stage at the far end were stacked the birthday presents, bunches of well-meant gladiolus or chrysanthemum and bottles of forbidden vodka. Food and drink were of course served from trestle tables, and in the middle of the room, on a smaller table, stood the cake. Tamara Karsavina was seated in her wheel-chair in front of the stage. The only other two chairs in the room were placed on either side of her. I was amused to see who had gained possession of these, and wondered if there had been an

indecent rush. This thought made me look upon the party
in terms of a ballet – just such a bitter-sweet *divertissement* as
Boris Kochno might have devised, with Proustian under-
currents of rivalry, sadness and spite. I had missed the very
beginning, but I could imagine it: and as I drove back later to
London with the Goslings I invented names for the successive
'numbers' to amuse Nureyev, who was joining us for supper.

1 *Jockeying for position.* Which two ladies – for men were
obviously disqualified – were entitled to occupy the chairs
on either side of the great ballerina, to join her in a seated
pas de trois, as it were the two girls in white whom Fokine
had linked with Chiarina to circle like the Three Graces in
Schumann's *Carnaval*? I had always guessed that the sin of the
rebel angels was snobbery; that Lucifer was a kind of Duc
de Saint-Simon, obsessed with precedence and determined
to assert his right to be placed at dinner nearest to the throne
of God. I was sorry to have arrived too late for the skirmish-
ing, hand-to-hand fighting, mopping-up and consolidation.
Phyllis Bedells certainly had a claim, and three Dames of
the British Empire were present. (I had tried twice to have
Karsavina made a Dame: first, through Kenneth Clark, at
the time of the Diaghilev Exhibition; next, at the prompting
of Lady Gladwyn, through the agency of Lord Drogheda
and Lord Goodman.) Well, Rambert was the eldest – only
three years younger than Karsavina – and had known her
longer than anyone else in the room. Even if in 1913 she had
barely qualified for the *corps de ballet*, and was not particularly
close to Mme Karsavina, she had earned her place. (It
occurred to me that Mim was the only person present
besides Karsavina who had seen Nijinsky married in Buenos
Aires.) *She* sat on the right hand, and Dolly Watkins whom
Tamara loved, sat on the left. I was delighted to observe that
the fine Shetland shawl over Mme Karsavina's lap was
mauve-pink. I knew her favourite colour-scheme; and the
Victorian posy I had ordered and brought with me was

Three Dames of the British Empire drink a toast to the Queen of Shemakhan. Tamara Karsavina with Marie Rambert, Alicia Markova and Ninette de Valois. Photograph by G. B. L. Wilson.

composed of crimson, pink and purple flowers; the deep red rose in its centre being intended as a reference to the most celebrated of all *pas de deux*. Pat Dolin, who was dressed as a golf professional in a white coat and loud check trousers, had appointed himself unofficial Master of Ceremonies. When I kissed Mme Karsavina, he bellowed at her as if she were deaf, which she wasn't, and in case she did not know who I was, which she did, 'That was Richard Buckle, the critic of the *Sunday Times*.' Aside, to me, he murmured, 'She probably doesn't know who you are.' Dolly assured me that if she herself had not fallen ill in the previous year it might never have been necessary for Mme Karsavina to leave Frognal. Later in the evening, another old and cherished friend of Karsavina's, Grace Lovat Fraser, took Dolly's place. Her husband Claud had designed Karsavina's own ballet *Nursery Rhymes*; and Mrs Lovat Fraser, when still mourning his early death, had made some of the costumes for Diaghilev's *Sleeping Princess*.

2 *Spotting the Absentees*. I looked round to see whom I did and didn't know. I supposed that all the huge strange women with teeth were teachers of dancing. Nik Bruce, tall with grey side-whiskers, introduced me to his wife, whom I had seen only once at Frognal when the whole family lived under one roof. Next I met their Etonian son in his black school suit. He had a Bruce look: the set of his eyes in the oval face, like that of his father, his late grandfather and a cousin to whom I was also introduced was distinctive, but their dark colour was inherited from Mme Karsavina and the Byzantine emperors. I remembered Karsavina comparing his photograph with the miniature of Benjie as a boy, and telling me with amusement that he had coined the word 'loonigan'. I also remembered Peter Williams confiding that he was having difficulty in explaining to the Trustees of a charitable fund why Karsavina was in need of a pension, when she was paying her grandson's fees at Eton. Hadn't Peter been asked to the party? Perhaps his kind endeavours had been anonymous. Ninette de Valois, in a crisp scarlet organdie shirt and black skirt, was looking smart and pretty, and I told her so. Idzikovsky was as dapper and pleased with himself as when I had watched him teaching Edalji in the 1930s. Where was Arnold Haskell? He was having a pace-maker fitted to his heart. Markova, beneath an Antonine beehive of black hair, wore a plain dress to match. Her sister Doris was in waiting. But where was Margot? It was rumoured that she was on tour. So were Yehudi and Diana Menuhin. Rudolf had a rehearsal, and although he longed to come as soon as it was over, the Goslings had assured him that he would never find the way. He had sent a case of champagne. No critics, no press. But G. B. L. Wilson was, as ever, busily taking photographs. Mary Clarke told me afterwards of G. B.'s complaint that whichever way he turned Idzikovsky stood plumb in front of the camera. (Stas died in March 1977, and at his Memorial Service in St Paul's, Covent Garden, Tchaikovsky's Blue Bird *pas de deux* was played on the piano.) It was

315

surprising that Lifar had not got wind of the affair and flown from Paris. And where was Fred?

3 *Getting a speech in edgeways.* Certain dancers and choreographers have a mania for speech-making: perhaps it is natural that they should wish to break the rule of silence imposed on the stage. Ninette de Valois had a genuine gift for speaking impromptu and organizing her arguments, the exercise of which in committee had certainly contributed to her establishment of the Royal Ballet. Marie Rambert just liked baring her soul in public. To Lifar's love of the sound of his own voice I have already drawn attention. Dolin also liked to speak. On the other hand, Frederick Ashton, who enjoyed the incense of applause and was as ready as Pavlova to prolong his curtain calls, could not sleep for days before he had to make a speech, and shook with nerves. Yet it was Fred who was due to speak in praise of Tamara Karsavina at this birthday party, and he had not arrived. Kathleen Gordon convened a hasty conference. Nigel told me afterwards that he had suggested I should speak, but Rambert said No, it must be a dancer. It would be Dolin, after all; but first John Gielgud would improvize a few well-chosen words about his memories of Karsavina in younger and happier days, spoken with the tears which came so readily to his eyes. He told me that he and Arnold Haskell had played truant, when they were at Westminster School, to attend matinées of *The Sleeping Princess*. Their top-hats and tail-coats had made them conspicuous in the gallery. Dolin found an easy way out. He procured a sheaf of congratulatory telegrams and read them aloud. He began with the critics and official bodies; and ended what seemed a long time later with the Queen Mother. As Pat announced the august name, then paused and swept his gaze round the room with the commanding air of a town crier, I felt sure – perhaps wrongly – that Fred, who was very thick with the Queen Mother, had prompted the sending of this telegram; and it amused me to see Pat stealing

the show. As he finished reading each telegram he handed it to Kathleen Gordon, who received it with a dour expression. 'So wish we could have been with you. Maggie sends her love.' 'Ever so many congratulations and our heartfelt blessings.' 'Thinking of you with deep affection on this great day.' Even when signed Yehudi or Margot these good wishes became monotonous in the extreme. Banalities fluttered and fell in the alcoholic air, 'thick as autumnal leaves that strew the brooks in Vallombrosa'. Oh, *where* was Fred?

4 *The Cake*. Mme Karsavina was now seated in the centre of the room, facing her cake. A man I did not know began to light the ninety candles. This was a slow business, and Mme Karsavina stared fixedly at the spreading radiance as if reliving her long life year by year. Learning to walk; 'Fat Nannie'; first reading of Pushkin; Father's farewell performance; early dancing lessons . . . We had hardly reached her acceptance by the Imperial Ballet School when it became clear that without a church taper – and with match after match having to be laboriously struck and disposed of – the first candle might well have burnt out before the ninetieth was lit. I therefore procured a second box of matches and started on the other side of the cake. The crescendo of heat on the face of Phyllis Bedells, following a glass or two of champagne, made her hysterical. Cassandra-like she issued, every few seconds, bulletins of doom. 'You'll never do it!' 'Take care!' 'They're beginning to melt!' 'Look out! The cake's on fire!' But all the candles were lit; and we blew them out together. Karsavina cut the cake.

5 *Tempers are frayed: late arrival of Sir Fred*. Ninette kept asking Kathleen Gordon 'Where *are* they? There must have been a terrible accident.' Miss Gordon was indeed very annoyed. Maria St Just, who had driven down with John Gielgud, asked me if I knew Woizikovsky was dead. I said the Goslings had just told me so in the car. 'Did you ever hear any more from him after the last time we saw him?'

'No.' (That was over three years ago, and the poor man had been in need of money. In fact, after some doubt and embarrassment, I had tipped him £5.) 'Nor did I,' she said acidly, 'except for a short sarcastic note.' Ronnie Mahon, widower of Lydia Sokolova (who had lived for over ten years with Woizikovsky), was present at the party, accompanied by a tall, sweet-faced girl with short hair; and they told me they were going to be married. I confessed that I had seen them together arm-in-arm at Charing Cross Station and thought how happy they looked. So life went on. Ninette rushed at Nigel Gosling and began to abuse him for what he had written in the *Observer* about Kenneth MacMillan's *Four Seasons*. 'You can't dismiss a new ballet in a few lines like that. It's disgraceful.' (Nigel kept thinking it was me she should have been angry with.) Ninette always pronounced ballet 'bally'. Suddenly Fred Ashton appeared at the door with Michael Somes and Leslie Edwards. Kathleen later wrote to Mary Clarke, who showed me her letter, that 'Michael was so shattered my anger dissolved.' Michael had been driving, and as he got more and more lost, he and Leslie had talked in whispers for fear of upsetting Fred. They had gone almost to Reading. 'Fred, trembling as if with ague, asked, "What did the Dame say?"' We formed a circle once more as Ashton delivered his long-awaited eulogy. During this Pat Dolin ran round the outside of the group, making mischief. He could not get over the fact that he had never been knighted (presumably because he spent the war years in America), and found it hard to be civil about those, such as Rambert and Ashton, on whom honours had been bestowed.★ 'Do you see that?' he whispered. 'He's *reading* his speech! *Reading* his speech!'

6 *Exit of the Ballerina.* It had been a long evening for Mme Karsavina and the time had arrived for her to return to her nursing-home. Suddenly Keith Lester came into his own.

★ Anton Dolin was knighted in 1981.

Even before Ashton had supported Karsavina in *Les Sylphides* on the tiny stage of the Mercury Theatre in 1930, Keith had toured Europe as her partner. (In 1935 I had admired his ballet *David*, given by the Markova-Dolin Company, with décors by Bernard Meninsky and a curtain by Epstein.) Now he was principal teacher of the Royal Academy of Dancing. Still upright and handsome, though grizzled and limping, he seized the chance to be Karsavina's final cavalier. Taking possession of the handle of her wheel-chair, he propelled her towards the door. His expression was determined, even disdainful, as he looked neither to right nor left; and the crowd parted like the waters of the Red Sea as he gathered speed for a brilliant finish to the *coda*. 'Good-night ladies. Good-night, sweet ladies. Good-night. Good-night.'

Phyllis Bedells discovered that her mink coat had disappeared – and she had not paid the last instalment on the insurance. A very inferior waist-length coat was discovered on the back of the chair Grace Lovat Fraser had occupied. (After many telephone calls and taxi-rides on the following day an exchange was effected.) Maude Gosling told me on the way home that when she had wished Karsavina 'Many happy returns!' the reply came, 'Not *too* many!' There would, in fact, be three. My little bouquet had remained on Tamara Platonovna's lap throughout the evening. This may have been just because it was small and of the right colours: I chose to interpret a signal of love.

One thing was certain: Boris Kochno would outlive us all.

In 1961 I had received a startling letter from him. He told me of the existence of some fragmentary memoirs of Diaghilev, written on the Lido in 1928. These he had translated from Russian into French, and he suggested that I should put them into English and sell them to a London newspaper. Of course I was delighted at the idea.

The handing over of 'the papers' took on the character of a cloak-and-dagger romance. On 5 October 1961 I was to

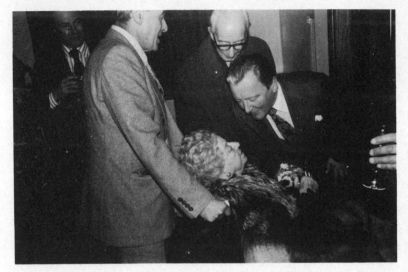

Last goodbye to Mme Karsavina. Leslie Edwards, Keith Lester, Tamara Karsavina, Dr Lawrence Heyman and the author. Photograph by G. B. L. Wilson, 10 March 1975.

take the train from Lunel, where I should be staying with the Hugos, to Marseille. At 7 p.m. I was to meet Boris at the Grand Hôtel de Noailles. This I did. He showed me the envelope containing the typescript of his French translation. I told him that if my English version met with approval I should employ an agent to sell – I hoped – three serials to a Sunday paper. We drove to dine with Comtesse Pastré, with whom he was staying at the Château de Montredon. I still had not seen Diaghilev's text; and when Boris drove me back into Marseille, we sat drinking at a café on the Cours Belsunce, where I was somewhat distracted by the beauty of the passers-by. I said that I supposed we should share the proceeds of the publication fifty-fifty. Boris said no: the money must be divided in three parts, mine, his and Diaghilev's. The two latter were his by right. When the time came to say goodnight, Boris could not bring himself to part with the precious envelope. I left empty-handed about one in the morning to console myself by a search for adventure. Boris said one should never look for adventure: one should wait till it came to one. I wandered the streets in vain; and as I returned to my hotel on the Vieux Port the only human being in sight, seated alone outside a deserted café, was Boris, waiting for adventure to come to him.

From my Diary:

> *Friday 6 October.* Noise awakes me about 4. Shut windows. Sleep till 9. Deluge. Walk along port and get wet. Wait at café in vain for Boris from 11 to 11.45. Despair about taxi. Boris arrives at my Hôtel Méditerranée 12.10. Taxi comes 12.15. Everything settled in the street at 12.16. Panic about 12.30 train – traffic block and deluge. Catch train, which turns out to be 12.37. Excellent lunch. Arrive Lunel 3.10. Met by Lauretta and Joy [Murchie]. Sleep. Walk. Jean and three kids back from dentist at Albi for dinner.

I had not, however, been entrusted with the sacred typescript. It arrived in England on 3 December. The translation was easy, but a lot of rearrangement and editing were necessary. The text dealt mostly with Diaghilev's operatic ventures: there was disappointingly little about the Ballet. An agent sold an abridgement of my translation to the *Sunday Telegraph* for £1000. This was never published. However, the material was of value to me in later years.

In 1966 when Boris and I had both been staying with the Hugos at Fourques for Easter, I had a row with him. He had been so drunk that conversation became impossible – not only with him but, because of his growled interjections, with anyone else in his presence. After dinner a taxi would fetch him to Lunel, where he drank in a café, surrounded by the local boys (but he was not attracted by the young); then, when the taxi brought him back around midnight, I would hear him crashing into the furniture. Through the wall and throughout the night I listened to terrible altercations and imagined that Boris's servant Jean was fighting to remove the brandy. Boris did not like it when I complained. If some project relating to Diaghilev was mentioned he would grind out the challenge: '*C'est moi qui écrirai la vie de Diaghilev. Personne sauf moi ne connait rien sur Diaghilev.*' Yet, on Easter Day, when I offered him a Victorian moustache-cup – for he had taken to wearing a long Mongol moustache – he was touched and said no one had given him a present since the death of Bérard.

Every New Year Boris sent me a card, sometimes rainbow-inked, with greetings in his fantastic calligraphy. Juliet Duff had told me Cocteau compared this to 'forged bank-notes'. Boris's handsome *Le Ballet*, with cover by Matisse and lithograph by Picasso, produced in 1954, had been suc-ceeded in 1970 by *Les Ballets Russes de Serge Diaghilev*, the later chapters of which, in particular, were of great help to me in my researches. These were based on the documents Boris had salvaged from the wreck after Diaghilev's death. I had my eye on these documents for our future Theatre Museum, as well as on the designs and portraits which hung on the walls of Kochno's successive flats and accumulated in his portfolios. As I have related, I kept him regularly informed of the slow progress of my plans to found the Museum. It was at the opening party of the very imperfect exhibition of Diaghilev designs and costumes which I arranged for Venice in the summer of 1975, that the witch-like Irène Lidova rushed at me screeching '*Boris a tout vendu!*' I could have killed her. In fact, the French State had made Boris an offer he could not refuse; and all the Diaghilev material passed to the Bibliothèque Nationale, and was housed in the Musée de l'Opéra.

In November 1975, when I was discussing with George Weidenfeld the possibility of writing a life of Diaghilev, I was myself going through a phase of drunkenness and depression, and John Taras whisked me off to Paris in an attempt to cheer me up. At the preview of a small exhibition of Jean Hugo's stage designs at the Galerie Lucie Weill, near the Pont des Arts, I ran into Boris Kochno. He now looked like Genghis Khan, with a head like Moussorgsky's Bare Mountain: but he had exercised his considerable will-power and given up alcohol. It was as if Casanova had become a monk. I told him about the project for the biography, and asked him if he would mind my writing it. He said he would not, and promised to help me. His help turned out to be crucial.

In view of Boris's evident indestructibility I was astounded, a week after this encounter in Paris, when Joy Murchie, my old friend from the days of war-time Roman bacchanals, rang me up in London to say that Boris was dead. 'He can't be! I saw him last Saturday.' 'Oh yes, I've just heard from Mike, the friend with whom we both stay on Lake Garda.' I was horrified, and at once began telephoning Lauretta in the south, to ask if she could find out if the news was true. I hesitated to ring Boris's house. I began to compose a memorial tribute. When the rumour was proved false – it was the choreographer Boris Kniaseff who had died – I wrote to Boris that he had just missed enjoying one of the rarest of pleasures, that of reading his own obituary.

My own health was deteriorating. For the first time in my life I became asthmatic and bronchial. I vomited constantly and found it hard to sleep. As mentioned, I had broken my left thigh in September 1974, and although this mended and caused no trouble for a year and a half it then showed signs of developing complications. The story of my Great Depressions belongs elsewhere. Shortly after coming out of a so-called 'psychiatric hospital' in autumn 1976 I slipped on the staircase at Henrietta Street and broke my left arm. Over Christmas I was too fat to do up my trousers, and my mother battled in vain. I had given up hard liquor, but when I went to Paris in February 1977 to talk to Boris about Diaghilev I stopped at a café opposite Saint-Eustache to drink a Dubonnet.

Boris lived in a mysterious little house near what had once been Les Halles, the vast markets built under Napoleon III.

These had lately been demolished, and their whole area, as big as four football grounds, was surrounded by wooden screens, behind which orgies of excavation were taking place. There was still, however, a busy street market in the rue de Montorgeuil, along which it was necessary to pass in order to reach the lane where my friend had his hermitage. In the time of the Valois kings this area, just inside the city walls, had been noted for its whore-houses. When Boris, with his extraordinary ingenuity, cunning and luck, had discovered the house in 1962, it had been '*une remise à diables*', a store for the market porters' hand-carts, with an earth floor. He had transformed the tumbledown building into a cosy habitation, and filled it with such a miscellany of treasures that it reminded me of something in Balzac or Dickens. The ground-floor room, now tiled, where we usually worked together was intended solely for the reception of visitors: I don't think Boris ever used it when he was alone. We would sit on either side of a round grey marble table loaded with what he called his 'Stone Age' – a Roman tragic mask, a gold medal set in a lump of uncut amethyst, a Pharaoh's hand in granite, a stolen fragment of the Parthenon and a little painted pottery ram's head by Picasso – all presided over by the bust of a grotesquely grinning eighteenth-century faun. The sketch of a man's head by Géricault, bought at the Marché aux Puces for twenty francs, stood on an easel, and the walls were hung higgledy-piggledy with small gouaches and drawings by Bérard, Hugo, Mirò, Picasso and Bakst. There were also a pencil drawing of a reclining male nude by Despiau and a little pen-and-ink Beardsley: and I was not sure which of these two I coveted more than anything in Paris outside the Louvre.

Our first talk about my early chapters, which Boris read with care, lasted from twelve-thirty until five, and was not interrupted by an exquisite luncheon at L'Escargot, a pretty old restaurant of extreme distinction just around the corner. We had three sessions during that week's visit.

By the time I returned to Paris in February 1978 I had ceased to drink wine, and was a much happier man, but the join in my thigh bone had developed an arthritic condition, so that walking was not easy, and after sitting still at my desk for an hour or two I was bent double and had difficulty in carrying trays. My left leg was an inch shorter than my right. Lack of exercise had made me fatter than ever. However, I would not go into hospital to have my thigh fixed until I had finished writing the life of Diaghilev.

When I was beginning the biography in the winter of 1975 Ninette de Valois had exclaimed, 'Another book about Diaghilev! There's nothing left to say.' She could not guess that the survival of three amazing collections of documents would make it possible for me to solve many problems and chronicle Diaghilev's daily life and that of his company in· more detail even than Grigoriev (who, anyway, referred to no newspapers). One of my first actions on undertaking the task had been to make tables of dates, a foolscap page for every month of Diaghilev's life between 1909 and 1929, a line for every day. Programmes and newspapers enabled me to fill in details of what the Ballet performed on given days: the writings of Grigoriev, Benois, Lifar, Dolin and others supplied more information. Conversations with survivors helped me to separate truth from falsehood. The three collections to which I have referred, and which were almost untapped sources, told me more than I had believed it possible to find out. One of these, that of the Dance Collection of New York Public Library, housed at the Library and Museum of Performing Arts, Lincoln Center, New York, had already been useful to me when I was working on Nijinsky: at that time it had been mainly the Astruc papers, dealing with the pre-war years, that I had studied. In 1977 I found a stack of miscellaneous letters to Diaghilev written in later years, which had survived Heaven knows how, and had been bought for the Library by Lincoln Kirstein. It gave me a curious sensation to be reading the letters of people I had known, such as Diana Cooper, Christabel Aberconway, Sacheverell Sitwell or Anton Dolin, in a museum, but strangest of all to study a mass of affectionate, gossipy *business* letters to Diaghilev from my dear Juliet Duff, who had raised backing for his last two London seasons.

The second collection, also situated in New York, though in a private house, was even more extensive. Its founder was Parmenia Migel Ekstrom, Chilean on her mother's side, and married to a former officer and diplomat of Swedish descent who ran a successful art gallery on Madison Avenue. She had long been known as a historian of ballet from the sixteenth to nineteenth centuries, when the discovery of a hoard of Diaghilev papers and her purchase of these at thirty cents each had turned her into an expert on the Ballets Russes. To this nucleus she had proceeded over the years to add insatiably, and she had bought many designs and documents at Sotheby sales which our Friends of the Theatre Museum could not afford. Her collection had become the Stravinsky-Diaghilev Foundation. Lincoln Kirstein, who had never seen inside her cupboards, dismissed her 'Aspern Papers' as 'laundry lists', but I was eager to examine them. Parmenia was a small, *chic*, attractive woman, but she had a somewhat witchlike reputation and was known to look with disfavour on the Dance Collection at Lincoln Center, even though her name was, at that time, inscribed on its committee. I had met her and her courteous husband more than once in London, and liked them both: but a mutual acquaintance, sowing careless seeds of mischief, had given me to understand that Parmenia was suspicious of me.

It was therefore with a sense of bravado (and on an evening of euphoria induced by profitable interviews with Balanchine, Danilova and Doubrovska) that, on 7 May 1977, I rang her up. When I asked if I could explore her documents she said there was some difficulty at that time. (She later claimed that her hesitation was due to doubt as to how she could fit me in.) But I had a good card to play. 'In your

Introduction to the catalogue of the admirable Bakst centen-
ary exhibition which you arranged at the Fine Art Society
in London you stated that "students have free use of the
Foundation's resources". I hope you count me as a student.'
I heard a faint subterranean chuckle, and she gave me an
appointment, which was to be the first of six. In her discreet
pavilion of marble and glass on East 85th Street, near the
East River, very few works of art were exposed to view:
it was exquisitely empty in the Japanese manner. So when she
slid back one of the doors of an immense bookcase to reveal
hundreds of files, and asked me, 'Where do you wish to
start?' I was taken aback, and did not know how to reply. I
began copying at random Diaghilev's hotel bills, tailors'
bills and dunning letters: and was still working when it
struck me after five hours that I had overstayed my welcome.
Throughout this and subsequent visits Parmenia never left
me alone for a moment, so my research – which is to say
copying – was done while she sat talking helpfully on the
sofa beside me. Whereas Arne was openly a wit, Parmenia's
dark baleful eyes prevented many people from discovering
her very subtle and civilized sense of humour. I was touched
by the way they both doted on their clever son, who took
fine photographs. My own charms at that time were beneath
the surface – I was a fat old crock – but she seemed to like me
enough to cook me fairy meals; and I found her fascinating
as Circe. My book could not have become what it did
without her kindness. I copied several hundred highly
important telegrams and drafts of telegrams on her sofa, and
prolonged my stay with John Taras to do so.

The third extraordinary collection of papers was what had
once been Boris Kochno's own, now available for study in the
Bibliothèque et Musée de l'Opéra. Here I could read (and
accurately date) the backstage history of the Russian Ballet.
Otto Kahn telegraphed to Diaghilev about the release of
Nijinsky from Austro-Hungary in 1916, and advised him
that as the dancer was eligible for military service Diaghilev

must pull strings in 'Petrograd'. Debussy wrote to tell Diaghilev, in the course of his one war-time season in Paris, during May 1917, that he was harder to reach on the telephone than God; and recalled an evening they had spent at the Hermitage Restaurant in St Petersburg listening to gipsy songs. King Alfonso's secretary Torres was moving heaven and earth to help Diaghilev convey his stranded and penniless troupe across France to England at the height of the German offensive of 1918; and Diaghilev appealed to his English saviour, Oswald Stoll, for travelling expenses. Picasso, who called Diaghilev 'Zipa', wrote postcards from Saint-Raphaël to Venice, saying he had 'started work' (on *Pulcinella*); in March 1921 Falla telegraphed from Granada that he could not afford to go to Madrid to see the ballet, and begged Diaghilev to call *Le Tricorne* by its Spanish name *El Sombrero des tres picos* for Spanish audiences. Benois would leave Russia (where he was in 1921 Director of the Hermitage) to design *The Sleeping Princess* if Diaghilev would guarantee him, among other things, a further 30,000 francs-worth (about £640 or $2690) of work. (In the event Diaghilev gave the job to Bakst.) Stravinsky was sure that Bronislava Nijinska could not have *Les Noces* ready for the spring season of 1922, and he urged Diaghilev to put on *Renard* instead. Barocchi, Lydia Lopoukhova's first husband, bemoaned the fact that she was leaving both him and the company, and enclosed her letter asking for a divorce. Satie wrote that he was still 'licking his ears' after *Les Noces*. Poulenc described to Diaghilev how wittily Nijinska was including a sofa in her choreography for *Les Biches*. After the death of Radiguet, Cocteau behaved like the widowed Queen Victoria, and telegraphed that his musicians (Poulenc, Auric and Co.) were all that he had to live for. Lord Berners, composing music for *The Triumph of Neptune*, did not feel very inspired, but had just bought a delicious Renoir, so hoped things would go better. Diaghilev thanked Lord Rothermere for his guarantee of £2000 ($9700) for the

London season of 1927; but Rothermere was worried because he had heard some of the new ballets were ugly and
he thought 'beauty' important. Prokofiev would arrive in
London to rehearse *Le Pas d'acier* (one of these 'ugly' ballets)
on Tuesday, and asked for three rehearsals with Ansermet.
Dolin, who had left the company in a huff because of Diaghilev's increasing interest in Lifar, begged pathetically in
fluent but mis-spelt French to be taken back. Karsavina would
dance at His Majesty's for £120 (about $580) a week, and
asked 5000 francs for two performances of *Romeo and Juliet*
in Monte Carlo. But Constant Lambert, the composer of
that ballet, protested at Diaghilev's decision to give it on a
bare stage just because its subject was a rehearsal. 'It is like
putting sand on the stage in *Le Train bleu* because it shows a
beach.' Diaghilev gave Rouault a receipt for twelve pastels of
costumes and two of décors for *Le Fils prodigue*.

In 1929, when he died, Diaghilev was one of the most
celebrated men in Europe, and there was no composer,
painter, choreographer or dancer who did not aspire to work
for him. By repeating night after night his old favourites, he
could perhaps have stayed solvent – possibly even made a
little money. But that was not his way. Boris told me that
once a ballet had been produced to his satisfaction he was
bored with it. There was a telegram in Parmenia Ekstrom's
collection which Diaghilev, in Berlin, received from his Paris
bank on 21 June 1929, when a triumphant German season
was following a triumphant Paris one. 'Your account
overdrawn 75,000 francs (about £600 or $2900). Cheques
to the value of 20,000 francs have been returned. Cover
essential.' When Diaghilev arrived in London on the twenty-
third, Juliet Duff gave him some money she had collected
from guarantors, and he paid in £400.

Ninette had been wrong. These archives in New York
and Paris, of which the survival was so unexpected, provided
a very great deal more to say about Diaghilev – as Arnold
Haskell, his previous biographer, was quick to point out in

two generous articles when my book eventually appeared. Yet I was interested to notice that reviewers on the whole – Alexander Bland (i.e. Nigel Gosling) was an exception – were not particularly grateful for all the new information. Possibly they did not realize just how much of it *was* new. Most American critics thought I had provided too many facts and too few verdicts. Perhaps my objective treatment – so different from my flamboyant and self-revealing articles in the *Sunday Times* – was carried too far. I thought that my catalogue of Diaghilev's heroic achievements spoke for itself, and that his imagination and fortitude – the two characteristics I most admired in him – needed no rhapsodies from me to make them evident.

It was during my week's stay in Paris in February 1978 that I began to examine the papers at the Paris Opéra. A friend, Charles Murland (a member of the board of Festival Ballet), had taken a copy of the typescript of my book in its current state to Boris in Paris a week before my visit, and Boris had laboriously read through the entire work, making notes of inaccuracies and suggesting improvements. This was an incredible labour of love. I had arranged to see Lifar and Sauguet. I stayed for the first time at a little hotel with the misleadingly grandiose title of L'Hôtel des Tuileries, in the rue Saint-Hyacinthe, near the Marché Saint-Honoré. Its only spectacular feature were some fine carved Directoire doors. I had picked this hotel because it was between the Opéra and the Louvre and not too far from Boris; but my stay there made me aware for the first time of the 'village' around the church of St Roch, fashionable in the eighteenth century, and I fell under its spell. I have always had the urge to attach myself to a *quartier* – to eat, shop, make a nest and 'belong' – if only temporarily – there. The difference between my stays in Paris and those in New York – the two capitals I had visited most frequently in the last thirty years – was that in New York I had always been put up by friends, which was so much cosier (and cheaper), while in Paris I had never been invited to stay in a private house, with the exception of a visit to the Beaurepaire family at Neuilly in 1947.

On 11 February I drove up to Montmartre to visit Henri Sauguet, whom Diaghilev had commissioned to write *La Chatte* in 1927. 'I have written twenty-six ballets in my life,' the composer told me, 'but I have never been treated as well as Diaghilev treated me when I was working on my first.' He had not forgotten the quizzical way the world-famous impresario twice his age used to call him *'cher maître'*, and how tactfully Diaghilev led the conversation round to the suggestion of cuts in his score – which the twenty-six-year-old Sauguet violently resisted – by referring to the advice he had given Rimsky-Korsakov and Stravinsky. As I stood outside the house in which Sauguet had his flat, on the north side of the rue La Bruyère, I realized that it was immediately opposite the *maison meublée* where I had passed the latter part of my stay in Paris in 1938. There I had lain in bed, suffering from clap, which in those days few doctors had any idea of how to cure; there I had made a hundred designs for women's dresses in the hopes of selling them to Chanel and Schiaparelli; there I had eaten Camembert cheese with the rolls and hot chocolate or coffee, which was all that the room-service of that establishment could provide; and there I had been in love with the Yugoslav dancer. That was forty years ago, and here I was at sixty-two, back in Paris, still comparatively unfriended there, still living in a very modest hotel, still dining alone in the cheapest restaurants, but still thinking about Diaghilev. Although I had then been lithe and active, while now I was limping, stout and slow, I did not feel very different inside. Yet there was a difference. Whereas in 1938 I had lined up to buy a ticket to see Lifar dance at the Opéra, in 1978 I found messages from him when I arrived at my hotel; and only yesterday he had insisted on coming round to talk to me for two-and-a-half-hours. (Most of his stories I took with a pinch of salt.) Boris Kochno, Diaghilev's closest friend in his latter years, was now *my* closest friend in Paris. Igor Markevitch, to whom I had written on an impulse just before leaving my cottage, as I waited for the car to take me to the station, had telephoned from the South of France and was changing all his plans in order to travel to Paris in three days' time and help me with my book. When I went to see a Diaghilev Exhibition at the newly opened Centre Culturel du Marais (to which our Theatre Museum had lent costumes and the Picasso curtain), I was met at the door by its founder, Maurice Guillaud, and shown round in state. Yesterday, at the Musée et Bibliothèque de l'Opéra, the young director, Martine Kahane, with whom I had long been in correspondence, exerted herself to help me, and allowed me to remain copying documents beneath the huge chandeliers of the library long after it was closed to the public. By these courtesies, if I wanted to feel a big shot, could I measure my social advancement over forty years.

Boris was expecting me at one-thirty and if I took a taxi I should be early. (He was a late riser.) I walked slowly down the rue Pigalle, thinking of 1938. The meeting of ways in the open space in front of La Trinité brought a swarm of memories. Then I set off in a south-easterly direction, for Boris. I always felt that Baron Haussmann had made it very difficult for a pedestrian in Paris to take short cuts, for all his streets instead of running north-south or east-west seemed to intersect one's path at sharp angles, so that going too far to the left before turning right might lead one a mile out of the way. Crossing the rue du 4 Septembre I glanced right at Barclay's Bank, to which I had hastened when the franc 'fell' in 1938 to swindle France out of a few pounds. (It was on 5 May, and I went to *Goldwyn Follies* that evening.) Boris looked at me in amazement when I told him that in spite of my bad leg I had walked from Montmartre. His faithful Jean made me a bowl of coffee, and we worked till seven.

Next day, 12 February, it was snowing. Markevitch had arrived in Paris, and I was to meet him at the exhibition in the Marais at half-past-three. First I had to see Boris at twelve. It was our last session of work together on my book. His patience, seriousness and generosity were beyond my capacity to repay. I felt that we had been companions on a long journey. Boris had found the account he had written immediately after Diaghilev's death of the last days in that Venice bedroom which I had visited in 1945. His reading of this document – during which, as usual, I should take notes – seemed to have been planned as a little ceremony to crown our collaboration. Unfortunately time was short. As Boris read aloud (possibly for the first time) the moving words of which I gave the briefest précis in the first chapter of this volume, and as I covered pages with notes, I became aware that I was going to be late for my meeting with Markevitch, who had come from the south to see me, and whom I had not set eyes on for twenty-four years. Boris realized the awkwardness of the situation, accelerated his reading and interrupted it six or seven times to telephone, trying to find a taxi which would take me through the snow. At last he was successful. I put away my notebook. We parted with embraces. I was only half-an-hour late.

Markevitch had been sixteen in 1929 when Diaghilev fell in love with him and prophesied a great future for his music. He had obviously been unable to respond to Diaghilev's (last) great passion, even though the latter's demands, which Igor was frank about, were more sentimental than physical. Yet Diaghilev had exerted himself to be so amusing and instructive that Igor had sometimes broken into a run to arrive the sooner at his hotel. In defiance of doctor's orders Diaghilev had set off with him at the end of July 1929 on their musical tour of Germany and Austria; and Markevitch admitted that he had no idea how ill Diaghilev was at the time. But, as Boris had written, 'to appear carefree and young was Diaghilev's final *coquetterie*', and the effort probably hastened his death. I knew (from programmes George Harewood had produced for me) which operas Diaghilev

333

and Markevitch had heard together and on which days; in Munich *Die Zauberflöte, Tristan, Così fan tutte* and *Die Meistersinger*; in Salzburg *Don Giovanni*. *The Magic Flute* was the first opera Igor had ever heard. In the interval of *Tristan* (which was a matinée) Diaghilev had wept in a shady corner of the garden. When Markevitch asked him what was the matter, he murmured that it was 'the same thing as with his cousin Dima'. He was talking about hearing Wagner in the company of a lover. Although I had long known of the friendship and collaboration of Diaghilev and Dmitri Filosofov over *The World of Art*, and had read in Benois of their trip abroad together in 1890 in search of Western music, drama and painting, no one before had ever suggested to me that Diaghilev had been in love with his cousin – in fact, that Filosofov had been his first love, as Markevitch had been his last; and it was an important discovery.

It was odd that Markevitch should have married, seven years after Diaghilev's death, Kyra, the daughter of Vaslav and Romola Nijinsky. I knew and liked their son; and Derek Hill had sent me a snapshot of their grandson. He looked a dear little boy.

Back in Wiltshire, I polished my final chapters. Boris Kochno's letters continued to help me over details, and he passed on any afterthoughts that occurred to him. 'During our last stay in Monte Carlo D. took me several times to hear *Parsifal*. He seemed to be discovering Wagner's music, and was thrilled with the singing of Georges Thill. On the eve of his death in Venice D. spoke to me again of Wagner's genius . . . I doubt if D. loved Nijinsky in a 'carnal' way . . . As for cuts in your text, I think the details of the last part of your book are the most important . . .'

Indeed, the publishers had pronounced my book far too long. I cut twenty thousand words, then gave up. Nigel Gosling generously undertook to cut another fifty thousand. Then came the source notes, all two thousand six hundred of them, into which I tried to insert some of the information which had been cut. I had tapped so many sources over the years that I had forgotten what some of them were. I knew my life of Diaghilev was imperfect, but I also knew that there was no one living who could have written a book so nearly comprehensive, no one to whom Diaghilev's old friends would have talked as they talked to me. In May I felt able to go into Salisbury Infirmary to have a 'plastic thigh' inserted. Cecil Beaton had recommended the surgeon, Martin Brett, for whose skill I shall always be grateful. I had a room overlooking the spire of Salisbury Cathedral. Work continued in hospital. It was there I heard of Tamara Karsavina's death.

It was on 28 May, the day after I returned to my cottage where my mother had come to look after me, that the secretary of Markevitch rang up from Lausanne, where Igor himself was in a clinic, to say that Romola Nijinsky was very ill in Paris, and that Igor hoped I would do something to help. Even though he could not know that I was on two crutches, waited on only by my eighty-seven-year-old mother, I thought it strange that the celebrated *maestro*, who knew everyone in Paris, should turn to me, who knew almost nobody. I telephoned Boris, but there was no reply.

The reason that it seemed impossible to ring up Lifar was that he and Romola had been waging war over the body of Nijinsky. I have related how in 1953 Lifar had Vaslav's coffin disinterred and conveyed to Paris for reburial in a plot in the Montmartre Cemetery which he intended one day to share with him. His craving for publicity extended even beyond the grave. Markevitch had told me that Romola had recently bought a plot in the same cemetery, and not unnaturally wanted to lie beside her husband: but Lifar would not give up the body. Although Markevitch was only Romola's *ex*-son-in-law he was to be one of her executors, and she had persuaded him to go and discuss this matter with Lifar. Serge was adamant. Igor told him that if he would not see reason Romola was determined to go to law. A cunning smile then came over Lifar's face and his eyes sparkled with anticipation as he exclaimed, 'In that case we shall have the biggest law-suit in history!' He and Romola at least had a love of litigation in common.

Romola Nijinsky died at the Hôtel Lotti, rue de Castiglione, ten days later. Boris wrote: 'Here the death of turbulent Mme N. has passed entirely unnoticed: no newspaper reported it, and I only heard the news from you.'

The exhibition in the Marais had been the first (slightly premature) sign that the world was going to celebrate in 1979 the fiftieth anniversary of Diaghilev's death. In New York Diana Vreeland was planning an exhibition of Diaghilev costumes at the Metropolitan Museum to run through the winter 1978-9. I had never met this famous former editor of *Vogue* and queen of New York's fashion world, but Cecil Beaton had told me years before that she kept repeating my name: 'Dickybuckle, Dickybuckle – it's so euphonious.' In May 1977 I had seen a show of costumes from Russia she had arranged at the Metropolitan Museum, which included Catherine the Great's wedding dress. I had rung up to congratulate her, but she had flu; so I wrote a letter suggesting that she should exhibit Diaghilev costumes in 1979. I forgot all about this, and she never mentioned my letter when we eventually met, so I do not know if it was I who first gave her the idea for the show. Our Theatre Museum lent many costumes, and Pip Dyer went over to keep an eye on them. Mrs Vreeland invited me to write a piece for her booklet (it was not a catalogue), and she paid my fare to attend the opening of the show in November 1978. The Friends of the Metropolitan Museum's Costume Institute were to have a dinner. As I thought I should know none of the Museum's rich patrons I asked if I might sit next to Mrs Stravinsky, who had been helpful to me over my book. She went nowhere without Robert Craft, so they were both invited.

I was alone in John Taras's house on West 69th Street on the day before the dinner, for John was on tour. It was a

Sunday, and I was painting a would-be cover for the *New Yorker* which included a bust of Mrs Vreeland, whose appearance had impressed me when I met her for the first time on the previous day. A lady called Hélène Obolensky, whom I pretended to remember meeting with Nureyev, rang up to say that Lifar had been staying with her for a 'choreographic conference' – indeed, I was aware that Balanchine had failed to escape being photographed with him on the stage of the State Theatre. He was on the point of returning to Paris, but had just heard about the dinner at the Metropolitan. He was sure that the Friends of the Museum would like to ask him if they knew he was in New York. Could I help? I said I believed tickets were two hundred dollars. Oh, well. I telephoned to Diana Vreeland. She laughed: in Paris Lifar had refused to lend anything to her show. Shortly afterwards, Mrs (or Princess) Obolensky rang in rapture to say that Lifar had received his invitation. 'Hold on, he wants to thank you –.' 'I can't talk now, I'm having a shower, I'm terribly late,' I lied. Before long Pip Dyer rang from the Museum to say he had seen the seating plan, and Lifar was at my table. As Lincoln Kirstein remarked (quoting Andrew Mellon), 'No good deed goes unpunished.'

The next evening I called for Vera Stravinsky and Robert Craft in Fifth Avenue. She was looking incredibly attractive for her nearly ninety years, with a big neat coiffure and a printed green and white chiffon dress designed by herself. They were studying an advance copy of their new, fascinating and voluptuously illustrated book on Stravinsky. In the vast entrance hall of the Metropolitan Museum, which had been transformed by lighting, flowers and *buffets* draped in brown and spinach-green cloth, we had to walk several miles in a southerly direction to find a chair for Mrs Stravinsky: we thus missed the sight (described to me later) of Lifar receiving the guests. Hot nuts were served in baskets by seductive waiters who appeared to be out-of-work actors, or call-boys on the game.

The dinner was very well done. In the museum's restaurant, from whose pool rose candles as big as trees, dinner for four hundred was served at forty round tables. Each table-centre was different. Ours was cauliflowers and orchids. I sat between Vera Stravinsky and Alexandra Danilova. The latter had ruined her appearance by substituting for her smooth chic hairstyle a golliwog 'bubble cut'. Opposite, Felia Doubrovska was next to Lifar, and every time she caught my eye she cast her own heavenwards and shook her head despairingly.

When dinner was over, the guests were to transfer themselves to the Costume Institute, which was in the basement at the opposite (northern) end of the Museum, and to admire Diana's exhibition. Two thousand others had been asked to come in after dinner for drinks. Unknown to anyone except a French television *équipe*, Lifar had made plans. As we got up from our table he seized Mrs Stravinsky by the arm. Now, my attractive guest was no lightweight and obviously unaccustomed to violent exercise: yet Lifar propelled her northwards at such a speed that Craft and I were quite unable to keep up with them. I don't know how he did it, and I wondered if their sprint, which was, after all, at least as far as from 81st Street to 83rd, two whole blocks, might not be the death of Mme Vera. Off they shot, through the glory that was Greece and the grandeur that was Rome, traversing · several millennia of Egyptian and Chaldean culture, to arrive – down an escalator which was intended to bring infirm people *up* from the lower galleries, but which Lifar had ingeniously arranged to have put into reverse – at a point where the television cameras of France and the press photographers of America awaited them. Three-quarters of an hour later, after battling through dense crowds of celebrities, none of whom I knew even by sight, I found Mrs Stravinsky quite alone, grey in the face, slumped on a sofa in a little ante-room near the office, begging to be taken home.

On 17 March 1979 I was working at my desk in Wiltshire

Leonide Massine rehearsing *Le Tricorne* at the Dance Centre, Floral
Street, Covent Garden. He is miming the alarm of the Corregidor.
Photograph by Bryan Wharton, 1 March 1973.

when I had a telephone call from Borken in West Germany.
Mary Ann de Vlieg, whom Massine had brought to dine
with me in London a year before, was ringing to tell me of
his death that morning. She had informed the press in France
and America. Would I announce the news in England? It
was a Saturday. I telephoned David Dougill and asked him
to pass the sad news to Mary Clarke, Nigel Gosling and
Reuters. He acted quickly; and an hour or so later, still at
work on the index of *Diaghilev*, I heard Massine's death
announced by the BBC on the one o'clock news.

During our last dinner together (on 6 February 1978) I
had been touched by the fact that the eighty-three-year-old
Massine was obviously head-over-heels in love with the
very young American girl, whose hand he held, when he
was not eating oysters and *sole meunière*, throughout dinner.
Mary Ann was indispensable to him in his work, he told me;
and he was so anxious that I should like her that he confided,

when she was out of the room, that she was descended from President van Buren. To hear Massine talk of Diaghilev you would have thought the latter was a saint, which I knew he wasn't; and it was in vain that I led the conversation gingerly to a discussion of the Doistoievskian dramas that had resulted from Massine's falling in love in 1920 with Vera Savina, his first (English) wife. 'Wasn't Diaghilev very jealous?' 'No, no!' Christian forgiveness could be carried no further. The last words Massine spoke to me were on the telephone a few months later. As he was on the point of hanging up he said, 'Don't put too much into your book, Dicky. You'll only have to take it out again!' I laughed, uncertain whether he was referring to the exigencies of lawyers or publishers: but, by God! he was right.

In May 1979 Jean and Lauretta Hugo were to be in Paris for a few days. I planned to stay two nights at the Hôtel des Tuileries, to see Boris, to visit yet another Diaghilev exhibition based on Boris's former collection, then to motor south with the Hugos. It was years since I had been at Fourques. I arrived in Paris with an advance copy of *Diaghilev* for Boris. On Tuesday the twenty-ninth I dined at the Hugos' fourth-floor flat in the rue de Chanaleilles, south of the river. It was a lovely evening, and the windows were wide open on a view of the chestnut trees of Mr Niarchos's garden, the grey roof-tops of the silent quarter, the distant twin spires of Ste Clotilde and a green sky. I walked back to my hotel across the Pont de la Concorde, and as I turned off the rue de Rivoli up the rue de Castiglione it struck me that I had never entered the Hôtel Continental, where Boris Kochno had first dared to call on Diaghilev on 27 February 1921, and where a few days later he had been engaged as secretary. I walked round the galleries which surrounded its covered courtyard, and although the hotel was now called the Inter-Continental and its clientèle seemed to consist largely of American children in raucous shirts and blue jeans, the décor was still heavy with Grand-Ducal gilt.

The exhibition of Boris Kochno's collection at the Bibliothèque Nationale, with some additions from other sources,
was held in a beautiful long room, the Salle Mazarine, whose
eighteenth-century stonework had lately been cleaned. I
was to meet Jean and Lauretta there on the morning of 30
May, and I arrived early. In the previous winter I had
photographed a huge flapping scarlet banner inscribed with
Diaghilev's name on the façade of the Metropolitan Museum
in New York: I now photographed his name written large
on two boards flanking the arched entrance of that proud
institution to which Victor Hugo had bequeathed his manuscripts, and which he prophesied would one day be 'the
Library of the United States of Europe'. The poet's great-
grandson, Jean, was not feeling well, and had decided to wait
for Lauretta in the church of Nôtre-Dame des Victoires; so
she and I went round the latest Diaghilev Exhibition alone
together, as we had gone round so many other exhibitions
in the past forty years. It was odd to think that the Edinburgh
Festival, which had put on my own show in 1954, was this
year to make Diaghilev the principal theme of its celebrations.

In the piece John Drummond, the Festival's new Director,
had asked me to write about the legacy of Diaghilev for his
programme, because the Edinburgh Festival was mainly
one of music and because our Theatre Museum was presenting an exhibition of costumes (at my old haunt, the
College of Art), I dwelt chiefly on Diaghilev's revelation of
Russian music in the West and his commissioning of Stravinsky's and Prokofiev's first ballets, but suggested how the
1954 Exhibition and the 1968–9 Sotheby sales had led to the
foundation of the Theatre Museum. I might have written
that because Diaghilev had re-established the tradition of
classical dancing, metamorphosed by Russian magic, in the
West where it was born, that because of the great dancers
and choreographers to whom he had given such shining
opportunities, and that because of his 1921 *Sleeping Princess*
in London (that 'disaster'), there were classical ballet

companies in Great Britain (five at least), France, Germany, Italy, Belgium, Holland, Portugal, Switzerland, Turkey, Israel, Japan, Cuba, Brazil, Argentina, Peru, Australia and Canada. There were more than twenty in the United States. Having stated this, I should have liked to drop a little Angostura bitters on the sugar in my champagne cocktail by adding that Diaghilev nursed no ambition to extend his influence in this imperial way. He was a lazy, selfish man, who cared not a damn for posterity, but stirred himself to epic exertions simply for the pleasure of devising works of art and seeing them take shape according to his will. One perfect performance was enough: then his questing soul would be greedy for new sensations. He did what he did because he would have been bored if he hadn't done it – which is the way of the true artist.

I could have added that the works of art which Diaghilev selfishly hammered into shape and which *obliged* people like Ninette de Valois, Marie Rambert, Leonide Massine, Boris Kochno, Lincoln Kirstein and George Balanchine to found schools and companies so as to hand on something of the vision they had shared before its phosphorescence faded, not only made inevitable the spread of the *classical* tradition of theatrical dancing, but imposed a *second* tradition of ceaseless experiment. Because Diaghilev, that improvident giant, had unthinkingly established a new code of honour in the lyric arts, no presiding *Intendant*, no knight-errant of a choreographer, could dare to rest comfortably on his laurels ever again. The inventions of Fokine, Nijinsky, Massine, Nijinska and Balanchine, whom Diaghilev sponsored, had pioneered the 'Modern Dance'; and future adventurers were committed to sail 'beyond the utmost bound of human thought'.

Before he had even turned his attention to ballet, Diaghilev had loved opera and symphonic music (he was a failed singer and composer). He never ceased, in spite of financial setbacks, to try to present singing along with dancing. The huge costly pre-war seasons of opera and ballet, sponsored

by Beecham, when operas of Moussorgsky, Rimsky-
Korsakov and Stravinsky were given alternately with new
ballets by Stravinsky, Strauss, Debussy and Ravel, could not
be repeated: but still Diaghilev had risked in the early
twenties the expense of choral ballets such as Stravinsky's
Renard and *Les Noces* and the little opera *Mavra*, for which
Kochno wrote his first libretto after Pushkin. Then the apathy
with which his 'French season' of 1924 was received, when he
tried to interest a pampered Monte Carlo public in little
known operas of Gounod and Chabrier, did not deter him
(though he had sworn as usual to abjure opera for ever) from
staging Stravinsky's *Oedipus Rex* in 1927. Diaghilev con-
soled himself, when he could not vary the diet of ballet, by
planning musical interludes, coaxing his audience to accept
a little new or unfamiliar music when they returned from the
bar. In this way several works of genius had their first hearing.
The high standard set by Diaghilev in the design and production of ballets had spread to opera. I could not help
thinking that in some roundabout way it was thanks to
Diaghilev that opera singers had grown younger and more
handsome to compete with dancers.

Between the years 1976 and 1979 – and this I did mention
in my Edinburgh article – while I was working on Diaghilev's
biography in the solitude of my Wiltshire cottage, I had
been tuned in, much of the time, to the excellent programmes
of music on the BBC's Radio 3. Often when I was writing
about Diaghilev's commissioning of a certain ballet, its
music would come to me, as if by sorcery, over the air; and
hardly a day passed when Diaghilev's name was not mentioned. Without the appetite for old and new music which
Diaghilev stimulated, should we, I wondered, have Radio 3?
Like Henry Wood he had been a benefactor of composers
yet unborn.

As for myself, who had swum – or drifted – for nearly half
a century in the wake of Diaghilev, although I could be said
to have achieved nothing solid in the world of ballet, that

343

penniless Maecenas, whom I so admired, who was too lazy for the most part to give his attention to a book and preferred looking at pictures or listening to music, had turned me, somehow or other, into a writer.

Lauretta went to find Jean in his church, and I walked to the Carrefour Gaillon, where I was to lunch *chez* Drouant with the publisher who planned a French edition of my book. Five streets met by the little Fontaine Gaillon, and I never passed it without thinking of Diaghilev and Boris going hungry in February 1922, a year after their first meeting. The London production of *The Sleeping Princess* had lost Diaghilev £11,000 ($49,500), and on the morning when, unable to pay his artists, he had fled the Savoy Hotel with Boris, leaving his scenery and costumes (some of which I later bought) to be seized by Oswald Stoll, his '*départ sinistre*' had been rendered more desolating by the disappearance, along with his few small pieces of jewelry, of Beppe, the Italian valet on whom he counted to be faithful unto death. 'The Hôtel Continental,' I had written, more or less at the dictation of Boris, 'could only offer Diaghilev a small room, high up, but with a sideways view of the Jardin des Tuileries. As he had no money he professed to like it better than any room he had ever had before. Boris was given a servant's room. Together they ate at a cab-drivers' restaurant, La Fontaine Gaillon. When they considered the *plat du jour*, they used to calculate if they could also afford soup.'

Boris was expecting me at half-past-three. On the corner of the rue de Montorgeuil and the rue Etienne Marcel I bought an armful of flowers. I was greeted with avuncular embraces. After I had arranged the flowers in three vases and stood them amid the treasures of the 'Stone Age', I photographed Boris seated at the round table among them. While we spoke of the exhibition at the Bibliothèque Nationale and deplored its commonplace poster, I felt an unfamiliar sensation in my left side: it was neither a sharp pain, nor even a fluttering of the heart, but a pervasive weakness which I guessed could

Above left: Banner advertizing the Diaghilev costume exhibition at the Metropolitan Museum, New York, November 1978. *Above right:* Entrance to the Bibliothèque Nationale, Paris, with the placard of the Diaghilev exhibition, May 1979. *Below:* Boris Kochno at his grey marble table, inspecting an advance copy of the author's life of Diaghilev, 30 May 1979, about 4 p.m. Photographs by the author.

345

only derive from a failure in that organ. I was on the point of asking if I might lie on the sofa, but instead I continued the conversation; and the feeling passed. Boris was taking Lauretta to hear *Wozzeck* at the Opéra that evening (it was no longer possible to drag Jean Hugo inside a theatre), and he needed time to get ready, so I left him at half-past-four, after delivering the life of Diaghilev which I had written with his help.

As I walked west along the rue Etienne Marcel, the feeling of weakness and fatigue returned more overwhelmingly than before. I was carrying my cheap little camera and I hardly had the strength to hold it in my left hand. There was not a taxi in sight. I imagined myself collapsing in the street and being robbed of nearly four hundred pounds-worth of francs, which I had in my pocket. (I had once seen a drunken man fall over in a Paris street, and a passing youth had whisked out his wallet and sped round a corner out of sight.) To telephone from a café, which would entail obtaining a *jeton*, looking up the number of my hotel and explaining everything to the implacable lady behind the desk, seemed much too difficult. I was sure Lauretta would be out and I knew no doctor in Paris.

There was a wooden seat beside a bus-stop on the corner of the Place des Victoires. I sank down upon it with relief, and felt a little better. I surveyed the equestrian statue of King Louis XIV in the middle of the circus, and considered taking a photograph: but to get a good angle I should have to brave the traffic and get closer to him. I decided I must push on, though I was very weak indeed. It was a hot day.

In the rue des Petits-Champs I noticed a little covered passage on the left, with steps leading downward. I remembered that this was an approach to the Palais Royal. I went down, crossed the rue de Beaujolais and passed under the arcade into the Gardens. There was an empty chair, and I sat facing the western sun, surrounded by children at play.

It seemed to me surprising that I should suffer from my

heart. In spite of the depression, which had been cured, and the arthritic thigh, which had been replaced, and the bronchial asthma, which was better, I thought of myself as tough, and now that I drank neither wine nor spirits I had looked forward to another twenty-five years of life. No doubt these seizures of the heart always took people by surprise.

In the 1920s Jean Hugo and his first wife, Valentine Gross, whose sketches of the Diaghilev Ballet he had given to our Theatre Museum, had lived in a small top-floor flat opposite where I sat. There Stravinsky, very drunk, had played his 'Ragtime' to Diaghilev and Massine on Mme Valentine's upright piano. There Radiguet, when he missed his last train back to the suburbs, sometimes slept on Jean's sofa. Years later Cocteau too had had a flat in the western gallery overlooking the rue Montpensier. Colette had lived in the Palais Royal, looking out on the gardens planned by Richelieu, but I was not sure on which side.

I thought of John Taras, who suffered from his heart, and was always taking pills and giving up butter. I thought of the Prince of Lampedusa who, in his dazzling semi-autobiographical novel, *The Leopard* (which, with Joy Murchie, I had watched Visconti filming in Palermo), was able to describe the approach of his own death. I thought of Proust's grandmother having her fatal stroke in the gardens of the Champs-Elysées. Then I thought of my own grandmother, Lily Buckle, and her little sit-downs on our shopping expeditions in Oxford – in a college chapel, in the Botanical Gardens or in the Cadena Café. I used to be indignant when her troublesome heart, which so often seemed to her to be on the point of beating its last, caused her to summon my mother and me to a death-bed which proved a false alarm. As I could hardly doubt that my own death was near, or to put it mildly, that I was beginning to die, I realized that what I wanted most was to be in England, in my own home, with those I loved around me; and I sympathized with Granny. I worried about the shock my mother was to receive.

It was a pity if I could not live to write my long-considered autobiography, but at least I had finished the life of Diaghilev. I had never minded going under an anaesthetic before an operation: oblivion did not alarm me. Now, I felt something like the relief I had experienced in youth on the eve of an exam, when I knew there was no more time to stuff my head with knowledge, and I could relax and take things as they came. I was amused to find I had no fear of death at all.

The immediate problem was to get back to my hotel.

Acknowledgements

One letter from Mme Tamara Karsavina is quoted by permission of her son Mr Nikita Bruce; several letters of Mme Lydia Sokolova by permission of her widower Mr Ronald Mahon; a number of letters from Lady Keynes by permission of her nephew Mr Milo Keynes; a few letters from Mme Romola Nijinsky by permission of her executor and son-in-law M. Igor Markevitch. Mr Lincoln Kirstein and Mr John Taras gave me leave to quote from their letters. Miss Kathleen Gordon allowed me to quote extracts from a letter she wrote to Miss Mary Clarke about Mme Karsavina's birthday party, of which she was the hostess. I am deeply grateful to them all.

Fragments from some of my own earlier books may be familiar to a few readers. In the Introduction and in Chapters 1 and 2 occur episodes described in *The Adventures of a Ballet Critic*, and in Chapters 5 and 6 others which occurred in *In Search of Diaghilev*. Sometimes the words are the same because I could not find better ones. Only a few phrases are quoted verbatim from my *Nijinsky* (Penguin) and *Diaghilev* (Weidenfeld, London, and Atheneum, New York) which are still in print, though I have described here the experience of collecting material for these. One or two pieces I wrote for the *Observer* and the *Sunday Times*, and which appeared in the selection entitled *Buckle at the Ballet* (Dance Books, London, and Atheneum, New York), are again quoted by leave of the proprietors and editors of those papers. In addition, a few sentences in Chapter 8 occurred in an article I wrote for *About the House*, the magazine of the Friends of Covent

Garden; and some paragraphs in Chapter 9 appeared in a slightly different form in Sotheby's catalogues of sales of Costumes and Curtains from the Diaghilev and de Basil Ballets (17 July 1968 and 19 December 1969).

The first critic of the early drafts of my text was, as usual, my friend Jane Harriss, who typed them. My second was Boris Kochno, who disliked my first attempt at an opening, and who pointed out errors, but steadfastly refused to censor references to himself. Robin Baird-Smith of Collins gave me his general impressions, suggesting certain cuts and rearrangements, particularly of the opening chapter; then Gillian Gibbins of Collins went through the emended text, line by line, in search of repetitions, obscurities and discrepancies. Even when we thought we had got everything right, my old colleague David Dougill, always the most vigilant of examiners, found many faults and omissions and wrote out pages of proposed corrections. Then Billy Abrahams of Holt, Rinehart and Winston asked me to suppress references to certain characters who had appeared in my earlier volume of autobiography, which had not yet been published in the United States. All these played a part in shaping the book.

M. Kochno, who had helped me with my life of Diaghilev, gave me information for the first chapter of this book, and his patient collaboration with me over the former work is described in the latter. Other friends who exerted themselves on my behalf were Mary Clarke, the late Nigel Gosling, Felix Hope-Nicholson and Alexander Schouvaloff, Curator of the Theatre Museum.

Artists who have generously made it possible for me to borrow and reproduce their work include Leonard Rosoman and Patrick Procktor. Mrs Maison of the Hazlitt Gallery and Mr Adrian Ward-Jackson obtained permission for me to reproduce drawings by Alexandre Benois for *Petrushka* which they had previously exhibited. I had hoarded many of the old photographs for years; but G. B. L. Wilson, who has photographed every ballet 'occasion' for longer than I can remember, produced precious unfamiliar records of the dinner party at Forbes House and Mme Karsavina's birthday party. The *Western Australian* kindly sent the print of Graeme Dalton's photograph, of which I had retained only a newspaper cutting.

Index

JA. BUTLER · HERBALIST & SEEDSMAN LAVENDER WATER